HEA

Higher Education Authority
An tÚdarás um Ard-Oideachas

C·H·I·U

Conference of Heads of Irish Universities

The University Challenged
A Review of International Trends and Issues with Particular Reference to Ireland

Malcolm Skilbeck

ISBN 0 - 904556 - 76 - X

Dublin

Published by The Higher Education Authority

To be purchased from the
Government Publications Sales Office,
Molesworth Street, Dublin 2.

or through any Bookseller

Price Ir£20/€25
2001

contents

acknowledgements

Information and advice, including comments on an earlier draft, have come from colleagues and friends, many with positions of responsibility in higher education institutions and systems. Particular thanks are due to:

Dr Per Olaf Aamodt, Director of Research, Norwegian Institute for Studies in Research in Higher Education, Oslo.

Dr Ian Allen, Deputy Secretary, Victorian Ministry of Education, Melbourne.

Professor Don Anderson, Research Fellow, Australian National University, Canberra.

Dr. Helen Connell, Education Consultant, Drysdale, Victoria.

Professor John Coolahan, National University of Ireland, Maynooth.

Mr Russell Elliott, Vice President Administration, Deakin University, Victoria.

Mr. John Hayden, Secretary/Chief Executive, Higher Education Authority, Dublin.

Professor Áine Hyland, Vice President, University College Cork.

Dr Mary Louise Kearney, Division of Higher Education, UNESCO, Paris.

Professor Elaine El Khawas, George Washington University, Washington DC, and formerly Vice President for Policy Analysis and Research, American Council of Education.

Mr Michael McGrath, Director, Conference of Heads of Irish Universities, Dublin.

Mr Sean Ó Foghlú, Former Head of Policy and Planning, Higher Education Authority, Dublin.

Dr Tom Karmel, First Assistant Secretary, Higher Education Division, Commonwealth Department of Education, Training and Youth Affairs, Canberra.

Sir William Taylor, Chairman of Convocation, University of London, and formerly Vice Chancellor, University of Hull.

Dr. Don Thornhill, Chairman, Higher Education Authority, Dublin.

Dr Alan Wagner, Principal Administrator, OECD, Paris.

Mr Richard Yelland, Head, Programme on Institutional Management in Higher Education, OECD, Paris.

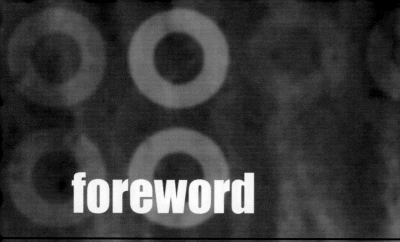

foreword

Over a century ago, British statesman Benjamin Disraeli told the House of Commons during the debate on the Irish University Education Bill that "a university should be a place of light, of liberty, and of learning."

This should still be the case but it is hardly likely that this definition would adequately encompass the missions and activities of our universities and higher education institutions today as they grapple with the many challenges of the 21st Century.

The university is no longer a quiet place to teach and do scholarly work at a measured pace and contemplate the universe as in centuries past. It is a big, complex, demanding, competitive, business requiring largescale ongoing investment.

In 1998, the UNESCO World Conference on Higher Education estimated that some 82 million people were enrolled in higher education institutions, a sixfold increase in the period 1960 to 1995. This rise has its parallel in Ireland where currently over 115,000 students study full-time compared to just under 19,000 in 1966.

As planners seek to address society's economic, cultural and social requirements, much of the current worldwide debate in the field of higher education is dominated by the imposing challenges of the new century. These include the impact of new technologies particularly in the communications field on higher education institutions and traditional modes of delivery; the changing demography in the student population particularly in the developed world; and the sources of funding for the ever increasing costs of investment in higher education.

Yet the history of universities and higher education institutions gives good cause for optimism. Universities have a proud and long tradition stretching back well over 1000 years. They have demonstrated their viability and durability over the centuries as well as the ability to change and to nurture progress in our world. They have adapted and adjusted to the great historical and societal changes brought about during the Renaissance, the Reformation, and explorations on this and other planets, the agrarian and industrial ages, world wars, the impact of new scientific discoveries and much more. As the 21st Century commences, they will have an even more vital role to play in shaping tomorrow's world.

We live in the knowledge-based society and no institutions are as well positioned to play an influential role as our seats of learning. Higher education and research are essential components of cultural and socio-economic development of individuals, communities and nations.

The demands and expectations that are being placed on higher education institutions by Government, industry, social partners, parents, students, professional bodies and other interested parties are formidable. It is essential therefore that we assess, review and explore performance and chart strategies so that our higher education system is equipped to deal with the new challenges of this century.

While all agencies have to cope with change, it is essential that our higher education institutions are strategically equipped to maintain that crucial distance necessary to offer objective insights and a critique of events and developments so that society in general can better cope and progress.

Nobody would now deny that education at all levels is central to economic, social and cultural well-being and a central part of self-development and personal empowerment. Worldwide, there is a growing demand for access to higher learning bringing forth new providers, new delivery modes and innovative methods of teaching and learning. The concept of lifelong learning is widely recognised, encouraging as it does a much greater diversity of the student body.

In this outstanding work, Professor Malcolm Skilbeck brings his considerable talents to bear on the myriad of themes, issues, challenges, threats, options, perspectives, patterns, policies and approaches that have surfaced in the recent international history of higher education.

Issues not only relating to teaching and research but questions of student and staff mobility, equality, transparency, quality assurance, and financing are explored in national and international contexts.

Prof. Skilbeck's work is a most important contribution to our knowledge and thinking in this area. It will repay careful reading and through its contribution to debate it will help to ensure that the proud record of public service of our higher education institutions will continue.

On behalf of C.H.I.U. and the HEA, we congratulate him on a superb piece of work and we extend to him our deepest appreciation. We would also like to acknowledge the financial support of The Atlantic Philanthropies for this project.

<table>
<tr><td>Roger Downer</td><td>Don Thornhill</td></tr>
<tr><td>Chairman C.H.I.U.</td><td>HEA Chairman</td></tr>
</table>

In all of the industrially advanced democracies across the world during the past three or four decades, universities have expanded and diversified. In adapting themselves to the demands and expectations of the emerging knowledge society, economic growth and rising human expectations, many are changing almost beyond recognition. They are now challenged to transform themselves still further, to avoid the threat of dilution of their fundamental values, or retreat into costly irrelevance. At the turn of the millennium, there is a continuing groundswell of demand. Individuals are seeking advancement while whole societies are looking to higher education and research to underpin economic growth, improve the quality of life and strengthen the social fabric. Universities have a vital role in helping to set new goals and directions for human development while maintaining a rich and ancient cultural heritage.

Forces in the industrialised world driving change in higher education

Several forces that are transforming societies, not only in the OECD countries but globally, are having a powerful impact on higher education policies and practices:

- Continuing **growth in demand** by individuals and by whole societies for ever higher levels of educational attainment, for credentials of value in employment and professional life, and for personal and community well-being;
- Increased recognition of the **economic returns** that follow investment in education and research that are of high quality and relevance to society's needs and expectations;
- **Expanding and shifting frontiers of knowledge** which both challenge established values, ideas, beliefs and institutional structures and have potential for numerous social and economic applications;
- Rapid development, pervasiveness and society-wide impact of **communication and information technologies;**
- **Economic globalisation and internationalisation** of many spheres of life;
- Continuing democratic quest for **cohesion, justice and equity in social** arrangements and for more **enriching and inclusive cultures.**

From their medieval origins and their renaissance in the nineteenth century, universities in the course of the twentieth century have demonstrated a continuing readiness and capacity to evolve. In changing direction, many have re-created themselves. There have been both fresh initiatives determined from within the institutions and statewide reform endeavours. The basic values of the intellectually free quest for knowledge and its diffusion remain intact at least as cultural ideals but in the evolution of the established universities and the creation of new ones, these values have been put in new contexts and given many different forms. There is also concern that the universities may not be providing the leadership in contemporary society that reflects their distinctive moral and intellectual stature.

Where are changes most acutely felt?

- Challenges and changes are **within institutions**, initiated by and affecting individual staff, departments, divisions and faculties, management and governing bodies, and students;
- Changes are **ubiquitous** - in teaching, learning, scholarship, research, administration and institutional culture;

9

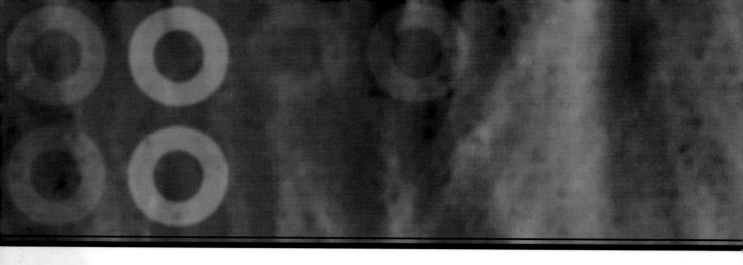

- Changes are *systemic*: through legislation, policy making, regulation, performance targeting, monitoring and funding;
- *Systems, structures and linkages, both formal and informal, are expanding,* from the state and national levels to cross-country regional and global groupings;
- Changes are **radical**: new kinds of institutions and processes (private and corporate providers, virtual institutions) staff responsibilities and new models of staffing (contract and performance based, entrepreneurial).

Expectations of universities

Drawn out of their once secluded, protected environments, universities, whether public or private, are now expected:
- To be **more outward looking** partners in the development of the learning society;
- To provide **leadership and service** at local, regional, national and global levels;
- To make **efficiency gains,** more effectively manage themselves to achieve performance targets in teaching and research, and be publicly accountable and transparent;
- To maintain **standards and high quality** with reducing unit costs;
- To demonstrate ability to obtain new and **additional sources of revenue**.

The pressures on universities and their responses to them have brought about a shift in orientation: less the scholar and teacher as source of canonical knowledge and more the student as learner and client; less the enclosed college, more the wide-ranging enterprise. The university is at the centre of a vast network of intellectual, social, economic, cultural relationships increasingly global in their reach. But the scale and the pace of change in a constrained resource environment require difficult decisions and strategic thinking of a high order. Some university leaders and policy analysts now question the survival of the university in anything like its present form, amorphous as that often is.

Action needed to meet the challenges: the human factor:

The test for universities is, essentially, their readiness to mobilise the enormous talent at their disposal. This requires:
- Policies and programmes both to bring in and provide opportunity for 'new blood' as well as for the continuing development of the capabilities of existing staff for:
  - Mastery of the new technologies in both teaching and research;
  - Improved resource utilisation with consideration for all members of the institution.
  - Strengthening and broadening interpersonal links with the wider community including industry;
  - Maintaining morale of staff and rewarding performance;
- Enhanced staff capabilities for strategic planning, performance targeting, monitoring and evaluating the quality of teaching and research, and achieving equity goals;

- Recognition by staff of the growing capacity of students to organise their own learning through a wide variety of sources including those of the Internet
- Creation and support of both on-campus and virtual environments that foster in students cultural and social values as well as intellectual proficiency and professional competence..

Action needed to meet the challenges : functions/activities of institutions:

Universities need to enlarge and improve their institutional capability:

- Improve governance and management through leadership programmes at the level of governing bodies, departments and divisions and for deans, senior administrators, presidents and deputies;
- Develop realistic strategies for lifelong learning in which undergraduate degrees constitute not an end but a stage in continuing education and professional development;
- Increase and diversify sources of university income: sale of services; consultancies; partnerships; management of intellectual property; rents from wider, year-long use of facilities; fee-paying students; and a wide range of entrepreneurial activities;
- Continue to build and strengthen partnerships and alliances: with other sectors; among institutions to achieve greater impact and economies of scale; internationally; and with other educational research and commercial bodies;
- Recognise and reward good teaching (more honour to teaching), administration and management, rather than concentrating their reward system on research;
- Balance current nationally competitive research concentration in the sciences, notably biotechnology and information technology, with support and encouragement for the advancement of knowledge and scholarship on a broad front and in all parts of the institutions
- Serve regional and local communities while extending their national and international outreach.

Action needed to meet the challenges: the university system and the idea of the university

- System-wide strategic planning and financial decision making, monitoring and reporting on performance including quality of processes and actions are of growing importance and need to be built into the norms of institutional life.
- Institutions, whether public or private, do not function in isolation but are part of intricate networks and systems. Policy makers, faced with the pressure of increasing enrolments, much more diverse categories of students, rising costs and socio-economic demand for applicable knowledge, are having to find ways to reposition universities within diverse tertiary or higher education systems; they need better data and to be able to make more comprehensive overviews of the sector.
- There is need for further development of an independent capacity by institutions for evaluative research, analysis and development of institutional culture, if the intellectual values of universities are to be sustained.

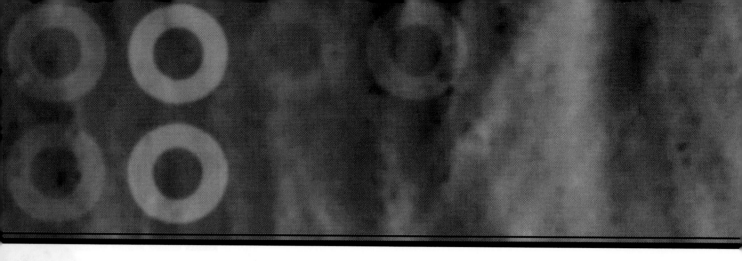

- Enhancing the collective voice and influence of university leaders is widely recognised as a necessary counterbalance to the 'corporatisation' of decision-making across the whole of society;
- The moral role of the university is in question and needs to be redefined to take account of rapid changes in the framework of knowledge, in the policy environment and in the multitudinous tasks the institutions are assuming.

It is against a turbulent international higher education environment that the **universities of Ireland** among other countries are now being challenged to meet the requirements of a fast growing economy and changing society. Irish universities have until recently operated on a relatively small scale, with very modest budgets. Largely state funded with augmentation from private sources for specific projects, they have been demonstrably effective, enjoying a high degree of protection while experiencing the effects of rapid growth in enrolments and highly constrained budgets. The swift, sustained growth of the Irish economy in the nineties, combined with a wide range of social, cultural and political changes, is resulting in a new dynamic. In an environment of national goal setting and strategic planning a traditional society and economy is being transformed into a modern, knowledge and information-based society. University reform and development are seen to be key factors in this transformation. There is a challenging new environment:

- Economic dynamism: the new Irish economy;
- Secularisation of society: new values and lifestyles;
- International links beyond the old nexus (UK, USA): Europe and the world;
- A decade of intensive policy development: social, economic and educational reform measures and proposals and legislation;
- Calls from all quarters for responsiveness, flexibility and innovativeness by the institutions;
- Recent national policy focus on research with substantial augmentation of funding;
- Positive responses by institutional heads to proposals for national development
  (are these matched within the institutions?)

In order to meet these expectations to play new and more diverse roles, the universities - while maintaining the tradition of free inquiry and the disinterested pursuit of knowledge - need to:

- **Review and appraise** their policies, structures, practices and capabilities with reference to the national directions being set in a succession of strategy documents, major reports and policy initiatives;
- **Reposition** themselves as a strong system not just a collection of separate, individual **institutions**;
- **Define missions and strategies** to achieve greater strength in an increasingly competitive international higher education market;

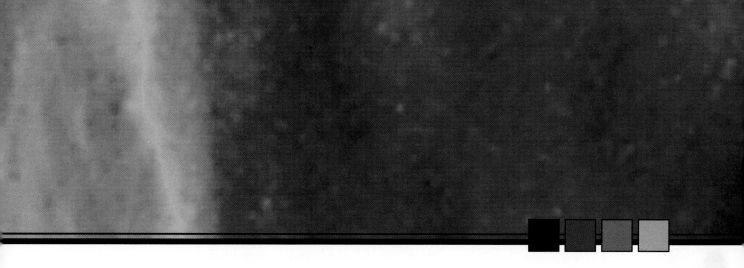

- **Appraise the quality of their teaching, research and service roles and set standards including international benchmarks** for their continuing development;
- **Broaden and enlarge their student intake,** to increase the proportion of mature age and post-graduate students and better meet access and equity targets;
- **Adopt more flexible teaching** to facilitate part-time study, developing in all institutions a lifelong learning mentality;
- **Strengthen links and partnerships** with industry, the community and the institutes of technology to achieve a more open style of operation and closer integration with the community;
- **Seek to diversify funding sources** through increasing the sale of services on the international market, closer links with industry and the extension of fee-paying courses;
- **In strengthening their collective capabilities and action,** to rethink the balance between competition for resources and co-operation for impact.

While it is not evident that there is any threat at present to the survival of any of the Irish universities, there are major changes in orientation and style that are called for. There are opportunities and pressing needs for change to strengthen individual institutions and to steer the system as a whole into closer alignment with the development strategies for a highly competent, knowledge-based society that are now being pursued across the wide spectrum of recent and current national policy concerns.

The challenges are not to any single part or operation of the university but to the whole institution. They are as much to teaching as to research, to study as to the dissemination of knowledge, to what is taught and learnt and to how the university sets its goals, defines its targets, develops its strategies, deploys its resources and monitors and assesses its own performance. To gain strength and impact and to maximise their human and financial resources, the universities need to work more closely together, in various partnerships, yet with more entrepreneurial flair. The readiness to address the challenges creatively and effectively, while maintaining the intellectual and moral values of free inquiry and the disinterested pursuit of truth, will be a demonstration of the Irish university's continuing relevance and vitality.

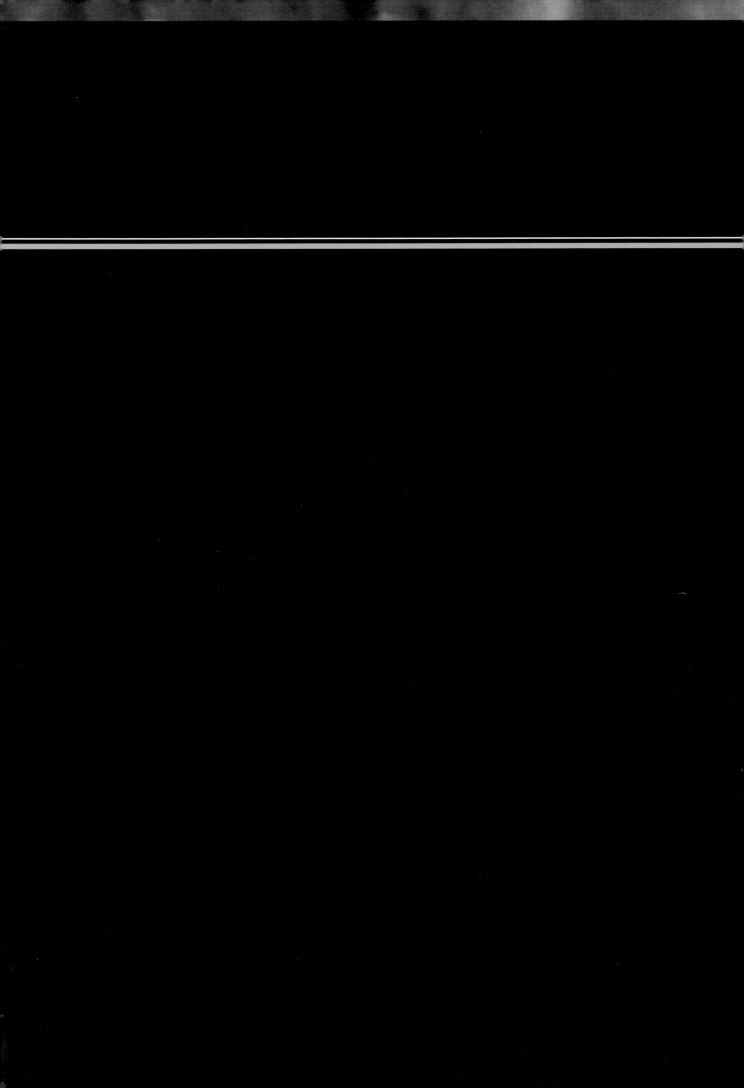

introduction | The Nature of the Enquiry

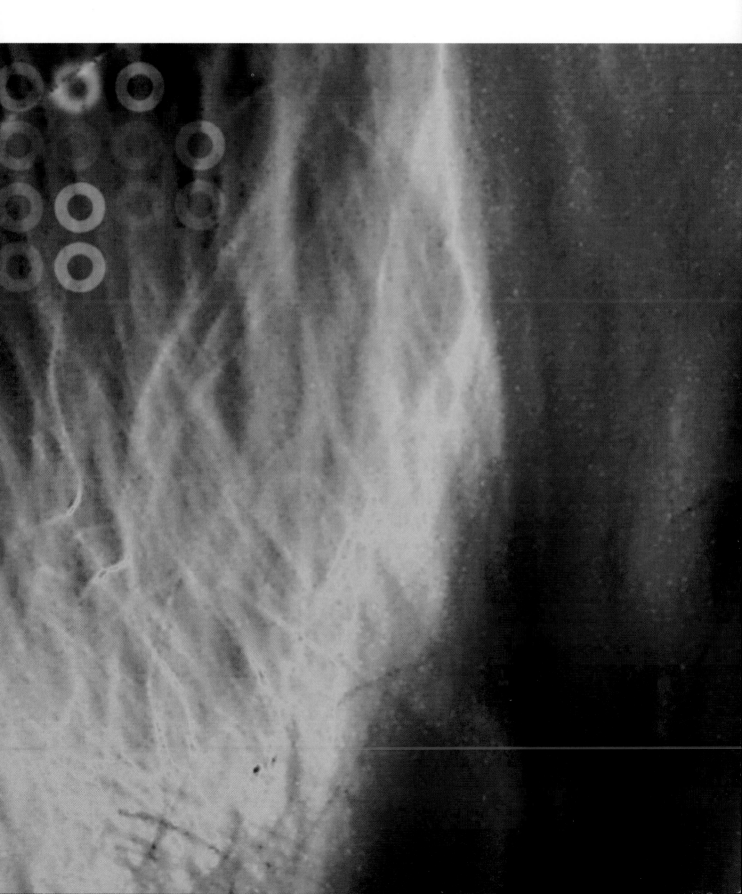

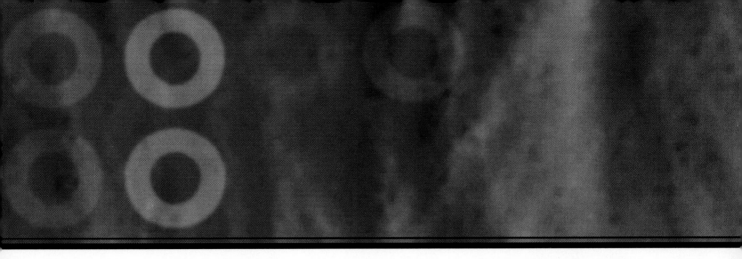

Why should we place our knowledge infrastructure in institutions which are separated from their surroundings by financial, organisational and cultural walls?
(National Advisory Council for Education, ARO, 1994, p. 3.)

What happens when a proud, prestigious and ancient institution, the university, is rapidly and unceremoniously brought to the hurly burly of the market place, subject to unprecedented societal pressures and demands from which in the past it has been largely protected when not almost entirely detached? In the course of little more than a generation the tradition of the detached scholar engaged in self-determined, disinterested inquiry and the pursuit of truth has been consigned to history. The image of the secluded ivory tower now belongs to the realm of romance; the 'cultural state', it appears, is being displaced by the market place.

The changes that have overtaken the universities, or been initiated by them, are of course more complex and variable than are suggested by the stark parameters of a drama of extremes: assault; turbulence; and a quest for rebirth. Nor is the 'cultural state' another lost illusion: it is neither wholly illusory, nor is it altogether lost. Universities, of course, never were wholly detached and aloof from the issues of the day; they have always been major players in professional education and a recruiting ground for the public service. Their scholarship and research findings have historically played decisive roles in cultural consciousness as in the underpinning of social and economic development. They continue to do so. Through networks of their graduates and links with governments, the professions, business and cultural institutions, the universities have very often been able to set the terms of their external relations. They still can, to a quite large extent, but only through systematic penetration, not to say mastery, of the very forces that are transforming social and economic life.

The changing visage of higher education provides the subject matter of a thriving industry of research and analysis - a substantial and relentlessly increasing body of reports, reviews, and action programmes. Trends and issues are documented and debated in innumerable articles, research studies, conferences, and meetings. Through legislation, regulations, and policy initiatives of many different kinds, governments are seeking to steer greatly expanded and diversified systems, bringing universities into the mainstream of national economic and social development and international relations. In responding the universities are forging, or endeavouring to set, new directions for themselves. Altogether, in the course of three or so decades, a new world of higher education has been created, on the still visible foundations of the old.

There are, within the academic ranks, many who regret or deplore the impact of several contemporary social and economic forces on institutional values and culture. Transformations of an irreversible kind have occurred; they are set to continue

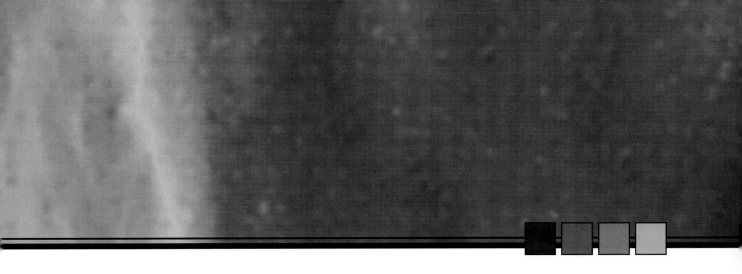

in the world's higher education systems. The scale and pace of change can be disturbing when it is not invigorating. Understanding the forces at work is a first step towards steering or moderating them to take advantage of the opportunities they provide.

In the preparation of this report, two purposes have been paramount: first, to offer an overview and appraisal of trends and issues arising in the international domain of university education, broadly defined to include the functions of teaching, learning, scholarship and research; second, to focus these trends and issues in possibilities for action for consideration by the Irish university system. The intent is less to survey the field than to identify concerns and issues that are at the heart of current international debates. It is hoped thereby to assist universities to further their ideas and plans for their own future development by holding a mirror to the changing world of higher education.

Inevitably there is a speculative and subjective element to such an approach, however well grounded it may be in material from both academic and policy sources. Any attempt to portray trends and issues in their full complexity is doomed to failure while reduction to a short, simple outline would be nothing more than a mirthless caricature. In the burgeoning field of research and scholarly writing on higher education and the proliferation of journals and online sources, there repose tens of thousands of items. With the number increasing by the day, there are far too many to encompass in a single overview. In making a selection relevant to higher education in Ireland, it has seemed desirable to concentrate on (a) literature and data sources which help to identify and illuminate by example widely agreed major international developments and trends and (b) material mainly from the early '90s onwards to illustrate current and emerging concerns. As a most valuable aid toward correcting distortion and bias, higher education leaders and specialists from several countries have kindly commented on an earlier draft (see Acknowledgements). Even so, a degree of arbitrariness in the selection of source material is inescapable.

Material for this study has been drawn from a wide variety of published and unpublished sources and from different country experiences. But this is not a global overview: the main thrust of the report relates to the advanced economies and stable democracies of the OECD membership and to those kinds of institutions that seem to the author to be most relevant to contemporary higher education in Ireland.

Given that institutions, policy makers and the agencies that have system-wide responsibilities are faced with ever more demanding challenges and, very often, difficult decisions, the overall thrust of the report is towards decision-making and policy action. In the current international debate there are numerous cross currents not to say contrary directions. Options

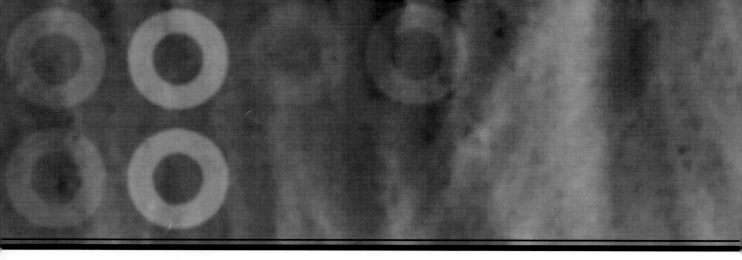

are being canvassed and considered; tradeoffs are being made; on several important issues, there is no certainty, no consensus of informed opinion. We are, for example, well launched into a period of fundamental renegotiation of relations between the state of the university and the university and the wider community. It is not a settled situation with clear and definite outlines that sets the scene for future action. It seems important to draw this out rather than to suppose that growth and development will be merely incremental, a kind of trajectory along familiar and well trodden tracks.

The text falls into three parts. **First,** there is a general overview, a sketch of the main trends and recurring issues. In the **second** part, while the more general approach of trend analysis is maintained, a set of specific topics and key issues is treated in greater detail and with reference to a wide range of the literature of research, scholarship and policy-making in higher education. The **third** part aims at a crystallisation of issues and concerns that have either surfaced or been implicit throughout the report, in order to sharpen the focus on questions, challenges and opportunities for the Irish universities collectively and the Irish university system. The international evidence examined in the second part and the strategic policy environment which is progressively being established for higher education in Ireland provide the underpinnings for the position taken in this final section.

In the constant and necessary endeavour to sustain the vitality and relevance of universities, new directions are being sought. The new is often superimposed unceremoniously upon the old with little understanding of what is likely to emerge. Values, as well as institutional arrangements often of long-standing, are being reconstructed. The very concepts of 'the university' and 'university education' are challenged, and not only by the sheer growth of numbers and the great diversity of institutions and programmes of study and inquiry. There is a loosening of the bonds among teaching, learning, scholarship and research and some guiding, authoritative institution. Resources and priorities for their use are everywhere at issue. It is upon the success of their efforts to meet the challenges facing them that the universities must stake their future, some say their continued existence.

A Note on Terminology

Several terms, which recur in legislation, policy documents and the research literature are at times used interchangeably and can be a source of confusion. The issue of terminology becomes more complex when translations are made from other languages into English and vice versa. For the purposes of this study, the following terminology has been adopted:

- *University:* An institution, whether public or private, which aims to: advance knowledge through inquiry and research; educate students for entry into careers with a high knowledge base and requiring intellectually demanding competences and skills; strengthen cultural values; foster responsible citizenship; and provide service to the community;

- *Education:* Systematic processes of learning and teaching aimed at the continuing growth and development in individuals and society of skills, knowledge, values, standards of conduct and understanding;

- *Research/scholarship:* Rigorous and structured inquiry in the pursuit of knowledge, understanding and truth to the most advanced levels through widely attested designs and procedures for data gathering, analysis, testing, demonstration and discourse;

- *Tertiary education:* In the sequence of primary and secondary, the tertiary level requires standards of learning and teaching derived from the frontiers of knowledge, together with advanced applications and uses whether in more theoretical or more practical spheres. The term 'tertiary' has been adopted by UNESCO, OECD and others, for purposes of international comparative statistics, with types of courses, teaching and teachers serving as proxies for distinguishing university and non university tertiary levels.

- *Tertiary institution:* A college, institute, university or other academic agency functioning at the level of tertiary education; elements of scholarship and research in the tertiary institution may range from permeation of the whole institution, its ethos and practices, to an explicit recognition of their value but with limited applications within the institution's own practice;

- *Higher education:* Sometimes used interchangeably with 'university education' in this report (as elsewhere), 'higher' also refers in the literature (and at times in this report) to tertiary institutions other than universities.

part I | Directions: An Overview of International Trends and Issues

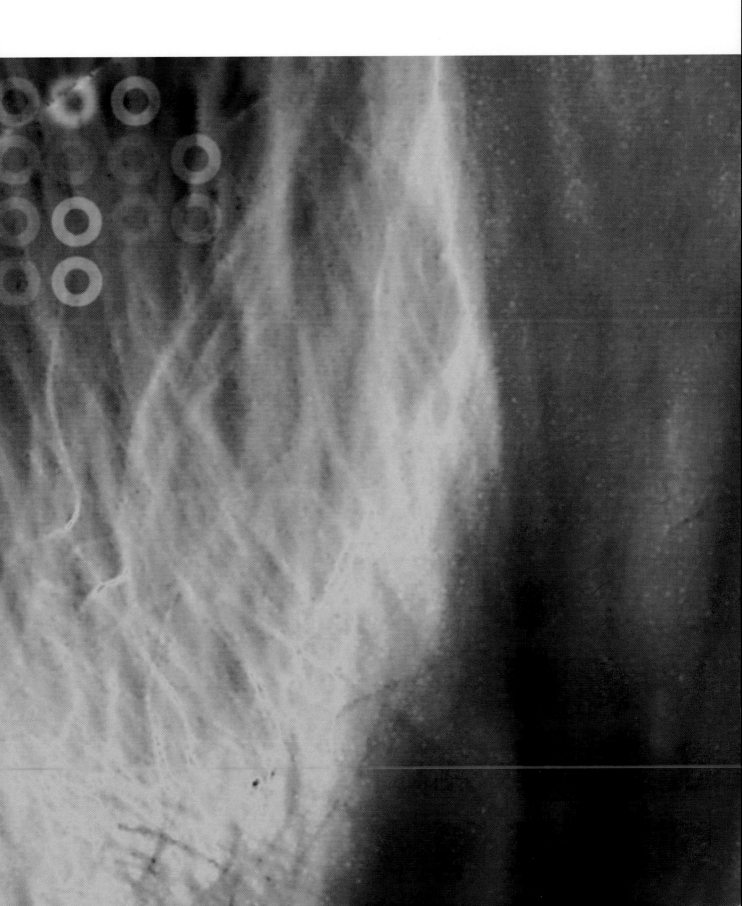

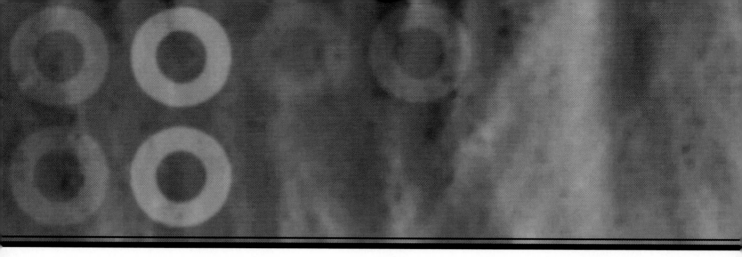

The university has become one of the great institutions of the modern world (Perkins, 1966, p. 3.)
The universities of the world have entered an age of endless turmoil (Clark, 1997, p. 291)

Delivering the Stafford Little lecture in 1966, the former President of Cornell University located the university at the very centre of national life. He saw it as the most sophisticated agency for advancing knowledge through scholarship and research, crucial in the transmission of knowledge and its application to the problems of modern society.

For Perkins, as for a long train of academic leaders and thinkers, there is a distinctive set of attributes and functions that legitimate continuing use of the generic term 'university' despite the enormous diversity of institutions it encompasses. There are values and processes centring on the quest for knowledge, and a culture of scholarship and learning that, from their mediaeval origins to the present day, have defined the activities of universities however varied in time and place. But these attributes, the values and the culture now take many different forms in practice. Nor is there a sharp line between the functions of universities and other education institutions and agencies, which might justify privileged treatment or structural rigidities and barriers. Old boundaries are becoming permeable.

Whether any or all of the functions performed by universities - in teaching or research, the advancement of learning or community service - might best be separated from the institution and dispersed through other agencies, is an issue lurking just beneath the surface of current debates. One conspicuous example is the erection of research institutes independently of universities and competing with them for funds. Another is the separation of funding for research and for teaching with targets for each independent of the other. Yet another is the emergence of the 'virtual' university which delivers resources for learning and teaching but may have practically no academic staff of its own and makes no claim to undertake research.

In his lectures, Perkins drew out the historical continuity of the university as a many-faceted centre of learning. Attributing the success of the multi-purpose American university to its being heir to the ideal of research and the graduate school from Germany, to the nurturing of undergraduates from Britain, and to the uses of knowledge in service of the community from Jefferson, he nevertheless expressed concern for the future: *'Is the university's autonomy and integrity inevitably compromised by its growing involvement with society and by the increasing necessity for state, regional and national planning'* (Perkins, 1966, p. 4). Perkins also observed some paradoxes: the clamour for admission, yet mounting dissatisfaction with conditions of student life; the high regard for research, yet the risk of research monopolising intellectual life; and a discernible overall loss of principle and of direction.

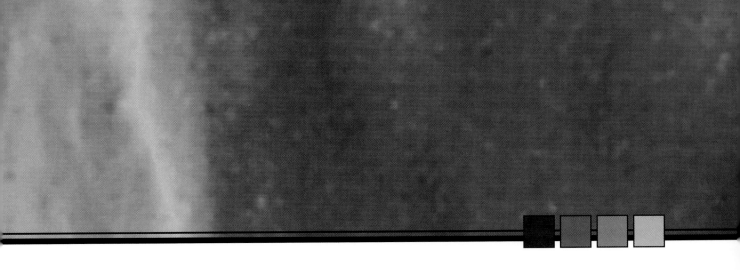

Universities are changing profoundly...

During the third of a century since Perkins gave his lectures, higher education worldwide has experienced changes on an unprecedented scale. These have resulted in waves of critical self analysis and tireless efforts at renewal, affecting institutions everywhere. As Burton Clark, one of the leading authorities on higher education in North America and Western Europe, says: 'endless turmoil'.

In common with all other major social institutions and agencies, public universities and higher education institutions generally have been subject to the forces of modernisation. Thus they have felt the impulse of the new economic and social realities that are transforming enterprises everywhere, whether public or private, big or small.

Universities are increasingly brought under external scrutiny and appraisal. Procedures are required of them that correspond to new regulatory environments as well as to public expectations that are increasingly diffuse and variable. The logic of production, productivity, results, performance in the market place and accountability has been superimposed on that of the dispassionate quest for knowledge and the disinterested pursuit of truth. There are those who take the scale and significance of these changes to the point of querying whether universities have a future at all. Hence the title of an American book edited by Ronald Ehrenberg, *The American University - National Treasure or Endangered Species?*

Universities thus face an uncertain, unclear future. They have not been immune from such basic change forces as a huge growth in demand for access affecting all levels of education throughout the 20th century. Qualities and capabilities in graduates that better match labour market needs and opportunities, and meet civic objectives, are in high demand. Institutions everywhere, the best endowed and financed no less than the most needy, public or private, are having to seek new sources of funding, improve their efficiency, resource utilisation and overall management and decision-making. They are having to learn to communicate more effectively with the wider environment.

No longer the province of intellectual and social elites, the universities collectively are open to a much greater proportion of the population than ever before. There is, too, a wider cross-section among the academic staff with a corresponding diversity of backgrounds and interests. The opening of the universities to the world, together with the scale, the resources needed and the impact of their operations, has meant that governments are increasingly attentive to their costs, procedures, and results.

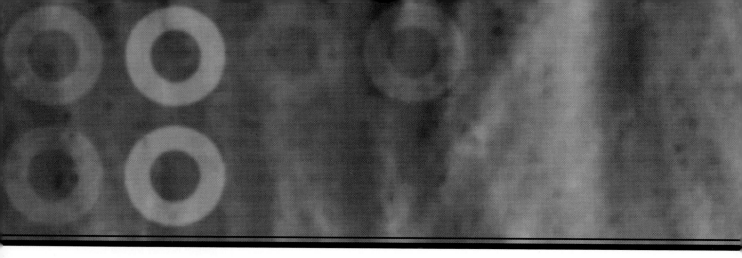

Six factors in the modern period that are reshaping long-held values and institutional practices stand out:

- Continuing increases in individual and social demand for access to study at all levels;
- Insistence by governments and employers on more economically and socially responsive education and research;
- Pressure to improve quality and achieve higher overall standards;
- Changing fiscal policies and priorities for public expenditure;
- Requirements to improve efficiency and raise productivity;
- A progressive shift from formal, institution-bound teaching to technology-facilitated learning.

(Frankel, 1968; Roszak, 1969; Taylor, 1987; Neave, 1995; McGuinness, 1995; Association of European Universities (CRE), 1995; OECD, 1998d).

The impact of these factors is discussed in the following chapters.

Long-held academic values and formulations of the ideal academic life, deriving from the writings and actions of Wilhelm von Humboldt, John Henry Newman, Ortega y Gasset, Karl Jaspers and others in a classic corpus of European academic literature are, as a consequence, under acute pressure. But it should be recalled that this highly influential and still much admired, aloof, scholarly and morally earnest tradition is but one part of the historical legacy. There is more than one corpus. Alongside the austere classical tradition is the appeal to utility, witness to another strand of life in the nineteenth century.   Progeny of this strand in England include the great metropolitan university of London and the civic and industrial universities of the provinces; in the USA, the enormously influential land grant agricultural and mechanical accredited universities; in Germany, the powerful and prestigious technical institutions; in France, the specialist professional institutions and the post-Napoleonic *grandes ecoles*; and many others.

There is no single 'idea' of the university, but many 'ideas' (Rothblatt, 1989, p. 19). The great diversity of universities (and other tertiary institutions) in the United States reflects successful resistance to a single idea, to a unique essence. There are those today who assert that it is impossible to find any grand organising principle of operation other than 'market responsiveness' (Smith and Webster, 1997). This seems unnecessarily obtuse or pessimistic. What is it that is responding and is there no sense of purpose, value and continuity? Some would answer that there is not: 'We use the term 'university' but we no longer have any clear sense of what it might stand for: we no longer have a concept of 'university''(Barnett, 2000, p.115). It is on the forging of a new concept, entailing radical change, that the contributors to a recent study have set their sights . (Scott (ed.) 2000). But this concept denotes restless diversity and shifting patterns, not clear, unequivocal procedural principles and criteria.

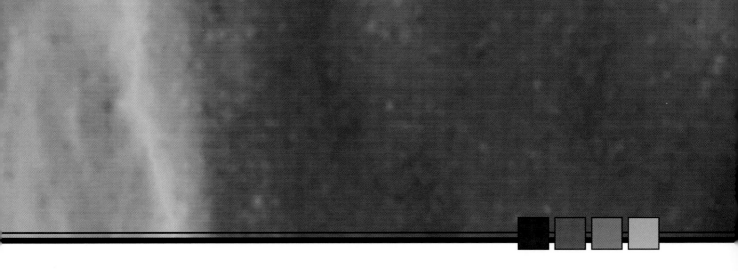

The classical ideals - of autonomy and scholarly independence, the unity of teaching, study and research, the collegial authority of the community of scholars and knowledge as its own end - are of course not static. Nor is the utilitarian tradition. Both have been continually reshaped from the time of their birth. The emergence, from the mid 20th century onwards, of the mass university serving community needs and defining new directions in research and scholarship is perhaps the most visible recent expression of this reshaping. There are many other manifestations, not least new contractual relations with the state and new partnerships with industry and the community. In all of this it is important to keep hold of the idea that the quest for knowledge is critical and creative and that the advancement of knowledge is entwined with the development of civilisation and quality of life for all.

In recent decades, the intellectual and cultural 'space' occupied by universities has been reconstructed by a succession of critical events: the radical critiques of the sixties; the economic crises of the seventies; huge volume increases in enrolments; the growth, specialisation and attempted reintegration of knowledge; the new global movements following liberalisation of trade and investments; the re-awakening of the Asian region; the redrawing of the map of Europe - west, central and east; the technological revolution; the growth of industry-higher education partnerships. Higher education is caught up in all of these changes and visibly contributing to many of them.

In these swirling cross currents, the processes of teaching, learning and assessment retain certain architectural features: the systematic, rigorous structuring of knowledge by teachers for purposes of communication; the requirement of student familiarisation with and cognitive mastery of new content; the eliciting of performance in written exercises, practical assignments, tests and examinations. But the infusions of communication and information technologies, together with the development of new settings for study whether in the workplace or the home, are beginning to modify and sometimes transform the long familiar processes of the lecture, seminar, laboratory, demonstration, field trip, written assignment and examination. More open, flexible, diverse partnership-based and self/group managed learning systems are testimony to an interest in more active, student-centred learning.

And are everywhere facing radical challenges...

It is not simply that the specificities of institutional life and conventional education practice are under challenge: indeed, while many are changing, others retain their familiar contours. Rather, the change is one of key, of context and orientation and this gives new meaning to familiar practices: these are a consequence of both a wide range of reform measures, of addressing expectations, simply expressed as 'the knowledge needs of society' (Lynton and Ellman, 1988), and accepting 'public accountability for public funds' (Ball, 1996).

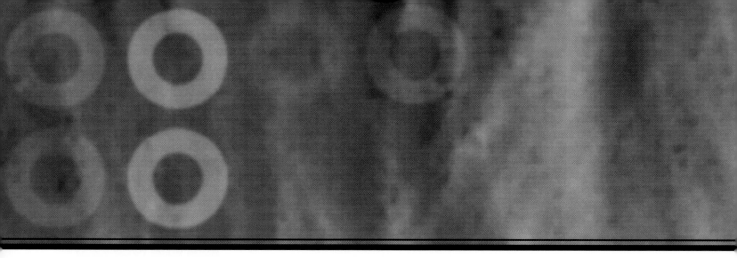

Universities both public and private have entered new relationships with government. The long-established requirement of accountability in the use of public funds has, in the course of the nineties, been strongly reinforced by a more broadly based demand that public universities and other higher education institutions systematically appraise themselves, attain clear targets, and demonstrate the overall quality and efficiency of their activities whether in teaching, research, service to the community or institutional management and accept external evaluation or audit by public agencies.

Nor is demonstration enough – there is a clear expectation, usually articulated by government and its agencies, of ascertainable improvement in both productivity and quality, for example in the value of research output and its utility and in graduation rates and other measures of teaching performance. In some instances, no improvement means no funds. Quality and efficiency, however defined, are two key elements in the steering role that governments have increasingly assumed in the wake of devolution of financial and other responsibilities to individual public institutions. For private as well as public institutions, there are also policy and legislative requirements in fields as diverse as health and safety, equity, research ethics, personnel management and many others.

The pressures and reporting requirements are a potent force for change in institutional governance and decision making, summarised as the need for universities to become more entrepreneurial in style and operation (Shattock, 1996; Clark, 1998) with calls by the Association of European Universities amongst others for a better dialogue between the universities and policy makers. As Peter Scott remarked: *"In nearly every country universities have ceased to be regarded as privileged institutions rightly immune from political pressures and the push-and-pull of the market"* (Scott, 1993, p. 46). This changed condition is reflected not only in accountability measures but also in the targeting of funding to meet specific policy objectives.

Not even the most prestigious universities feel secure in the face of challenges to improve the overall quality and social relevance of their work, to make continuing efficiency gains in a highly competitive environment. Competition comes increasingly not only from other higher education institutions within the same jurisdiction but from beyond national borders through the internationalisation/globalisation of higher education.

No less significant for the academic institution is the gathering challenge of non-academic providers – whether in access to knowledge and information, in professional recognition and upgrading, or – through various cross-border partnerships – in the awarding of formal academic qualifications. The American corporate university movement whereby large business corporations, often in association with conventional universities, provide for the continuing education and training of their

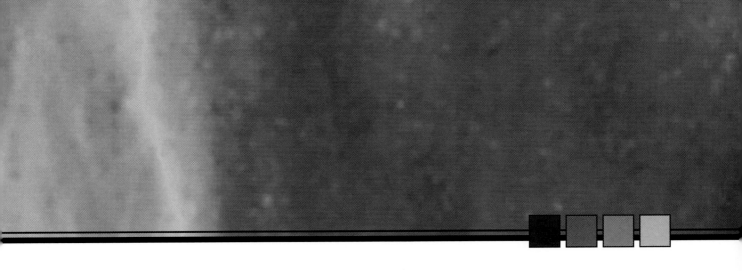

workforce, and sell their services to others is an example of a challenge - and an opportunity. The emerging global virtual university movement is another.

Despite the celebrations by some of Europe's ancient seats of learning on achieving their five hundredth, eight hundredth or even nine hundredth year of age, a question now beginning to surface is whether, indeed, the university as a relatively stable, well-defined centre of teaching and research **has** a future. The ability to connect students with sources of knowledge and to enable them to acquire and use advanced knowledge through the new technologies is sometimes seen as a fundamental challenge to the substantial monopoly enjoyed for centuries by higher education institutions. The licence to teach, which gave the mediaeval universities a powerful position in society, has been enormously broadened through the multiplication of degrees and diplomas over which monoplistic control has been largely sustained thus far. But for how much longer?

In a commentary on the UK, equally relevant to other countries, Webber (2000) affirmed that competitive forces are uppermost in shaping the agenda of universities. *"The next few decades will be very different. Some of the protective monopolies maintained by the state are starting to weaken; the relationships between universities and their students are becoming overtly commercial; the number and range of existing providers has already increased to the point where the higher education cartel is fragmenting; future growth in the student market seems likely to be strongest in new market segments that existing universities may be poorly positioned to address; and technological change is enabling new entrants to challenge the traditional economics of higher education provision and to offer substitute products via new distribution channels"* (Webber, 2000, p. 58).

In considering this kind of comment it must be remembered that universities have never had anything resembling a monopoly in research, or even been able to control the research agenda, except in piecemeal fashion. Specialist research institutes and industry-based centres play major roles. Universities are competing with one another. Such cartels as exist have a limited scope, although recent groupings, notably of research ambitious universities in some countries, may herald a new cartelisation. But universities have enjoyed either a monopoly or dominance in the award of credentials of various kinds. The emergence of qualifications authorities, independent of institutions, could be the beginning of a new competitive environment.

The trends toward specialisation not to say fragmentation of research and of teaching within universities, are a far remove from the ideals of von Humboldt and Newman or more recent theories of liberal education such as those advanced in the

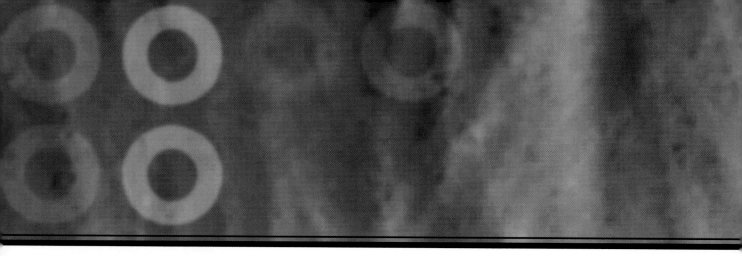

celebrated Harvard Report on *General Education in a Free Society* (Harvard Committee, 1945). Modularisation of courses, models of competence, and extra-institutional mechanisms established to recognise competence and award qualifications all mean that specific learning and research needs can indeed be met in a multiplicity of different ways. These are not of necessity dependent upon the setting of a large, complex, costly institution - the university. Within universities, they have borne witness to the decline of classical - and modern - concepts of liberal education.

What, then, is the future of what to many of its advocates still appears to be - and has been - one of the more stable, and enduring of society's institutions? Mindful of the challenge implicit in this question, universities have begun to see their roles and to set their missions with reference to distinct orientations which, on the one hand, connote a high degree of institutional specialisation and differentiation but, on the other, link them integrally with mainstream intellectual, social, economic and cultural developments.

Through a combination, then, of distinctiveness of type and close alignment with selected socio-economic-cultural trends, and through close practical attention to its own survival and growth requirements, the university at the dawn of the twenty-first century optimistically sees a future for itself. But this future, while it builds on a tradition and past strength and achievements, requires a massive, fresh investment of imagination, thought and energy. New sources of funding are also needed. Neither their whereabouts nor the means of tapping them are obvious. The challenges faced by higher education in the final third of the twentieth century were but a prelude to those that lie immediately ahead.

Authorities differ in what they take to be the key challenges, questions or issues confronting higher education although certain themes recur frequently in the literature. Taylor, in a review of trends and issues in the context of the first years (undergraduate level) of higher education prepared for the OECD study *Redefining Tertiary Education* (OECD, 1998d) posed six questions:

- What is the appropriate **scale of participation**
- How should tertiary education be **funded**
- What changes are needed in **boundaries** (different levels, types of education institutions) to facilitate access and maximise resource effectiveness
- How is **quality** best measured
- What are the implications of the **new technologies**
- How can **accountability** be best handled

(Taylor, 1996).

28

From a European-wide perspective, the Association of Rectors of European Universities (CRE) in its *Strategy for Action 1995-98* outlined five key areas of challenge:

- Improving **quality**
- **Restructuring** the university
- **Financing** the university
- Linking with **society**
- Reinforcing **cohesion** among universities

(Association of European Universities, 1995)

In elaborating the restructuring challenge, CRE alluded to demands for accountability and to intensifying competition to the once information-privileged position of the universities. This comes mainly from new technologies and through open and distance learning opportunities made available by private providers. According to CRE, this competition is *"the single biggest issue confronting universities"* (*ib*. p. 4). Many universities have yet to heed this wake up call.

Academic administrators and officials with financial and funding responsibility have specific perspectives on the challenge to universities. For them there are essentially two issues: the diversification of sources of funds; and the readiness of academic staff of universities to come to grips with what is often characterised as an impending funding crisis. Declining levels of "core" funding from public sources relative to costs have resulted in a great array of commercial and quasi-commercial activities whose implications are often poorly understood by academic staff. Where universities are heavily dependent on fee income, political pressures to moderate fee increases mean that ever closer attention must be given to cost management.

Such developments as the recruitment, internationally, of full fee paying students, the sale of intellectual property, tendering for contracts and the operation of a range of commercial services have come to be seen as not just attractive options but as essential means of raising revenue. Entrepreneurship in these directions is not always being matched by sound management for which many of the staff involved have had little preparation. Cost consciousness and financial management are singled out by senior administrators as major problems in Australian universities requiring attention across the whole institution (Elliott, 2000; Karmel, 2000).

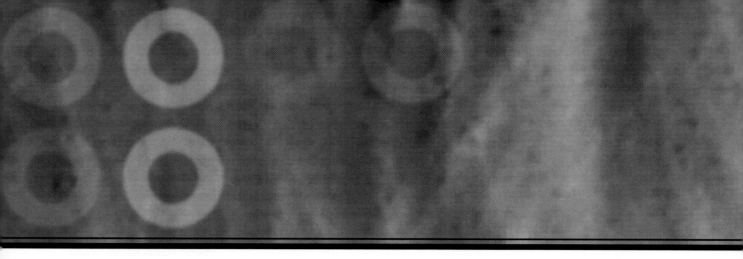

Challenges which entail system-wide approaches

The key challenges to the universities are not confined to the above sets of substantive matters or to single institutions. They entail a reorientation of the whole system. Indeed it is reasonable to ask whether what may be needed is the very creation of a system out of the existing diffuse collection of individual, competitive institutions.

System-wide policies and collective action by universities are said to be called for: to address national needs and priorities; to provide assurance of standards and quality; to ensure public accountability; to achieve synergies and economies of scale; and so forth. Such policies already exist, for example, in setting entry requirements, or in funding formulae, but in some countries, Ireland included, they have not gone far beyond that. Recent Irish legislation and a series of moves to strengthen the policy environment are steps toward a more co-ordinated, systemic approach. The Irish universities will need to prepare themselves for a more pro-active role if they are to have a significant input to these developments.

A leading Australian academic administrator and former head of the Tertiary Education Commission, Peter Karmel, referred to the systemic perspective as a paradigm shift that occurred in Australia in the late '80s with the establishment of a unified national system from the two separate streams of colleges of advanced education/ institutes of technology and universities. The shift had two aspects, first, the creation of a **system** with specified objectives and priorities centrally determined by government, i.e. 'an environment of compliance', and, second, an increasing emphasis on education as an instrument of economic policy (Karmel, 1993). Both points are highly apposite to widespread developments across the OECD countries in the course of the 90s. There is an evident need both to increase the power or capability of universities, through more and stronger partnerships, cooperative ventures both national and international to achieve critical mass, and to further develop system-wide priorities and strategies. Karmel's language reveals that it was not the universities that were in control; it is significant that in these developments (including Australia in the late '80s) the universities often find themselves ill-prepared, deficient in vital information and a grasp of the politico-bureaucratic realities.

...In face of emerging public policy priorities, both economic and social ...

Systems, once established as such, have increasingly been brought under the spotlight of public policy priorities. The reports of the Mjoes Committee in Norway, the Dearing Committee in the United Kingdom and the West Committee in Australia are recent examples of national strategic goal setting. The Swedish concept of a knowledge society is another and European ministers of education, in the Bologna Declaration envisage an emerging knowledge region: Knowledge Europe.

In a government-initiated (but independent) higher education management review, some seven years after the Australian unified system was established, the 'academic enterprise' was enjoined to take a fresh look at itself and (*inter alia*) to:

- 'balance the traditional benefits of collaboration and collegiality with an environment of increasing competition for domestic and overseas students, staff, research funds, industry support and status...'
- take into account the shifting emphasis of government priorities towards the expansion of the vocational education and training sector ...
- [recognise] ever-increasing attention to quality assurance mechanisms and the repositioning of the student as a customer or client ...
- focus closely on flexibility in curriculum development and delivery ...
- balance the incentives for more applied research while preserving the traditional role of university research as the
- independent pursuit of basic knowledge'

(Committee of Inquiry, 1995, pp. 2-3).

In Ireland, after a decade of intensive policy analysis, there are now legislative frameworks, a broad set of national goals and priorities, a substantial augmentation of the national research budget, targeted funding and an array of specific policy initiatives, to which the universities can relate the strategic planning that they are now called upon to undertake (see Part III below).

The bending of higher education priorities to meet explicit national economic policy objectives was already becoming apparent in several countries in the '80s: *"The most visible new demand falling on higher education in the United States is the need to be more effective in an economy that is for the first time truly international. .. The jolt of growing completion ... the importance of research and new technologies and the growth of jobs; the need for scientific and technical talent ..."* (Newman, 1985 p.xiii) were among the agenda items (correctly) forecast for growing attention in the nineties. Reference to the internationalisation of the economy was also a foreshadowing of one of the contemporary preoccupations of higher education, namely globalisation, its impact and opportunities.

...For which a succession of international reports provides a focus...

The economic pull is everywhere apparent in discussions of university priorities. It goes a long way towards explaining the systemic thrust in the paradigm shift Karmel had in mind and it gives impetus to the steering role that governments are seeking to adopt. As a challenge to universities, the economic imperative has for decades been strongly and consistently argued by the OECD, representing Member governments in Europe, North America (now central America as well),

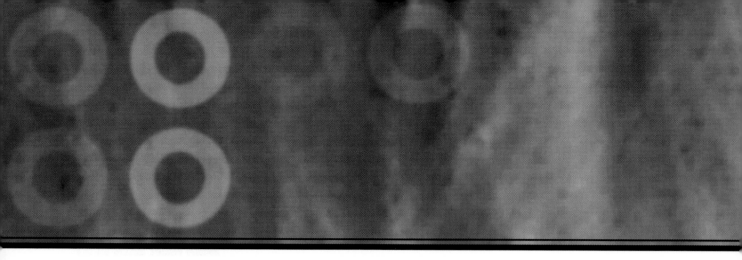

Australia, New Zealand and, in Asia, Japan (now Korea too). At an international conference in 1981, the rapid growth of higher education in the post war years, together with the need to maintain and further develop its dynamic, led the report authors to the prescient observation that *"in the period ahead, governments will be led to adopt more active roles and explicit policies in the development of higher education"* (OECD, 1983, p. 21). Comparison is instructive on this point with perspectives and the tone of the 1974 OECD report *Policies for Higher Education*, arising from the 1973 International Conference on Future Structures for Post-Secondary Education. Whereas in 1974 the OECD document (parts of it written by Martin Trow), retains a strong flavour of the self-contained university world, its needs and expectations; by the '80s it is the government's and the public's needs and expectations and the economic agenda that had come to the fore. They have remained a dominant motif to the present day, a necessary but not a sufficient condition for the future well being of the universities.

A major consideration for the OECD in the report of its 1981 international conference was how to mediate between the inner working of the university and external factors like overcoming the economic crisis of the '70s. In part this was to be through more industry-related higher education research and meeting skills-for-employment needs. Expectations for higher education were that it:

a) respond to new needs at local and community level;

b) contribute to revitalising the economy by producing the 'right' kinds of highly qualified manpower and contribute to the further training of the labour force in the context of rapidly changing technologies;

c) sustain adequate levels of technological innovation through scientific research;

d) help to promote greater social equity, at a time when the more deprived sections of the population are hardest hit by the economic situation (OECD, 1983, p. 13).

A key point was what was termed *"an internal crisis of purpose"*. In his subsequent study, for the OECD, William Taylor spoke of *"the catholicity of a university's mission, the variety of roles that it performs, the many different functions that it serves"*, as the crux of the problem of identity. But he also remarked that these characteristics have contributed to the university's remarkable ability to survive the vicissitudes of the centuries (Taylor, 1987, p. 14).

The 'catholicity of mission' - or 'supercomplexity' (Barnett, 2000) - is a timely reminder that there are considerable risks in a one-sided devotion to an economic agenda however important that is within the overall mission and activities of the university. The diminution of a broader cultural role and of a capacity to sustain an independent critical role would be a serious loss to society as well as a threat to the institution's adaptability to changing social circumstances and priorities (Coolahan, 2000).

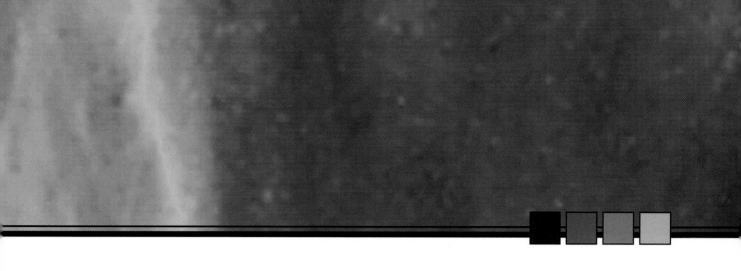

Meeting at ministerial level in 1990, the OECD Education Committee issued a joint communique on the major challenges for education and training for the '90s. Without singling out higher education, ministers felt that the systems were insufficiently responsive, too slow in adapting to the new landscapes. They declared a need for greater:

- recognition of the centrality of education and training in economic and social progress;
- awareness of the impact internationally of global environmental and health problems;
- awareness of the changing international environment affecting the movement of labour and migration;
- awareness of the newly industrialised economies outside the OECD area;
- development of an educated citizenry participating in 'information' societies.

(OECD, 1990; Skilbeck 1998).

In the latest of the OECD line of international studies of higher education, in 1998 the authors of *Redefining Tertiary Education* examined the consequences and implications of the massive increases in enrolment for the 'first years'. One conclusion was that, despite enormous pressures, the tertiary education systems of the ten countries reviewed in the course of the study had demonstrated flexibility, initiative and a robust approach in addressing major problems of growth and adaptation. These qualities, it was suggested, would be even more in demand in future (OECD, 1998d).

A more disturbing picture, world-wide, emerged from the voluminous reports and studies prepared for the 1998 UNESCO World Conference on Higher Education. While the relatively small number of countries in the 'industrially advanced' sector, and some others were showing a great capacity for mastering the challenges, in many poorer, less developed countries there is a gathering crisis of resources, quality, sustainability - and confidence. This is not irrelevant to universities more fortunately placed in thriving economies and stable societies - such as Ireland. The global crisis of higher education means that national and international development projects and programmes are at risk, mobility becomes one way, research partnerships are jeopardised, expectations of a global sharing of ideas and information cannot be fulfiled, and gaps widen (Kearney, 2000; The Task Force on Higher Education and Society, 2000; Joint Working Group, 2000).

But there are many cross currents and concerns to be resolved...

For the OECD countries, the trends of policy or practice have neither been uncomplicated nor free of confusion and uncertainty. In the words of the former Minister for Education in Finland Olli-Pekka Heinonen, there is in reality *"a crossfire of expectations' - promoting the economy and meeting high level employment requirements; devising solutions to global environmental problems; serving as strong cultural centres - and others including meeting social equity goals, ...trail blazers in society as*

33

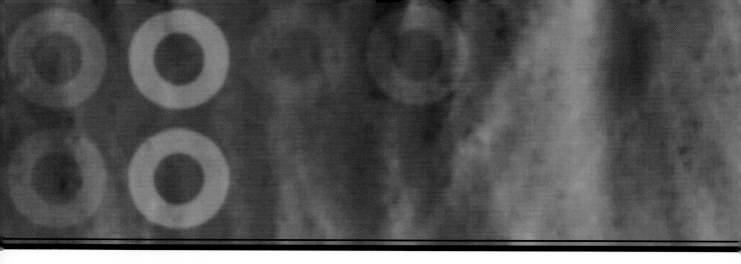

well as social critics; [universities] should change and preserve; they should promote both national culture and the economy; they should create optimism in the face of resource cuts; they should have faith in research and education at a time of high unemployment; they should be regional, national and global at the same time." (Heinonen, 1997, p. 17).

Commenting on the contemporary cohabiting phenomena of strategic steering, devolution and accountability, a Norwegian analyst remarked: *"The reforms in state governance structures are full of contradictions. Decisions and responsibility are delegated to institutions, but the state does not lose its authority. Traditional state bureaucratic regulations are broken down, while management on institutional and departmental levels is strengthened. Reforms in the higher education governance structure are characterised by both increased academic self-regulation and increased managerialism. This is the ambiguous arena in which evaluation systems are introduced"* (Smeby, 1996, p. 14)

Not so much featured in the literature of the nineteen-nineties as in that of the nineteen-sixties and-seventies, is the theme of 'more means worse', jeremiad of the critics of major waves of expanding enrolments of that period. Their argument usually posited a limited 'pool of ability'. 'Worse' meant that quality of (average) learning standards of performance would fall with an enlarged student intake. Since the so-called 'Golden Age' of funding in the sixties, universities in most countries have experienced steady, sometimes very large reductions in the 'unit of resource' whereby much larger numbers of students are being taught at a lower cost per capita. Thus the argument has shifted from the unsustainable claim about a fixed 'pool of ability' to the impact upon the quality of service that universities can in reality provide their large intakes of students in the wake of eroding funding levels.

In 1994 Frans van Vught, at the time head of the Centre for Higher Education Policy at the University of Twente, one of Europe's leading centres of its kind, drew pessimistic conclusions in a study of participation rates and funding levels in seven OECD countries (France, Germany, Great Britain, Japan, the Netherlands, Sweden, USA). Notwithstanding the infusion of new, mainly private funds into research, universities were experiencing critical funding problems for teaching: *"the teaching function will bear the full burden of future reductions in public higher education funding, as it has already done in the recent past. Combined with the trend to increasing participation this will lead to catastrophic effects in the foreseeable future: institutions will no longer be able to provide adequate education as available funds, under unchanged circumstances, will become absolutely insufficient to provide the necessary infrastructure of staff, support services and teacher-related developmental research"* (van Vught, 1994, p. 5).

This dire warning has been heeded - although without real appreciation of the additional capital and recurrent costs entailed - but in quite diverse ways, rarely if ever including a restoration of earlier funding levels. Some countries have

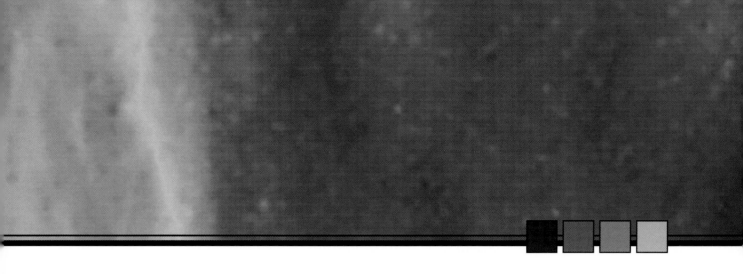

tightened limits on enrolments. Many have begun to take the possibilities of technology assisted or augmented teaching and learning more seriously. Student tuition fees and other charges have been introduced or increased, and grants-in-aid of various kinds reduced. Advantage has been taken by institutions of cross-funding, made possible by high fees for international students and the sale of services. Many systems have moved to establish more formal ways of enhancing efficiency including financial penalties for unduly protracted study or attrition and new procedures for assessing the cost effectiveness and the quality of the education provided by institutions.

There is a widely held view that, despite all these and other efforts to increase revenue and contain costs, there is a continuing financial crisis. It is not possible to say, on the basis of systematic evidence, whether in fact 'adequate education' is being provided. There are conflicting views and the evidence is inconclusive. On the one hand, defenders (usually in ministries of higher education) of performance-based funding and other efficiency measures are apt to claim that there has been no loss of teaching quality or decline in standards of student learning. On the other hand, the literature provides many examples of mounting pressure on staff through increased teaching loads and more numerous reporting and administrative requirements, with concern expressed about the impact on the quality of teaching and learning.

Class sizes for undergraduates particularly have increased; very often staff-student contact has been reduced. Attrition rates, insofar as they can be ascertained, are often high and there is evidence of some increases in countries which have enjoyed low rates in the past. Attrition is difficult to estimate since statistical returns seldom acknowledge completion of courses or units as distinct from years or whole degrees and rates are affected by the proportion of part-time, distance education students who have higher non-completion rates and by mature age students who aim to complete only part of the programme. Allowing for all this, rates of dropout, failure and standards are cause for concern. Despite the frequent, ominous warnings from university leaders about a threat to overall quality of teaching and learning the lack of well researched evidence on standards means that on this important question answers must be tentative pending the studies that are badly needed.

The increasingly competitive research environment and the role of research in determining institutional status in many countries means that staff are under great pressure to strengthen their research profiles. There are not the same incentives to improve teaching. However, universities have aimed to respond to these situations through a series of innovations including the better preparation of academic staff for their teaching roles and the strengthening of various student support and service facilities. There is further discussion of these matters in the chapter below on 'Encounters'.

...In light of the multiple functions of higher education...

It is important in assessing the continuing debate over expansion and the resourcing, efficiency and quality issues to bear in mind the multiple functions of higher education and the increasingly varied and numerous ways these are being resourced. In an account of international trends in higher education, Swedish educator, Torsten Husen enumerated five main purposes of universities in the contemporary world:

- Training professionals;
- Providing a repository for wisdom;
- Generating new knowledge;
- Serving as a 'public utility';
- Helping protect free speech and democratic practice.

(Husen, 1994).

There is a tension in recent debates about directions universities should take: between their traditional and much prized cultural critical/liberal education roles and their constant adjustment to socio-economic pressures, particularly workforce preparation and economic returns to research. This is not a new tension - it has been apparent since early in the nineteenth century with the parallel development of the intellectual theories and the establishment of new universities already referred to. Any worthwhile scenario for the future of universities must incorporate cultural space for this debate and provide for the continued vitality of a broad range of academic values and not just those perceived to be of immediate relevance and utility.

But a declaration of the importance of cultural critiques and breadth as well as depth is not enough. It is reasonable to ask whether university specialisation and professionalisation do in fact provide sufficient scope for critical debate and inquiry on the great issues of the day: the impact of globalisation; the uses of technology; the ethical and social frontiers of bio-technology; the exploitation of people and of natural resources; increasing inequality within and among nations and so on. Such issues may be raised in certain conferences and symposia and in some journals, and in debates about liberal arts curricula and general education courses, mainly in the USA. However, more often than not they receive scant attention in the policy literature and in what students actually study. The universities may not be adequately performing the roles of intellectual leader and moral critic in the public domain and framework of general culture. There is a sense in the community that too often they remain preoccupied with their own needs, especially for public funds, and their specialist interests.

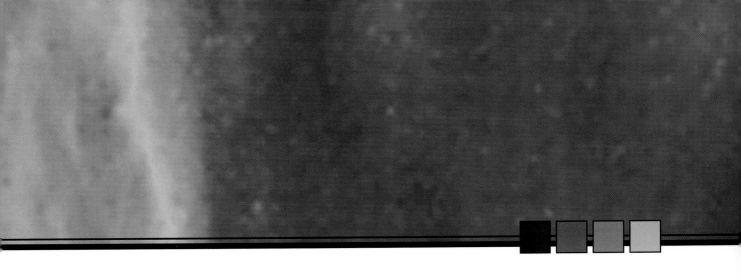

Cultural criticism, intellectual and moral leadership tend to run counter to the predominance of economic concerns. As already indicated, the mainstream of OECD thinking has been centred on the economic or 'utility' function, of developing human capital in part through technology and other applications of knowledge, in part through continuous upgrading of skills and competences, and in the solution of social problems. This preoccupation derives from the specific role of the Organisation - economic and economic-related data collection and policy analysis. But it also reflects the dominance of economic considerations in much of contemporary life.

Universities are naturally and unavoidably significant economic players and their economic roles are receiving ever closer attention. Thus there is an interest in demonstrating how they generate economic activity, notably in their regions. To illustrate: an independent study of the impact of higher education on the economy, commissioned by the Committee of Scottish Higher Education Principals, showed that higher education in Scotland in 1993/4 generated gross output of £2.47 billion, £1.2 billion of which is the output of higher education institutions and the remainder the multiplier output generated in other Scottish sectors (McNicoll, 1995). In a survey of sixteen studies conducted over a 20 year period, Brown and Heaney (1997) documented substantial benefits of tertiary education institutions on local economies, including their impact on jobs, regional incomes and the skills base.

Assuming the accuracy and reliability of these and similar findings, it is coming to be recognised that a major function of higher education is to serve as an economic catalyst and generator. Universities materially contribute, through research, technology transfer, the education of highly skilled personnel, industry partnerships, sale of services and other ways of fostering innovation, increasing productivity and sustaining a range of economic functions. Increasingly, they are expected to demonstrate capability in these respects. This is certainly the view taken in Australia and the United Kingdom, for example, in respect of the economic impact of the higher education 'industry' including as an export earner through the sale of services via fee paying international students and contracts.

Important as new and more diverse sources of revenue can be - and they have been relatively under-utilised in Ireland - the general line of argument is more broadly based. With governments moderating their own level of inputs - which they have been doing since the '70s (Millett, 1978, p. 17) - industry and the universities have combined forces to argue for a better appreciation of the economic value of higher education in the competitive international environment: *"to compete in the global market place the UK economy must rely primarily on translating human brain power into advanced processes and high added-value on goods and services. This means that trained minds are needed to inject creativity, analytical ability and inventiveness across whole organisations"* (Smithers and Robinson, 1996a, p. 3).

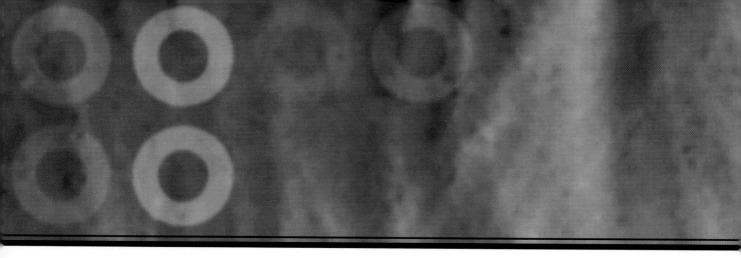

Similar sentiments have been widely expressed throughout the '90s and continue to resonate in the corridors of power. When so many countries are taking this line, they are competing with one another, in seeking to raise the standard of their educational systems and the performance of institutions. For any one country (and institution) this underlines the value of benchmarking and a constant endeavour to effect improvements. For Ireland, the implications are clear. It, too, is competing in the international market place and the quality of its human resources must be judged not against purely internal criteria or past levels of attainment, but by international standards.

And what of the tradition of detached, untrammeled inquiry ...?

How well the implications and consequences of this utilitarian approach mesh with longer established expectations and viewpoints about the functions and values of universities is, as already indicated, a matter of debate. Knowledge takes different forms and its values and varied uses are not all immediately apparent. It is worth returning to the debate since further consideration of the issues will show that what may appear to be conflicting conceptions of the university and its mission may be based on a false dichotomy.

The two most notable figures in the establishment of the by now classic, European-derived concept of the university, are the intellectual and state official, Wilhelm von Humboldt in Germany at the beginning of the nineteenth century, and the intellectual and church leader, John Henry Newman in England and Ireland in the middle of that century. Both grounded their views about the purpose and nature of universities in the pursuit of knowledge as of value in itself. But knowledge is of many different kinds and forms as they very well understood.

Although these luminaries differed in the meaning they attached to knowledge and the forms taken in the knowledge quest, the ideal in each case was inquiry, in a calm setting for detached reflection, analysis and creative thought. Members of universities, whether staff or students, were to be united in pursuing knowledge which is a function alike of research or scholarship and of teaching and learning. The value and uses of knowledge in society were seen as integral to the quest. The knowledge workers, however, required the freedom and independence provided by the university as a place of inquiry.

Thus von Humboldt and Newman recognised a multitude of linkages between the university and the wider society, including practical applications and uses of knowledge. But the university was conceived as having its own, distinctive mission. It enshrined values that stood in their own right as part of the mosaic of structures and processes in an essentially pluralistic concept of culture. Their conception of the mission and role of the university in society has become canonical embedded in what are now, however, struggling concepts of untrammeled inquiry and liberal education which are in danger of being submerged because they are taken to be self-serving and irrelevant.

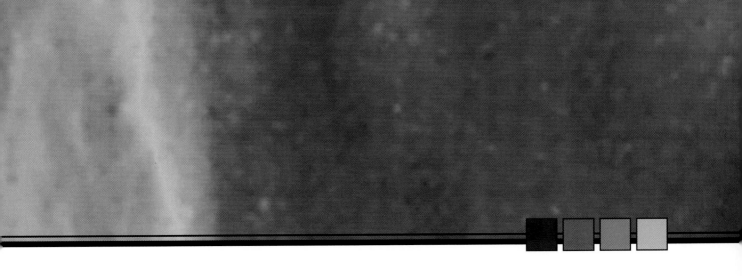

Particularly for the Humboldtian view the autonomy of the university and freedom of inquiry – to teach and learn – were of fundamental importance (Pritchard, 1998; Rothblatt, 1989; Sorkin, 1983). For Newman, writing at a time when the two ancient English universities of Oxford and Cambridge were distinguished neither for research nor teaching, it was critically important in the establishment of a Catholic university in Dublin – to whose end he devoted his *Idea of a University* – that the youth be nurtured through an idealised or elevated version of the Oxford tutorial system in an environment of high intellectual and moral culture (Newman, 1856, 1943; Ker, 1988, ch.9).

Appeal to Humboldtian or Newmanist ideas and principles has featured in the history of universities in many parts of the world to the present day and cannot be dismissed as an appeal to the authority of the past. Burton Clark (1995), for example, has continued to take up the cudgels on behalf of 'the development of knowledge' as the primary mission of the universities. As mentioned above, the impact of other concepts of higher education – whether civic, economic, or nationalistic – have often prevailed in practice, but they do not provide an alternative. Instead the various purposes and uses of the university need to be continually informed by intellectual and moral standards for which other sources than current social needs are required.

The university is not only an idea – or rather a complex of interwoven idea and ideals – and a set of processes of learning. It is quintessentially also an institution and a way of life for its increasingly numerous members and those it serves, with recognisable forms and patterns of behaviour. Scholarly detachment is not for the purpose of aloofness but an essential condition of inquiry and the growth of knowledge from which the whole society stands to benefit. The claims for academic freedom and university autonomy are not absolute but require a recognition of obligations and the relation of the university to the wider society (Moodie, 1996).

...The tradition of free enquiry has evolved

Late in the nineteenth century, in Germany, science and education were explicitly recognised as the 'fourth factor of production' alongside land, labour and capital (von Brock, 1991, p. 273). This foreshadowing of contemporary theories of the knowledge-based economy was most visibly expressed in Germany in the strengthening and regularising of higher education and research, and the emergence of the concept of science policy (*Wissenschaftspolitik*), developments which also, however, imposed much greater government control on the universities. In the USA the German influence led to the establishment of the great graduate schools based on ideas assimilated by the thousands of Americans who studied in Germany post Civil War. At the same time, in the land grant colleges and universities for example, new forms of professional and technical education of great social and economic significance were developed.

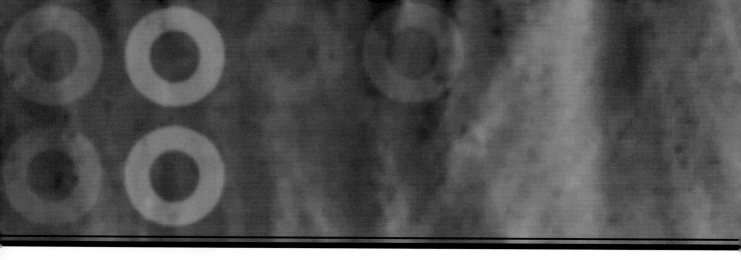

It must also not be forgotten that one of the architects of the classical canon, Newman, acknowledged the educational value of the varied, sophisticated culture of the metropolis: the libraries, academies, journals, meetings, places, scientific congresses, parliament and so forth that he designated a 'sort of necessary university'. He added - anticipating a piece of late 20th century usage - that we cannot do without such 'virtual universities' (Newman, 1856, p. 14).

Many features of the classical canon are now seen in some quarters as not only arcane but irrelevant. From several sources they are under quite fundamental challenge. The challenge is a mixture of specific developments and theories of culture. It includes technologies for the assembly, storage and transmitting of knowledge, specialised non-university institutions of research and scholarship, segmentation and specialisation of knowledge, the commercialisation of discoveries through patents, the dominance of economic goals and purposes, and a transformation in modern society and culture expressed in Lyotard's view of the 'post-modern' condition as 'the temporary contract supplanting permanent institutions'. The contemporary university, often defined as a modern institution (and not a post-modern one) (Barnett, 1992a) is thus vulnerable to those changes and developments which are fragmenting institutions and relationships across whole tracts of contemporary social, economic and cultural life.

The university in question?

How solid, durable and permanent is the huge concentration of intellectual capital, the lecture halls, laboratories, offices, libraries, social and recreational spaces that are today often a landmark - sometimes centuries old in semi-rural parkland or privileged urban sites? Can they retain their hold on the imagination and command the respect and resources so necessary for their continued vitality? Will they withstand what some see as a crisis of confidence, others as a steady erosion of their central role in the formation and application of advanced knowledge? If the form remains, how different will the substance be? Does the concept of university find equal expression in the latest virtual university or private business college as in Bologna, Oxford, Harvard, Trinity?

These questions - whether in the radical form of an incipient questioning of the meaning or substance of a term so variously applied, or of the need for universities at all, or of a growing concern about their role and means of support - are now quite definitely on the agenda. The universities themselves have not shirked the questioning and have already begun to map out a variety of scenarios which will, they believe, underpin their fundamental role in society and ensure their future. But the university of the future will not any more be able to claim the whole realm of advanced knowledge which Newman regarded as their domain - nor the intellectual pinnacle so prized by Humboldt, as their *raison d'etre*. While many universities will survive and prosper, it is not at all clear that all will or need do so. Many are languishing or in sharp decline in some parts of the world, and everywhere pressures are mounting.

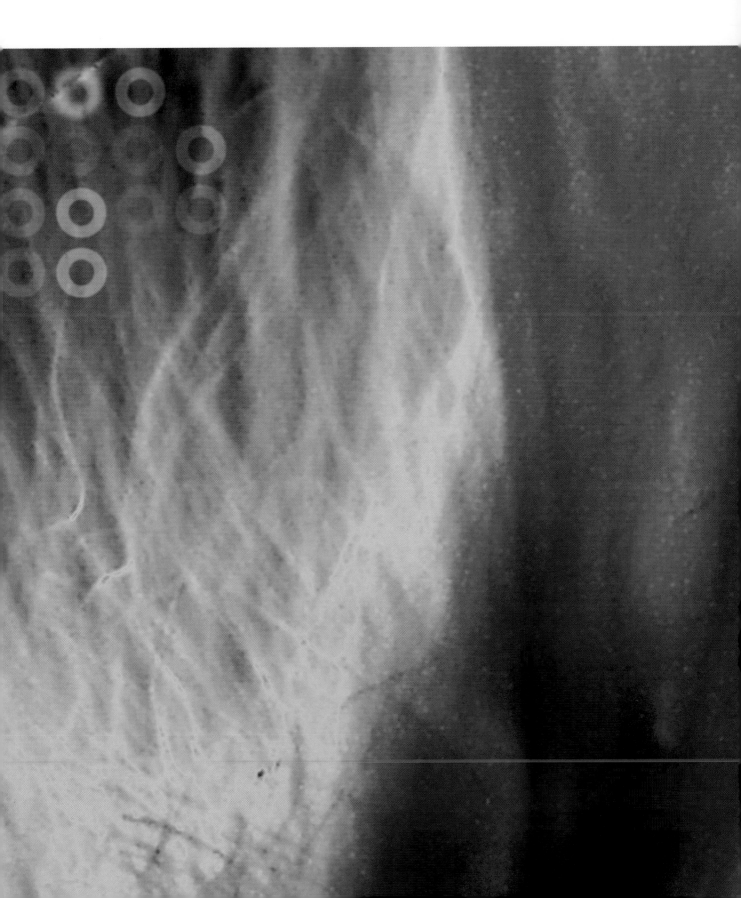

part II | The Trends and Issues Examined

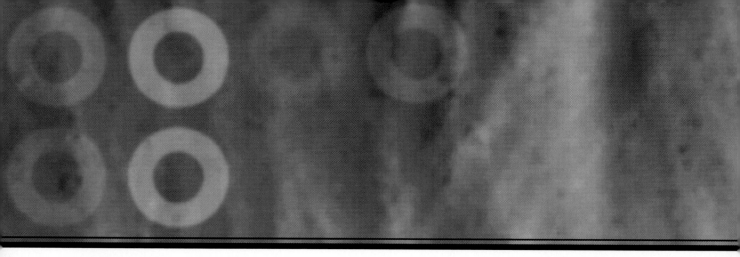

Expansion

'In the mid-nineteenth century approximately 100 names a year were added to the Register (of graduates of the University of London). In 1999 there were nearly 30,000' (University of London, 2000, p. 10)

The OECD review of trends in the first years of tertiary education in ten (later twelve) Member countries (OECD, 1998d) singled out increasing enrolments and expansion of the sector as the most decisive change of recent decades. It has far-reaching policy implications and has swiftly changed the institutional landscape.

The main factor driving expansion of enrolments in OECD countries is not population increase but higher participation rates, as shown in the following chart (and see Appendix).

■ Contribution of changing population size
■ Contribution of changing enrolment rate
◇ Absolute change in tertiary enrolment

Chart C3.3. Index of change in the number of students at the tertiary level between 1990 and 1997, and contribution of demographic changes and changing enrolment rates to the change in tertiary enrolment (1990=100)

The absolute change in tertiary enrolment since 1990 (diamonds) is a result of changes in both population size (light bars) and enrolment rates (dark bars).

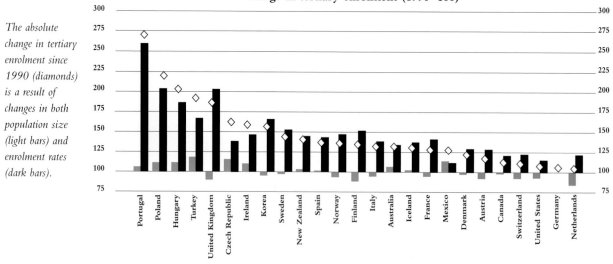

Countries are ranked in descending order of the absolute change in enrolment. Data for 1990 and 1997 follow the ISCED 76 definitions.
Source: OECD (2000) Education at a Glance. OECD Indicators Education and Skills. Paris. OECD. Chart 3.3 p. 154.

Ireland is one of the countries with the largest increases in the period 1990-1997 and also the one country with Belgium/Flanders where entry to university typically occurs immediately after the completion of upper secondary education. In others – Australia, Iceland, Hungary, Norway, Sweden and New Zealand – more than 20% of first time entrants to university are 27 years of age or older (OECD, 2000, pp. 154–156). Mature age participation is highly significant for a variety of social and economic reasons and in the framework of lifelong learning and professional development policies is set to increase.

While numerous forces have been at work over several decades, in generating enrolment increases, three that are closely inter-related stand out:

- The aspirations of individuals in the 'education century';
- Socio-economic demand for a highly skilled, competent work force and citizenry;
- Growing recognition of the role of advanced knowledge and its applications in underpinning modern civilisation.

The OECD review of tertiary education was designed, not only to document and analyse growth and reflect on its causes but to pinpoint issues and problems countries were experiencing and ways of addressing them. Among problems that were identified were: the mounting pressures exerted on the traditional university; on its resources, and capabilities; its priorities in teaching and research; its capacity to adapt and diversify; and its readiness to enter into partnerships and other innovative ways of responding to demand, both social and individual. Similar issues, on a global scale, were the subject of the World Conference on Higher Education organised by UNESCO in 1998. But no simple causal model suffices to explain the scale and nature of growth. What is more, that growth is not simply a response to socio-economic change, it is a source of further change (Aamodt, 2000).

Enrolments have dramatically increased...

The growth of enrolments in the second half of the twentieth century is often singled out as giving rise to the most complex and crucial issues in higher education. It represent a profound qualitative change not just quantitative growth. As expressed in the words of Martin Trow, a leading American authority on international trends: *"Since the Second World War the central problem for higher education in most Western industrial societies has been how to transform the small elite university systems of the nineteenth and first half of the twentieth centuries into the systems of mass higher education required to meet the growing demands both for wider access, from segments of their societies, and for more highly trained and educated workers for their labour markets"* (Trow, 1994b, p. 111).

Similar comments were made, in the early '70s by Bereday (1973) and in the course of the major studies of higher education conducted under the auspices of the Carnegie Commission on Policy Studies in Higher Education (1980). Lionel Robbins, himself chairman of the committee which produced the celebrated expansionist report on higher education in the UK in 1963, remarked on the phenomenon of growth, in a preface he wrote to a book which linked the

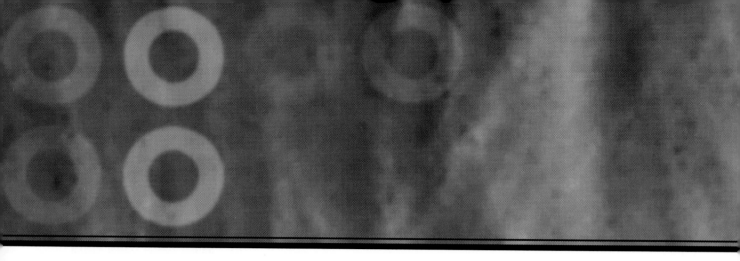

Carnegie findings to Western European experience. He called the rate of increase in enrolments 'prodigious', finding in expansion *"the centre of gravity of the main problems with which both the labours of the Carnegie Commission and this commentary upon them are concerned"* (Embling, 1974, p. x).

In 1974, reporting on an OECD conference on post-secondary education, Martin Trow produced a model of student enrolments in higher education systems designed to capture the expansion then in full swing in many countries and to explain a number of qualitative changes as percentage figures rose. Higher education is at the **elite** stage, according to Trow, when its student population is less than 15% of the relevant age group; it is at the mass stage when the percentage rises to between 15% and 35%; and it is at the **universal** stage when the figure reaches 35%. Trow expected that in this progression over time, higher education systems would *"expand their goals, diversify their structures and attract clientele from increasingly diverse segments of the population"* (OECD, 1974; Trow, 1976b). 'More' in this context, does not mean more of the same. With a greatly enlarged clientele drawn into the institutions, new and different subjects, courses and ways of organising teaching and new cadres of teachers and researchers, are introduced. Nor did more students usually mean correspondingly more money as institutional administrators dealing with marginal funding and declining unit cost regimes have discovered.

Absolute growth in numbers is only part of the story. Whole new cohorts have entered universities: mature age; part-time; specific equity categories; huge numbers of first generation tertiary level students, and so on. Growth has also come in waves: a '60s wave, a '90s wave, and it has affected different subjects and institutions differently. Old institutions have expanded, new ones been established, a multiplicity of types of provider has emerged, private and public.

...And there is a new *Zeitgeist*

As telling as were the Trow percentages of the '70s - now completely overtaken by events - is the Zeitgeist: *"mass higher education countries are defined as those in which a spirit of universal attendance prevails, even though there is not always enough tenacity to enforce this spirit"* (Bereday, 1973, p. 3). The three decades since these appraisals of trends and needs were made can be characterised as a steady, albeit at times uneven cultural shift whereby in the industrially advanced nations at least, participation in tertiary education in one form or another, at some time in the life cycle, will become the norm, the common expectation across the whole society. This is a signal that expansion in enrolments is not simply a function of the demography of the school leaving cohort and the level of qualification attained at that stage. It is set to continue, and policy and resource planning need to be well grounded in a framework of lifelong learning for all (OECD, 1999, ch.1).

Few people thirty years ago anticipated either the rate or the nature of expansion, whereby across much of the OECD membership universal participation on Trow's model would be either attained or within reach at the turn of the century. To the contrary, there were firm predictions of a downturn in line with demographic decline (Barblan and Sadlak, 1988, p. 4). It was not well understood at the time that expansion would be achieved in ways other than a continuing increase in the volume of the 'age relevant' cohort. Indeed the term 'age relevant' has already lost utility in a number of countries. Four factors are important in understanding the mix of quantitative and qualitative changes in participation rates: a substantial rate of increase by mature age (adult) students studying part-time; in several countries, a clear majority of women enrollees; greatly increased retention and success rates in upper secondary education; and the redefining of entry streams into higher education to include so-called vocational and general streams. In addition, from the late '50s and '60s onwards, there were the stirrings of significant equity and social justice movements which were to lead to policies designed to increase participation rates of several categories typically and severely under-represented in higher education (Skilbeck, 2000).

A consequence of growth, still to receive adequate attention, is the implication that those not gaining access to tertiary education will be, somehow, disadvantaged. While the practicality and value of everyone receiving tertiary education can be questioned, as participation rates increase, and the benefits of tertiary education become more apparent, the issue of those not participating becomes sharper.

The demographic profile in Ireland has led some to predict a decline in tertiary enrolments at a time when there is continuing labour market demand for highly educated and trained personnel. These predictions may prove incorrect since there is scope to further improve secondary level completion and success rates, to vary entry requirements, to increase enrolments of mature age students and to increase enrolments of fee paying international students. Several of these options are under active consideration (Conference of the Heads of Irish Universities, 1998; Commission on the Points System, 1999). Experience of other countries suggests that there is a range of policy directions to pursue in both generating demand and diversifying the supply of tertiary education. These include a reconceptualising of the 'age relevant' cohort and a broadening of the socially responsive and service roles of the institutions.

In the country that pioneered the expansion move, the USA, already in the 1970s massive enrolment increases were being experienced. Between 1969 and 1979 there was a 42% increase in the number of college students from 7,976,834 to 11,669,429 (data from the US National Center for Education Statistics, cited in Levine, 1980). The same data sets showed a significant increase in part-time enrolments, from 31% in 1969 to 41% in 1979; moreover, more than half of all

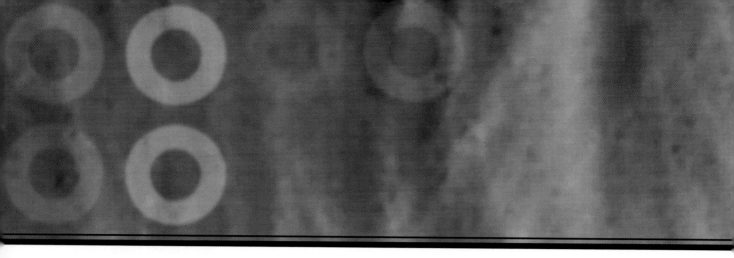

undergraduates worked at jobs while attending college. Such figures presaged trends in many countries as well as the US in the following decades, to the present day.

...Which has grown out of the factors promoting access

As mentioned above, no simple causal model of a one-way growth is adequate. What is important to understand, though, is just how, through the growth process, universities in many countries have greatly extended their linkages, the degree to which they are entwined with a complex of forces in contemporary society. A series of educational reforms and initiatives helps explain the increased demand for access and, in turn, reflects higher participation rates:

- The progressive raising of the permitted age for leaving school and associated pressures and incitements to youth to 'stay in education';
- The restructuring of upper secondary education, increasing and clearing pathways from school into some form of tertiary education;
- Financial inducements to families and students for whom protracted study has been an unacceptable alternative to paid employment;
- Programmes to assist and enable defined equity groups to complete secondary and embark on tertiary study;
- Bridging and special access programmes to help students attain the standards of learning appropriate to tertiary entrance;
- Improved counselling and guidance services;
- Adjustments to tertiary admission requirements and more flexible arrangements regarding attendance at tertiary courses;
- Concentration of tutorial and support services in tertiary institutions on 'at risk' first year students;
- Provision of support services for specific categories of students, such as those with disabilities;
- Programmes designed to enable adults with low levels of formal education attainment to 'return to education';
- Improvements in statistics and records of student attainment and progression which facilitate targeted action and evaluation of special programmes.

These and other measures aimed at extending access to groups previously participating in tertiary education at low levels are discussed in a review of international experience of access and equity policies and programmes (Skilbeck, 2000). Conclusions in that study are drawn for higher education in Ireland and an equality review under the terms of the 1997 Universities Act is expected to be launched by the Higher Education Authority in 2001. Despite intensive efforts, major inequities in access and participation persist in all countries: low socio-economic groups; rural and isolated students; mature

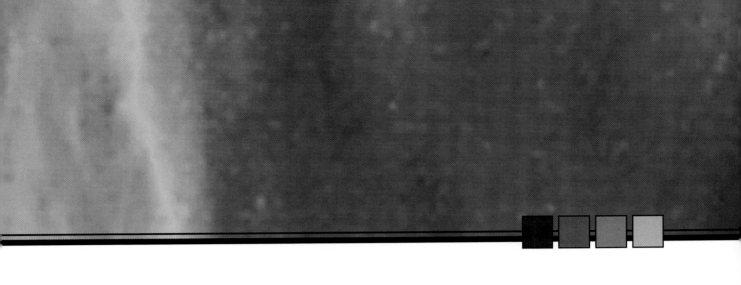

age students; women in certain professional courses; post-graduate study; positions of senior management in universities; ethnic minorities - and so on. Specific needs and programmes in Ireland are addressed in several recent reports (Commission on the Points System, 1999; Clancy and Wall, 2000; Osborne and Leith, 2000).

...The entry of whole new categories of students reflects varied sources of demand ..

Growth rates internationally, while generally strong, have been uneven across countries. They were rapid in the USA as noted above and in Japan, for example, from the 1960s and from the 1980s in a large number of countries, among which in the OECD region are Australia, Denmark, France, Italy, the Netherlands, New Zealand, Norway, Portugal, Spain, Sweden, Turkey and the United Kingdom (OECD, 1998d, ch. 2). Overall increase in rates of participation sometimes masks significant decline in particular fields which vary by country - physical science and engineering for example. Enrolment levels continue to grow, not, as noted above, as a result of growth in the size of the so-called 'age relevant' group, but because of pipeline effects from the substantially increased levels of upper secondary completion rates, and through the growing variety of vocational and technological as well as traditional academic routes (OECD, 1997a, ch.5).

Of particular significance for the future is the revision of ideas about 'the relevant age group'. In the past this has almost always referred to school leavers, entering higher education between the ages of 17 and 22/4 (older in several Continental countries). It is necessary, now, to approach the issue differently. Figures are increasingly quoted in terms of participation at some stage in the life cycle. On this basis, several countries are quoting projections in the order of 80% of the population taking tertiary level courses but not necessarily completing degrees and diplomas. In the UK, while enrolments of the 18-24 age group have been capped by the government at the level of 30%, on a life cycle basis it is anticipated that 60% of the population will in the years ahead have some direct experience of higher education with 50% by age 30. Even the cap of 30% for the 18-24 age group (introduced because of rapidly expanding levels of demand with heavy cost implications and acute pressure on the quality of provision) has been challenged, for example, by the Confederation of British Industry, reflecting socio-economic demand for high levels of skill (Smithers and Robinson, 1996a). In the UK, as in other countries, these figures also need adjusting to take account of full fee-paying international students (11% of total enrolments in the UK). They are an important source of revenue which, with other sources, enables higher education institutions to cross subsidize and soften the impact of continuing reductions in public funding.

Thus in both vertical and horizontal terms it is necessary to rethink concepts like 'relevant age group', and, indeed, 'student'. The vertical revision needs to take into full account the phenomenon of life-cycle or lifelong education, whereby - for purposes of both policy making and the expression of individual preference - access and participation refer

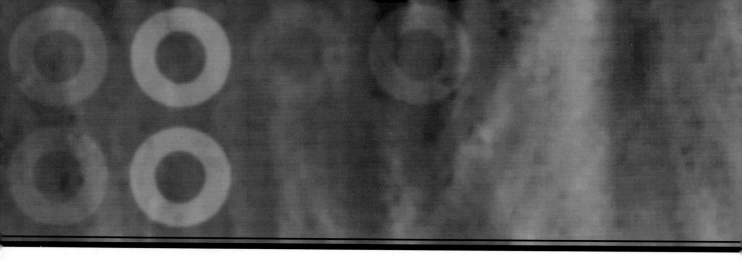

to enrolment and study at any age and include first time, second time and any other form of recurrent study. The horizontal revision needs to recognise that 'students' may be from any jurisdiction not necessarily that in which the institution is based and operates.

Moreover, the image of the student needs to be modified to be fully inclusive of all kinds of students including part-time, mature age, off – as well as on-campus, taking programmes for named qualifications and awards, short courses, residential and non-residential, enrolled in either 'visible' or 'virtual' institutions, and so on. These and other possibilities are opened up in the White Paper on Adult Education recently published by the Irish government (Department of Education and Science, Ireland, 2000). There are clear implications for the university to play a much larger and more varied role in meeting these new sources of demand in partnership with other tertiary institutions and agencies. But, for this to occur, adjustments in financial arrangements for and affecting mature age/part-time students are required, together with considerable changes in the organisation and content of study.

Necessary as is this enlargement and reshaping of concepts and categories, the enrolment and participation data sets maintained by national authorities and international bodies are frequently outdated, far from adequate and even misleading. Policy making often lags well behind the changed patterns and still often favours the 'traditional' student. There is likewise a big gap between common community understandings of 'studenthood' and the reality of participation. These and other mismatches between actual demand and participation rates on the one hand, and official knowledge and recognition on the other are a reflection of rapidity of change in a context of well-entrenched attitudes and expectations.

Since 1963, a celebrated if somewhat ambiguous, dictum of the Robbins Committee on Higher Education has characterised entry policy, not only in the UK: that courses should be available for all those qualified by ability and attainment to pursue them (Committee on Higher Education 1993). In several countries there have been disputes between national ministries and the university peak bodies as to the meaning of 'unmet demand', the former usually maintaining that all students wishing to enter higher education ultimately find a place somewhere, the latter challenging the data and pointing out that 'a place somewhere' may be a restriction of choice. This is a vexatious issue since while it is impossible to guarantee that any student can freely choose any course in any institution, equity demands that everyone should receive fair and equal consideration. Present structures and practices are often unnecessarily restrictive and will be increasingly open to challenge. Those countries which have advanced far down the track of open, flexible learning will enjoy a competitive advantage over those where restrictive mentalities prevail.

There is much uninformed opinion, still, about 'ability' and 'attainment'. The widespread use of public examinations at the end of secondary school for purposes of screening and selection has had as one of its effects a narrowing of our understanding of what people can and do attain in life. Heavy reliance on public examinations as an instrument for determining 'ability' and 'attainment' clearly brings into question their adequacy for these purposes, for example for groups typically under-represented in upper secondary education, and raises the issue of alternative entry routes especially for adults. These matters have been highlighted in the recent Irish report on the Leaving Certificate (Commission on the Points System, 1999).

Increasing rates of successful performance in public examinations have, paradoxically, been criticised, in France, England and Australia, for example. They are said to be indicative of a lowering of standards through 'easier' examination questions or more lenient marking. Standards over time are notoriously difficult to measure. Expectations change, as do curricula, teachers, teaching and the students themselves. While some targets may be lowered, acknowledging a much larger and more diverse student population, others may be raised. One of the more interesting of the studies of this phenomenon shows that in France, when the best entrance examination papers of candidates for the *grandes ecoles* over the past 40 years were remarked, it was found that standards had risen (Hughes, S., 1996)

Debates on the standard of attainment of the increasing number of students entering directly from school do however raise several issues. For the schools there is the challenge to demonstrate that all possible steps are being taken to prepare students to continue into some form of tertiary education and to experience success there. For the tertiary institutions there is a challenge to show that they are doing everything possible to provide for successful learning by all students, and not only those who display aptitude in meeting traditional requirements. A weakness detected in the review of the first years of tertiary education in a large sample of OECD countries is the frequently poor dialogue between secondary and tertiary education (OECD, 1998d).

The elite - mass - universal phenomenon in higher education has had its parallel in secondary education through rapidly increasing retention and completion rates, in the decades following the Second World War. As a result of the acute pressures at that level, not only were massive building programmes undertaken and very large cohorts of teachers trained and employed, there have been in most countries major structural changes in provision. Either in the form of better defined and articulated separate systems and streams, or school reorganisation along comprehensive lines, those changes demonstrate that substantial enrolment growth entails much more than providing additional places. As a result of different and more adaptable curricula and teaching methods more and more students have completed some form of full secondary

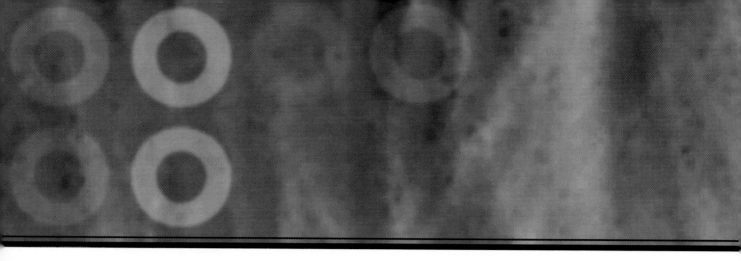

education, and are being certified as successful graduates. In some countries upper secondary school graduation rates are in the high '90s; many are well in excess of 70% (OECD, 2000, ch. 2C).

These levels of completion of second level education have more than compensated for demographic decline which, for a period in the 1980s, led some commentators and policy makers to predict overall decline in demand for access to tertiary education from the 18-24 age group. This decline has not in fact occurred although there is some unevenness in the trends. As noted above, recent Irish data on demographic trends has led to speculation about a crisis in enrolments in tertiary institutions. The 'crisis', in fact, presents opportunities which are discussed in Part III below. For several decades rising secondary school completion rates have been a major stimulus of demand for entry into higher education even allowing for the demographic shifts. As one commentator somewhat inelegantly remarked early in the 1970s, *"The increased number of secondary school graduates is the tail that wags the dog of tertiary enrollments"* (Bereday 1973, p. x)

Mature age entry and demands of tertiary education are leading to new kinds of provision and programmes
Mature age students are seeking more flexible study opportunities: part-time, work or home-based, of value in career advancement and in personal development (Berg, 1998). What cannot be emphasised too strongly is the shift now occurring towards an opening and broadening of educational opportunity to people of all ages.

Some countries report that in excess of 50% of new enrollees in tertiary education are or soon will be of mature age. In the United States, it is reported that 37% of all enrolments in higher education are aged 25 years or over (Choy, 1999). But as the data show, there are considerable variations among countries in mature age entry into higher education. Ireland has been and still is among a diminishing number of countries that choose to focus university admission policies for first degrees almost exclusively on the more able and successful products of a single end-of-school public examination. Few steps appear to have been taken to foster and facilitate either other avenues or mature age entry. There are exceptions, particularly in some study areas (including education, nursing, psychology) which actively encourage mature age students, but, overall, participation rates for adults in university programmes are quite low by international standards (Commission on the Points System, 1999, pp. 21-22). Until publication in 2000 of the White Paper on Adult Education, there had been a policy vacuum which combined with structural weaknesses and impediments to inhibit both systematic provision and participation. These are detailed in the report of the Points Commission.

The need for stronger equity policies is indicated by trends in enrolment data, not only in Ireland. While participation rates from low social and economic groups have increased (for example between the late '80s and mid '90s and in six countries studied by the OECD, at average annual rates of between 0.6 to 1.5%, overall participation increased as much or

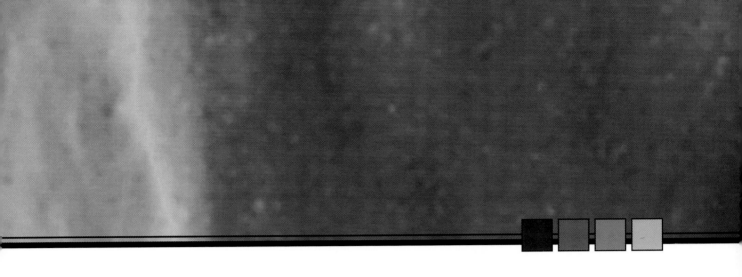

more. This signifies no relative improvement, a conclusion that can be supported from many different data sources including those for Ireland (Clancy, 1999; Clancy and Wall, 2000; Skilbeck, 2000). Age differentials in education qualifications in the whole population are very marked, a function in part of the much more limited opportunities and felt need for entry into tertiary education in the past. Unless decisive steps are taken to improve the supply of appropriate education opportunities, these differentials will continue in Ireland and all those countries where adult participation remains at fairly low levels - reflecting a policy environment which, for whatever reason, gives far more attention to the needs and interests of school leavers than (potential) adult tertiary level students.

Some countries and many institutions have developed attractive schemes and incentives for adult participation. North American, New Zealand, Nordic and Australian higher education systems, for example, have quite advanced procedures for facilitating entry for those who lack formal entry requirements. These include specially funded access and re-entry schemes, skills training e.g. in computer and literacy, financial incentives and a focus on just what is required to give confidence about their own capabilities and potential.

The picture of what is actually happening is both larger and more complex than appears from enrolment statistics in formal, award bearing courses. Students, for example, may be on track to enter university degree programmes, but not necessarily end on. In some countries sub-degree programmes have grown in popularity. In the USA, for example, there has been during the nineties a great expansion of specialist certificate programmes (Adelman, 2000). Several Australian universities have huge programmes of specialised professional training, including contracts with professional associations of engineers, accountants and financial planners, with government departments and large private enterprises. These may be post-graduate or available to people regardless of their formal qualifications. They are, incidentally, important sources of revenue as well as means for developing extensive contacts and partnerships with industry, commerce and government.

The growth of part-time, short course, work-related or work-based study, together with the diversity of providers of formal, award-bearing programmes has led to considerable confusion over nomenclature and uncertainty over statistical returns. Expansion and diversity of tertiary education have not been adequately captured in those returns. Hence the moves to redefine the international categorisation of levels of study used in their reports by UNESCO, OECD, the European Commission and others. But for useful international comparisons to be made and for effective policy making, countries will have to get a much better grip on adult education data than they now have.

At issue is the status comparability of a very large number and wide range of programmes and courses beyond the secondary level but below that of university (and other) degrees and diplomas. In addition to improvements that are needed

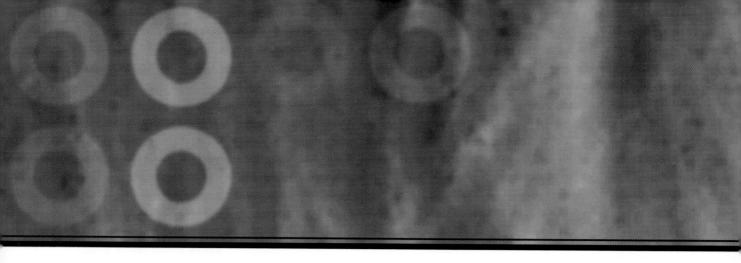

in the monitoring of these developments and their incorporation in national education statistics, are weaknesses to address in credit recognition and articulation. Although taxonomic analysis does not resolve policy issues, it certainly illuminates them. The concept of tertiary education, for example, and the roles of the various players would be further clarified by a better understanding of the standards of different study programmes, levels of attainment and ways of comparing them. These considerations of course require more than the revision of the international system of education levels. The emergence of qualifications frameworks is a significant step toward better understanding of what is happening and improved provision and articulation.

Of concern, internationally, is the comparability of the traditional Continental longer first degree and the shorter bachelor degree in (mainly) English-speaking countries. There have been moves towards convergence, for example the Sorbonne Declaration of a group of European Ministers of Education (25 May, 1998) and the reports prepared for the 1999 Bologna Conference of Ministers (Haug and Kirstein, 1999). A further complexity arises in efforts to establish comparability of 'university' level and 'college' level programmes – as between European universities and American community colleges, for example. Facing these difficulties – many still unresolved – and wanting to use a term that captured the variety of valuable and recognised types of provision, the OECD Education Committee in 1998 adopted the term 'tertiary education' (OECD, 1998d). Use of this term, however, means that further explanation is required for specific activities.

Let us consider, for example, the growing band of corporate providers in staff training and development (the so-called 'Corporate Quality Universities' of Motorola, Disney, Microsoft and others) in the USA and the UK. Their programmes range from the most advanced to quite basic staff training, and are delivered in innovative ways. This movement is evidence of powerful growth forces developing alongside those to which universities have traditionally responded (Kenney-Wallace, 2000). As mentioned above, many conventional universities are moving into partnership arrangements or simply diversifying their own programmes to meet industry demand for trained personnel.

But is demand being adequately met? And should anyone be 'in control'?

It does not follow, from the gross upward trends in participation and the overall increases in enrolments, that all needs are being met or even addressed. Figures from the Dearing Report in the UK indicate an increase in the age participation rate in formal tertiary level institutions from less than 5% in the early 1960s to roughly 35% overall, and more than 45% in Scotland. Impressive as is this rate of increase it raises further questions.

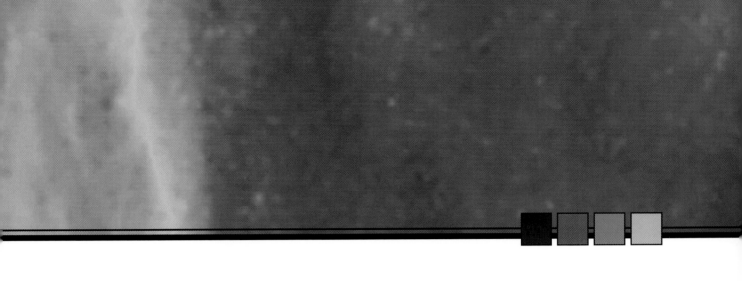

First, what are the comparative trends in rates of increase? Each country must examine its position comparatively, not for the purpose of what is often a quite misleading league table but as a means of asking whether it is satisfied with the rate and, if not, what lessons might be taken from countries that have performed better. Second, behind the figure of 35% (or 45%) is the question of the 65% (or 55%) not participating. Are the requirements for a highly educated citizenry and work force being met? Third, what are the targets both in terms of quantity (gross participation rates) and quality (rates of progression and completion, standards of performance, levels of attainment and so on)? It would be instructive to compare the Irish trends with, say, those in Scotland, an Australian state, a Canadian province, Singapore, and New Zealand, posing these and other questions (a benchmarking approach which goes beyond the usual Western European frame of reference).

While there is a growing interest in incentives to stimulate enrolment - especially of adults - a major issue remains cost, to the state, employers and individuals. Thus far, it seems that individual demand has remained fairly elastic in face of the apportionment of increasing levels of cost to students (less is known about adults than school leavers and students taking post-graduate degrees more or less end on). Other well-documented discouraging factors are inconvenience to students arising from the location of institutions and their timetables, lack of facilities especially for working parents and environments that do not sufficiently recognise the needs of quite diverse groups of students. Praise has been showered on the American community colleges that have systematically addressed deterrents and disincentives to study, especially for working or home-bound adults, and on student-friendly access programmes that move people from relative inactivity into continuing study and/or working life (Skilbeck, 2000; 2001).

A number of policy instruments widely deployed to regulate enrolments can be quite inhibitory especially to potential mature age students with a limited or unorthodox academic background. Numerus clausus has long been a screening device in European countries whereby enrolment targets for institutions and courses have been centrally set to regulate supply that is not sufficient to meet demand. France has a policy of enabling access to an institution and course of choice by all *baccalaureat* holders. But in practice this liberal policy is subject to a variety of constraints and operational restrictions, for example through the impact of selection procedures, and a general orientation which favours selection (OECD, 1998d). Quotas have been widely used to control entry to specific institutions/faculties and courses of study, and even lotteries - perhaps as a measure of desperation over the inability to find an acceptable allocation mechanism in a situation of scarce (or inadequate) supply. Examinations and tests are widely used as a screening device although, as noted above, higher levels of successful performance have meant that the proportion of an age group qualifying for entry in formal terms has greatly increased. Incentives in the form of price and funding mechanisms have been common not only in respect of entry but also retention. Grants-in-aid to students, loans and tuition charges are increasingly subject to

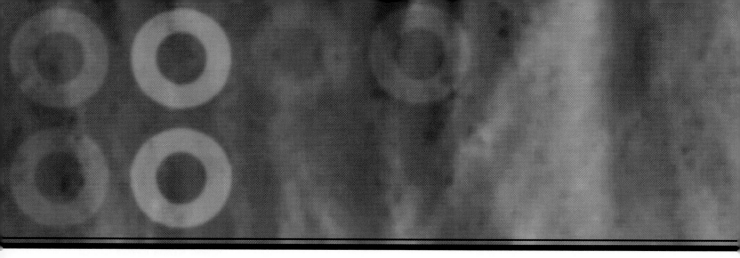

performance criteria and can be regarded as both an incentive to institutions and individuals and a potential deterrent to enrolment and continuing participation in study.

Policy instruments are one thing, their ability to manage and steer the situations for which they are designed is another.

Commenting at an OECD/Australian government international conference, Don Aitken said: *"We are in the midst of a large and enormously important social process, which seems common to the countries of the OECD and is plainly shared outside them: a rapid increase in the proportions completing schooling and seeking and gaining further formal education. This process started two generations ago (even earlier in the USA), and shows no sign of ending. No-one is in control of it"* (DETYA/ OECD 1993, p. 88). Since Aitken penned these words in 1993, a further force has emerged as a powerful new generator of both supply and demand - information technology.

Tertiary education for all at some stage in their life cycle is an emerging and realisable goal

Discussion in this chapter commenced with the perspective of Martin Trow in the 1970s. It is fitting at this juncture to refer to his reappraisal of the mass to universal scenario at the end of the century: *"Information technology now forces a revision of our conception of the conditions making for universal access: IT allows, and becomes a vehicle for, universal access to higher education of a different order of magnitude, with courses of every kind and description available over the Internet to people's homes and work places"* (Trow, 1999a, p. 327).

What 'allows' and 'becomes a vehicle for' does not inevitably come quickly into use. Trow observed that few European-university-based academics and administrators have fully appreciated its implications. These implications include strengthening students in relation to teachers, shifting the focus to learning from teaching, blurring the lines between education and entertainment, and a difficult set of resource and management issues for institutions, such as ownership of intellectual property and publications and the duties and responsibilities of staff vis-a-vis their employing institution. A further point is that the gap between adult learners and school leaver entrants to higher education has widened in that the latter are in many countries quite computer literate whereas many of the former are not. Just as, in the '70s, the volume increases in enrolment were seen to be the major factor of change, so by the end of the century, IT was, for Trow - and for many other commentators - 'the most destabilising or transforming development in higher education'. (See below, Part II Encounters)

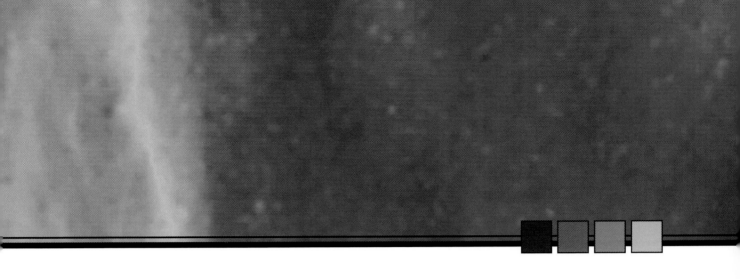

The facilitation of yet more increases in participation rates in higher education involves further questions. Trow lists four: the nature of the subject and subject matter being taught; the location of students (and hence conditions of study); the purpose of teaching (as to whether its focus is skills development or the cultivation of mind and sensibilities) and the academic talents and motivation of learners. To Trow's four, many other researchers and analysts would add the capability and interests of teachers in a technology-rich era and the resources and capabilities of institutions. There is also the claim that too many students are choosing or being directed into courses for which there is weak labour market demand. This does not mean that the courses are 'irrelevant' since they serve other purposes, but it is a situation that lends some credence to the criticism of 'over-educated' graduates (Keep and Mayhew, 1996).

Enlargement of tertiary education through massively increased enrolments has placed universities under enormous pressure. But it would be a mistake to suppose that only universities have taken up the challenge of numbers or that they can or should be expected to expand indefinitely. Enrolment increase whether through individual or social demand - the preferences and choices of individuals or the needs and expectations of society and the economy - raises the question of the suitability of existing institutions and systems to serve as the key instruments for sectoral growth.

Expansion of the university sector, voluntary or enforced, affects the balance and direction of the post-school or tertiary education system as a whole. This has recently surfaced in Ireland where, demographic trends indicating a substantial decline in numbers of school leavers, it has been suggested that it will be the institutes of technology, not the universities that will feel the impact of declining numbers. As already mentioned, increasing retention rates and increased provision for mature age entry could radically change the picture. The policy issue of an appropriate balance between sectors does, however, remain. For individual institutions, regardless of sector, the competition now common in many countries to recruit students especially when enabled to go beyond (system-set) targets without incurring penalties can have disturbing effects: those struggling to recruit in certain subjects may have to shed staff, even close whole departments whereas others, recruiting strongly, are thriving.

Despite the many difficulties, the necessity, ultimately, is to encompass all people of adult age in a well developed, comprehensive and multi-faceted system - or array of systems of education and training (OECD, 1996c). But we are a long way from realising that goal. Tertiary education systems and models of lifelong learning should be inclusive, attractive, accessible, well articulated, of high quality and relevance - and appropriate in their functioning, content and style to all learners. But how is this to be achieved and what, specifically, does further enrolment growth imply for the university?

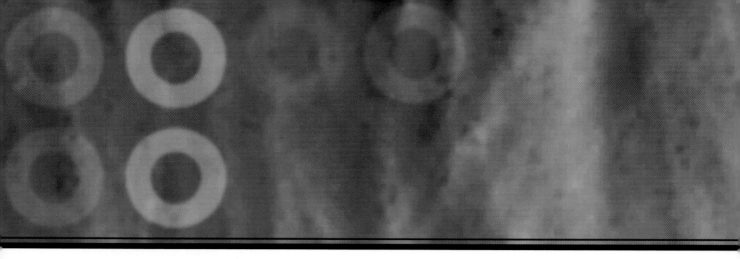

It is necessary to be cautious in predicting continuing rates of growth to saturation point – however that might be defined. For one thing, there has been a long term decline in incomes associated with degree qualifications relevant to other incomes (Marginson, 1992); although they still remain high, compared for example with investing equivalent funds in the market. There is an increasing proportion of costs of tertiary education borne by participants (Ireland is exceptional in having eliminated fees for undergraduate students). Yet there are penalties for not gaining credentials (not necessarily university), notably but not only for entry into and progression in the labour market. Generally speaking, the 'investment in human capital' argument is holding up even if the returns appear to many commentators to be variable. Policy initiatives and especially those associated with the message of qualifications needed for employment and 'lifelong learning for all', continue to encourage participation.

Taking all considerations into account, it seems likely that expansion of tertiary education including increasing enrolments in universities, both undergraduate and post-graduate, will continue. Preparations are needed accordingly. Since it is not participation per se that makes the difference, but the efforts students and teachers make to attain good standards, the preparations must address quality of learning and suitability of teaching for yet more varied cohorts of learners.

We turn now to the ways in which this ambitious enterprise is being or needs to be prepared for. This can be heralded as the third great education revolution which follows the first – universal primary education (nineteenth century) and second – universal secondary education (twentieth century): tertiary education for all (twenty-first century).

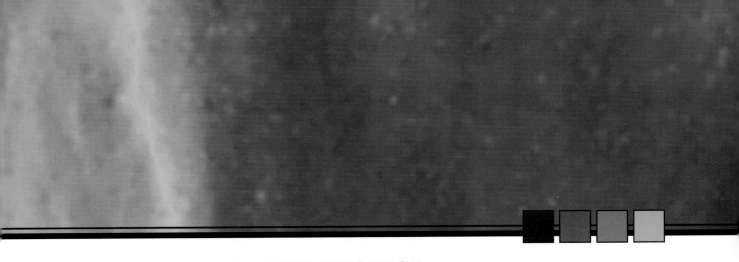

DIFFERENTIATION AND DIVERSIFICATION

Diversification: A fire brigade to quell the flames of massification (M. Hoffert, 1997)

It was realised quite early in the period of massive expansion that 'more' would inevitably mean 'worse' unless drastic changes and innovations occurred in curricula, teaching, study conditions and institutional management and organisation. The development over several decades of whole new sectors of tertiary education has marked the response to demand in many countries, Ireland among them. Already existing universities have expanded in size and new ones have been established. Across the OECD there are now numerous very large, multi-campus institutions with student enrolments in excess of 15,000 - 20,000 students (full-time equivalents) and some much larger still, with huge numbers of part-time and off-campus students.

There is growing variety in higher education

Sheer growth and/or multiplication of existing kinds of institutions alone has not generally been seen as the appropriate course to follow. The impressive enrolment increases that have occurred could not have been contemplated had there not been transformations in the provision of education. Although it is not the purpose of this review to survey trends across the whole of tertiary education as distinct from the university sector, it is necessary to pay attention to some of them. This is in order both to indicate where and how the universities are contributing to the overall supply (including a growing network of relations across the whole of tertiary education) and to draw out in a little more detail the impact of the 'pull' from socio-economic demand. This pull has, among other consequences, led many universities to introduce programmes of study similar or even identical to what is often regarded as the province of the so-called non-university or vocational sector.

...Both the system as a whole and in individual institutional provision

The terms 'diversification' and 'differentiation' have proved troublesome in attempts that have been made by a number of commentators to come to grips with the bewildering variety of responses to vastly increased demand and mass enrolments. Some authors have assayed a simple distinction: diversification referring to different types and levels of tertiary institution and differentiation to a variety of routes, course offerings and forms of study within any one tertiary sector. However, there is neither consistency of usage nor a sufficiently stable environment for clearcut distinctions to hold. What is evident is that there is not a tight, unified concept of higher education nor anything resembling a single model of the university. Instead there is a very loosely coupled family of multiple, varied routes and a great variety of forms, types or modes of higher education provision.

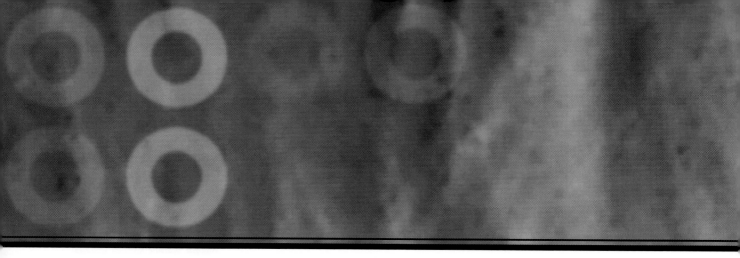

Leaving aside terminological details, what is encompassed by the calls for more responsive and flexible policies and practices? What kinds of differentiation and what sort of diversity, arising from the moves toward larger and more varied cohorts of students, are now in evidence? The answers, from different sources including an international seminar on diversification (OECD, 1997b) are numerous. Diversity and differentiation are to be found in:

- Characteristics of students and staff;
- Entry requirements and admissions procedures;
- Curricula, learning resources and study environments;
- Teaching and assessment;
- The variety of research and scholarly activities;
- Audiences being served;
- Networks and partnerships;
- Levels and methods of financing students and institutions;
- Conditions of employment and remuneration of staff;
- Types of institution, missions and modes of operation.

From such a list it can be inferred that 'diversity' and 'differentiation' are not simply a matter of different sectors and different study programmes. They have become a code for responsiveness, flexibility, variety, for niche marketing and greater entrepreneurship and initiative in designing and delivering education. It is obvious that fresh and indeed radical thinking is required about expectations of students and standards of student performance.

Fluid, seamless systems of higher education are a long way off, and most countries are still grappling with the structural (and resource) issue of a system comprising two (or more) broadly discrete sectors. During the past thirty years or so, alongside universities so-called 'alternatives' or 'non-university institutions' have been introduced or developed: *Fachhochschulen* in Germany and Australia; *Hogeskolen* in the Netherlands and Flanders; Polytechnics (now universities) and Further and Higher Education Colleges in the UK, Colleges of Advanced Education and Institutions of Technology (now universities) and Technical and Further Education colleges in Australia, Polytechnics in New Zealand, Regional Colleges in Norway, Institutes of Technology in Ireland, *AMKs (ammattikorkeakoulou)* in Finland – and many others. Essentially, three factors have been at work: increasing numbers of students seeking access; economic requirements including skills for employment; and the long-term upward thrust of institutions and courses of study from the secondary to the tertiary level.

In an OECD national education policy review (Finland) in 1995, the push from changes in secondary education was singled out as a major factor in the growth and restructuring of the tertiary sector, with positive socio-economic outcomes: *"The increase in the proportion of youth entitled to enroll for higher education was generally accepted as an investment towards economic growth, as providing increased opportunities for self-development, and as reducing inequalities deriving from socio-economic background, gender, region"* (OECD, 1995).

The OECD reviewers, generalising from the Finnish situation they were examining, attributed this higher education entitlement in many OECD countries principally to two factors: increase in the number and variety of tracks in secondary education including comprehensive forms of secondary education, especially at the upper levels; and policies which enabled young people pursuing (tracked) lower secondary or vocational education eventually to enroll in institutions of higher education, particularly, but not exclusively, in the non-university sector. Participation in tertiary education including routes and courses taken is significantly influenced by the structure of secondary education.

But the higher education institutions have had themselves to change their character, both individually and as a sector, in order for educational needs to be addressed. The impact of what has come to be politically unacceptable restrictive access policies (e.g. *numerus clausus*), bottlenecks at point of entry, and the repeating of examinations by students to allow higher grades (only to be penalised with point reductions for second and third attempts) is leading to major policy shifts. Many countries, not only those that now have a large college or non-university sector, have reformed curricula, modified the duration of courses and in other ways attempted to give force and prominence to a broad spectrum of tertiary education provision (OECD, 1998d).

The central question being addressed, in the words of a policy survey of the American scene, is: how to accommodate escalating demand in face of higher expectations for quality, severe fiscal constraints and the inflexibility of many existing institutional structures and policies. And, for the university sector: how to foster and sustain diverse institutions and programmes, from highly specialised technical training to major research universities, in the face of seemingly inexorable pressures for convergence toward a single model of the research university (McGuinness, 1995, p. 276). A common response to the first of the above questions is the creation of the separate, non-university sector, but in a number of systems there is an upward thrust coming from this sector, blurring the line with universities, a parallel to the convergence McGuinness identified within the university sector.

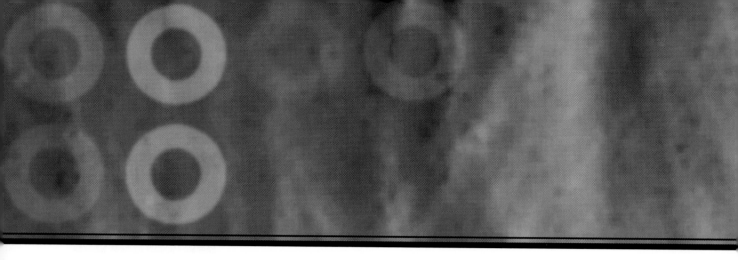

The Finnish example illustrates a sequence of changes common to many systems during the past two decades: a major problem of excessive demand in relation to institutional capacity and capability; a recognised need for high level vocational programmes not available through universities; a troublesome period of short term and ultimately unsatisfactory expedient measures; a bold new proposal; resistance by established bureaucratic and academic interests ('the time is not ripe)'; eventual acceptance and introduction of major reform measures including a whole new sector; a continuing undercurrent of scepticism and resistance - especially by the universities - to the newcomer which is seen to be competing for resources and status and to have a different understanding of tertiary level standards.

The Finnish authorities, having at first rejected the creation of a new tertiary sector proposed by OECD reviewers in 1981, established the *AMK* in 1991. By 1997 they were treating a differentiated or two sector higher education system as integral to a national policy of raising the overall standard of education, meeting economic requirements for high level skills, and promoting educational equality - to all population groups and regions of the country. This policy orientation was not only horizontal - different types of secondary and tertiary provision - but also vertical, bringing together academic secondary education, vocational education, universities and the *AMK* sector. In addressing an international seminar on diversification in Prague in 1997, the then minister of education, Olli-Pekka Heinonen said that the target figure of 65% of the age relevant cohort in higher education (including *AMK*) for the year 2000 was probably too low. Even the year 2000 target would not have been conceivable had the *AMK* sector not been introduced. Firm declarations by policy makers (and international reviewers) of the value of the new sector in addressing numerical demand and socio-economic needs may be contrasted with the reluctance of national authorities, less than ten years earlier, to initiate the much heralded reform.

The *AMK* story is but one illustration of the new roles being played by the sector of so-called alternatives to universities. The continuing development and strengthening of the regional institutes of technology in Ireland serves similar purposes. These 'alternative' systems, many of them in the European theatre deriving from the German *Fachhochschulen*, are not just vocational in orientation and spirit. They see themselves, and are seen by governments, as meeting multiple objectives: a key component of strategies to increase international competitiveness; to improve structural comparability across systems with very different historical origins; to meet growing access and study demands by students and expectations of employers; to strengthen regional development; to provide congenial conditions for the expansion of small and medium sized industry; to help rationalise the historically piecemeal patchwork of specialised, mainly short courses; and to expand overall provision at a reasonable cost. Continuing growth and strength of these kinds of institutions, whether in the context of binary systems or as part of a diversified unitary system, are necessary in order to address a wide variety of social demands and individual expectations.

Many institutions of this so-called alternative type now offer initial degrees in association with universities or independently, they undertake research and consultancy and play important economic and social roles in their regions. They have a potential for meeting future demands for many kinds of undergraduate study, possibly at lower unit cost levels than universities. But the craft-technician tradition is different from that which informs many university degrees; also their move into degree programmes has raised concern over potential neglect of middle-level skills training. The evolution of the tertiary sector will involve further realignments of the different component parts and institutions.

...But there are contrary forces and a blurring of lines at the system level

The establishment of the second tier, alternatives to universities, strongly encouraged and recommended by the OECD at the beginning of the '90s (OECD, 1991) has had some unanticipated or at least unplanned-for consequences. First, in many countries the development of a sector which might seem to alleviate some of the pressures for volume growth being experienced by universities was met by scepticism or downright hostility from that quarter (OECD, 1997b; Rhoades, 1990). Instead of being valued as elements of a complementary sector with which fruitful partnerships might be formed, these institutions have often been treated as rivals, competing for scarce resources, drawing away certain categories of students, and claiming a status for which it was asserted they were not adequately prepared. Second, as noted above, the second sector institutions have generally not been content to remain a kind of junior or lesser partner. Similarly, the policy emphasis on 'teaching only' has been widely challenged and many of these institutions now claim a research role, especially applied or industry-related research. These problems point to weaknesses in articulation policies - which are difficult to sustain not least because the institutions themselves often seem to prefer their own credit recognition procedures to system-wide approaches (National Board of Employment, Education and Training, Australia, 1995). In Ireland, these issues were pointed up in the application of the Dublin Institute of Technology, not accepted by the Higher Education Authority, for formal recognition as a university.

Different countries have approached the question of more (or less) differentiated forms of tertiary education in a variety of ways. From the 1960s onwards, in England, Ireland, Australia and New Zealand, the term 'binary' became firmly entrenched, to refer to the two institutional types of polytechnics and/or colleges of advanced education/institutes or colleges of technology/regional colleges and universities (OECD, 1997b). In Germany, there is a preference for the term 'multiple types' which seems apt and not only for that country, considering the diversity of kinds of post-secondary/tertiary level institutions to be found in most countries.

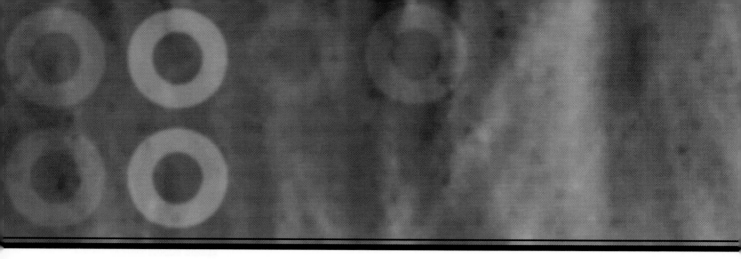

Within the university sector itself, there may be a bewildering variety of institutions - notably in the USA, from four year liberal arts colleges to research universities. In France, the *instituts universitaires de technologie* (IUT) provide short cycle vocational courses within established universities; other European countries also have encouraged the development of short cycle courses and institutions (Wasser, 1996). In New Zealand and France, university level courses are available in some upper secondary schools. Franchising arrangements are spreading, and there is a growing practice in several countries of courses for university credit in technical/further education colleges.

Whether or not this ever-changing profile of higher education is more accurately characterised as new forms of differentiation and diversification or fresh manifestations of old forms of status stratification, the 'inflation' of education credentials has been criticised (Hirsch, 1977) and the terms 'university' and 'higher education' have much broader, looser connotations that hitherto.

In Australia and England, respectively, late in the 1980s and early in the 1990s so-called unified systems were established through the adoption of the common term 'university'. However, in both countries, there is considerable diversity among the universities and a thriving sector of colleges of further/technical education remains, in part forming a bridge between secondary and higher education. Many of these institutions now offer degree level courses, usually the first stage of an associated university award; some have degree awarding status and many aspire to it. By recognising study in highly specialised vocational courses in these institutions, either directly in the form of giving credit or as providing advanced standing, universities have themselves become more diverse in their *de facto* course offerings.

Some commentators are concerned about the lack of clarity, the blurring of once well - demarcated sectoral lines in these developments through, for example, failure to maintain distinctions concerning level of provision, to control competition across (as distinct from within) sectors, and to ensure real opportunity for transition for students, across levels. Others are more sanguine or are reaching towards a new, more open structure of higher education. Peter Scott put it like this: *"binary systems were established in many countries to handle the inevitable and alarming heterogeneity which accompanied the rapid expansion of higher education in the third quarter of the twentieth century; as the inflexibility of binary systems has become apparent and the prospect of mass higher education has appeared less forbidding in the century's fourth and final quarter, a drift to more adaptable forms of post-binary differentiation has taken place"* (Scott, 1993, p. 45).

This statement was made in the aftermath of the abolition of the university/polytechnic binary line in Britain. What it did not anticipate was a press towards conformity (rather than the intra- and inter-institutional differentiation Scott had

in mind) consequent on the funding and evaluation structures for both research and teaching erected in Britain during the '90s. Moreover, in a number of continental European systems, where state control has in the past been much stronger than in Britain, it has not been conceded that binary systems are inflexible. It seems that 'inflexibility' is more apparent in systems, binary or otherwise, where there are not diverse and clearcut institutional missions, well-defined differences in the conditions affecting financing, course levels, qualifications on offer and teaching including remuneration of teachers, and well-developed linkages and articulation arrangements (see below).

Nearly twenty years ago, in his *The Crisis of the University*, Scott made another point about binary systems which continues to apply with equal force to tertiary education as a whole, namely that simple, category distinctions can all too easily disguise a multitude of variables. The polytechnic sector in Britain in the 1980s comprised diverse institutions: colleges of education; embryonic community colleges; institutions resembling liberal arts colleges and 'proto-polytechnics'. Similarly, the university sector was and remains diverse, comprising the ancient universities, London, the major provincial universities both older and newer, and a cross-sectoral institution (Ulster) (Scott 1984). There are clear echoes in this account of the most differentiated and diverse of all tertiary education systems - that of the United States.

Wherever more than one sector provides education at the tertiary level, there is a challenge to define relations between them, ideally in a well articulated structure which might include: study pathways in both directions; credit transfer; joint courses and study programmes; cross-sectoral institutions; joint R&D projects; agreed specialisation and concentration; strategic alliances; shared resources and facilities. Students, especially, need to be well-informed about study opportunities and pathways and opportunities for linked diplomas-degrees.

Policy statements often advert to flexibility and encourage better linkages. Pathways of a sort often exist but passage along them can be slow and tortuous even when families and students are fully informed about the maze that has to be negotiated. In Ireland, for example, a student entering a four year degree course on the basis of a good points score in the Leaving Certificate can expect to complete in four years. Another student, from the same year group but lacking sufficient points and therefore obliged to take an alternative route through a Further Education College and Institute of Technology, would require six to eight years before attaining the same degree (Hyland, 2000; Commission on the Points System, 1999, pp.149-150). Is it that the student needs all this time - or that the system is unduly rigid?

The main declared policy objectives in establishing or seeking to strengthen differentiation and diversification in tertiary education are: to break or curtail a university monopoly; to foster a culture of greater visible or direct relevance of teaching,

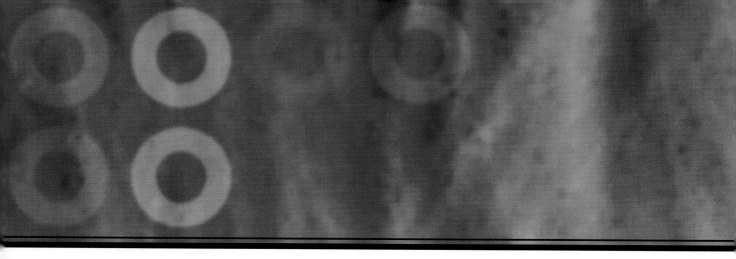

research and study to economic development; to broaden the range of study opportunities for different groups in the community; and to ensure that a substantial part of tertiary education remains under more direct social control. A major additional factor, not always explicitly stated, has been cost containment: universities have been regarded as too costly; differentiating institutional types (and hence cost structures) has become a major policy preoccupation, with definite implications for institutions of all kinds for subjects/ diplomas/ degrees that can be offered and for research concentration. While subscribing to these objectives, except perhaps those to do with control and costs, many of the institutions, not only the non-university ones, have bridled at the developmental caps imposed upon them.

At the beginning of the new century, there is a much broader concept of tertiary or higher education than ever before. Not only are there everywhere two or more sectors, there is a great array of types of institution and forms of delivery, including the open universities, private providers, institutions specialising in a very small number of fields, large-scale part-time study programmes, short course and single cycle institutions alongside research universities and others. But there are also forces at work and tensions that could lead to an implosion with reduced diversification and greater homogenisation as a result. At least, this is a possible outcome of tendencies in the state system of publicly funded and regulated institutions, characterised by academic creep in the non-university sector, for example and financial forces, evaluative practices and so on driving universities to conformity. Although there could well be efficiency gains, greater uniformity of structure and provision both within and between sectors would not be desirable, for a variety of reasons.

Varied needs are being recognised in more diverse kinds of teaching, learning and research...

Diversification is a strong feature of systems where public funding and controls are substantially moderated through the existence of a strong private sector of tertiary education with its own, quite varied funding sources and a legal capacity to develop its own norms. Account must also be taken of the diversification of the educational experience itself, whether in the public or the private sector. Diversification in this sense is achieved through the multiplication that has occurred of curricula and course offerings, different forms and patterns of teaching, variety in study opportunities, settings and experience, the different types of assessment and procedures for accrediting learning, and the structure of awards - degrees, diplomas etc and ways of meeting their requirements. All of these and others are apparent in the expanding university sector and may be regarded as evidence of its adaptability and readiness to address different needs.

Nevertheless, there are issues to address: should institutions and individual departments be encouraged to pursue a highly competitive approach, with rewards to the most successful, or is it preferable to seek to improve the research-capability of the whole system, all institutions contributing to strategic priorities and thereby achieving critical mass? The former

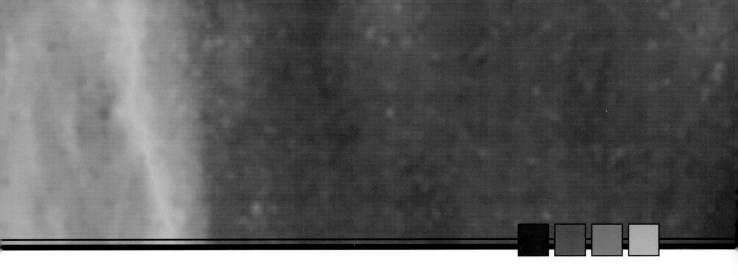

approach results in various within-system alliances and international linkages among self-chosen partners. The latter tends to see the national system as its target, all institutions contributing, albeit in varied ways, to nationally defined targets. As for the issue of diversified educational experiences within the university sector (and not only there), perhaps the most radical are those, of gathering strength since the 1990s, that enable students to qualify for awards through a large component of work experience, recognition of prior learning, independent study and self-designed study programmes and projects. A variety of motives attended these developments. In some institutions, equity issues and social justice prevailed; in others, the pedagogical need to provide for students of quite diverse backgrounds and study capability were uppermost. Overall, the tightening of relations between labour market requirements, student employment aspirations and institutions seeking closer identification with the changing needs of their regions have resulted in a wide variety of institutional profiles.

The gathering momentum of the movement to tie education more closely to the labour market is evident in the efforts made from the 1980s onwards to define study outcomes and successful learning according to 'competency'. Through the establishment of qualifications frameworks it is becoming possible, at least in principle, to separate the procedures for recognising competence and awarding diplomas, certificates and degrees from the designs for and processes of teaching and learning as defined by established colleges and universities. The creation of national qualification authorities, able to recognise levels of attainment quite independently of the institutions and settings that facilitated these attainments, could turn the principle into practice, a development not usually welcomed by universities.

Although there are rough precedents – the University of London external degrees, for example offered opportunity to students enrolled in accredited institutions or externally around the world with the university performing very largely an examining role – the qualification authority could be seen as a radical departure from the university tradition whereby the awarding of the degree – a virtual monopoly of the university – followed completion of a course of study designed, approved, delivered and examined by the same university. The recent establishment of the Qualifications Authority in Ireland, following the Qualifications (Education and Training) Act of 1999, while it does not entail a departure from the authority of the universities, does foreshadow more flexibility in the provision of study opportunities.

It is unclear whether the initiatives to establish national qualifications frameworks will result in any significant erosion of the degree granting authority of the university. The potential is there, but academic resistance where this has appeared to be a threat has been substantial and generally successful. Of far greater relevance, at present, is the multiplication of types and levels of university-provided and endorsed awards, courses of study, and types of course delivery. The ideal of a map

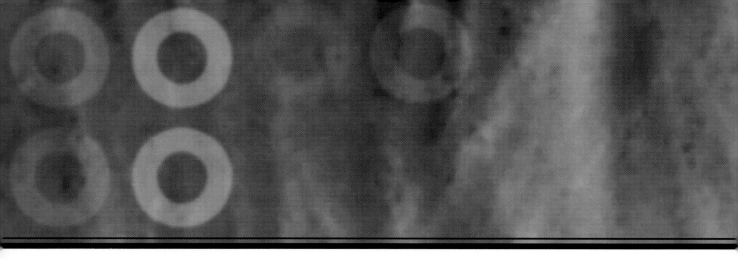

whose separate points could (with effort) be integrated in a unified knowledge field no longer commands much attention except perhaps among advocates of a classical canon. Organic, unified theories have been largely displaced by what Scott (1984, p. 64) characterised as 'the fissiparous knowledge of the modern university'. This is usually taken to refer to subject specialisation in teaching and research. However, in the perspective of university diversification it also signifies a broadening of the subjects, fields and topics available to study, a relaxation of rigidities and orthodoxies in disciplinary structures and the diverse procedures of knowledge production that go under the name of 'mode 2' science (Gibbons et al, 2000; Scott, 2000).

A more diverse student community, which includes a growing proportion of adult learners and whole categories of students once precluded from university study, clearly requires a more varied range of study offerings than hitherto. The fragmented map of knowledge is also the means to provide much more diverse study opportunities, relevant to the interests and needs of a more varied student clientele. Teaching and study systems such as self-contained units of credit, semester – long courses with in-built assessment, and the quantity of credit for prior learning, independent study and so on are highly flexible. But they raise the issue of how to maintain the coherence of study and enable students to integrate and make overall sense of their studies.

...Designed in part to meet a changing labour market

A powerful driving force in the diversification of study opportunities is the changing labour market. Since at least the mid to late '80s, preoccupation with the economic functions of higher education has re-ignited interest in the issue of the 'employability' of graduates which surfaced in the '70s and then languished somewhat, as confidence ebbed in employment forecasting and educational planning. In the late '80s and '90s, the rapid strides in the development and diffusion of the new technologies combined with the formulation of the so-called new growth theories, or knowledge-based societies, and a long period of buoyant economic conditions, to thrust the graduate employment agenda on to centre stage. This has resulted in such developments as work experience, improved career guidance and transition programmes, graduate destination studies and the statistics and the burgeoning research literature on graduate placement, earning ratios and career advancement.

These and related achievements notwithstanding, Teichler (1999a) among others has urged the need for better data and information flows between higher education and the labour market, better and more sophisticated analytical tools and improved institutional capability to assess employment opportunities for graduates. Students, too, in a UNESCO survey, expressed concern about their ability to sustain a reasonable standard of living through a stable working life (Kearney, 1998).

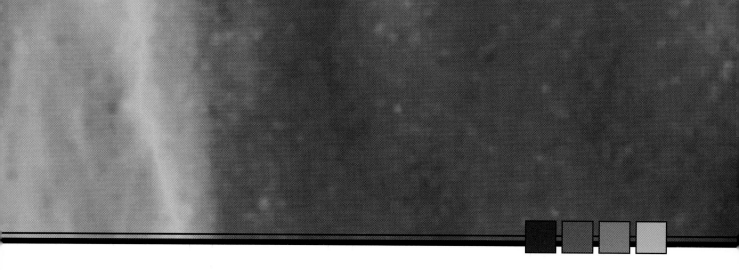

While universities have of course always prepared students for entry to the labour market, they have often done so indirectly, at arms' length, so to speak. Collaborative arrangements with the professions, industry and government in providing practical work-based experience and facilitating transition are not new, but they are increasing in range and intensity in many countries. It appears that the organisation of studies in many programmes in Irish universities does not readily facilitate the mix of 'earning and learning' that is beneficial to students financially and in their career preparation.

Without losing sight of broad educational goals and values, universities will need to demonstrate their efficacy in educating, orienting and preparing students for employment including self-employment. This is likely to weigh more heavily in the future, on the policy environment and on students' choices of institutions and courses. As Kivinen and Ahola (1999) remark: *"The transition from education to employment is no longer an exogenous variable in the art of proceeding from manpower forecasts to educational planning, it is an endogenous part of the new educational strategy aiming at quality and efficiency."*

Universities and industry have not been unresponsive. For example in 1996 the UK Committee of Vice-Chancellors and Principals together with the Confederation of British Industry and the Council for Industry and Higher Education and a number of other agencies declared a joint responsibility for extending career preparation, issuing guidelines for action to facilitate 'earning and learning' (The Council for Industry and Higher Education, 1996).

Instead of seeing occupational opportunity and preparation as a zone of conflict between the educational values of critical inquiry and independent thought, and employers' criteria for screening and selecting candidates, allocating jobs and maintaining a continuity of their own structures, universities generally have begun to accommodate, much more readily than hitherto, the requirements of employment for their graduates. Many have highly advanced procedures for this purpose. Nevertheless, the warning sounded by the OECD in its international study *From Higher Education to Employment* (1993) still needs to be heeded: efficiency and overall output are conditioned by *"the selection and streaming process; the duration or extension of studies; and the high proportion of failures and dropouts in higher education (in many, not all, member countries), particularly in the initial stages"* (OECD, 1993, p. 143.). The lack of flexibility in promoting short training courses, poor cross-sectoral links and other weaknesses in the structure of supply were also noted. Radical 'new concepts' would be required (p. 145).

As mentioned above, the requirements - or challenges - from the world of work have at times been questioned from within universities as 'instrumentalist' – a subjugation of academic to the utilitarian values of the market place. Paradoxically,

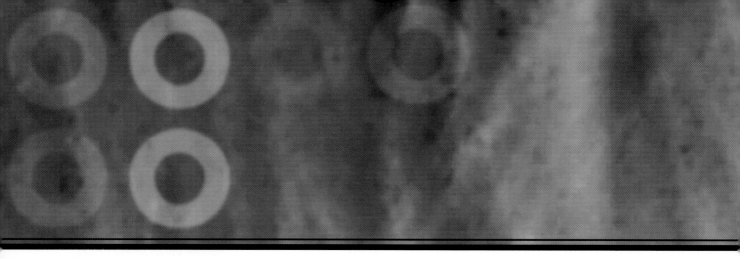

however, the qualities which are usually specified and the courses which are sought correspond in many ways to features traditionally associated with the ideal of a liberal, general education. They include the by now frequently cited attributes of a successful entrant to the graduate labour market:

- Flexibility and adaptability to new, challenging environments;
- Problem-solving capability especially in a team setting;
- Analytical capacity including the ability to produce written reports;
- Creativity and initiative;
- Communication skills.

Employer satisfaction surveys frequently indicate the value attached to such attributes. However, the idea (or ideal) of a well-integrated map of knowledge and intellectual coherence seldom emerges from such lists of desiderata. Issues of balance in the curriculum and the relationship of content to educational values are commonly submerged in catalogues of competency.

A further difference between such sets of attributes and those found in the historical literature on universities (leaving aside the desideratum of competence in at least one classical language) is a mastery of texts or least an aptness in referencing and a grasp of standard interpretations. Theories of liberal education have also generally specified a breadth of studies across several domains. From this quarter, critics of the competency approach reject the separation of generic competences and attributes from specific, domain-structured learning. While there is no agreement on just what domains to include, as against the competency approach the argument is made that students should experience a core of subjects in the arts and sciences. Too many of the statements about the need for graduates to possess generic skills neglect curriculum issues (OECD, 1998d). These and related concerns about the competency movement and the higher education curriculum are taken up in the following chapter.

The emphasis on team work, innovativeness and, to a degree, evaluation, in discussions of the broadening of study requirements, is very much a reflection of the perceived requirements of the professions and large enterprises, private and public into which graduates were (until recently) recruited in large numbers. There have been some attempts to adjust the stated expectations to the small and medium sized enterprises and to self employment which are of increasing relevance to the graduate labour market and to contractual rather than lifetime employment. However, there is still a sense that much of the prescriptive literature on competence envisages the past rather than the emerging labour market. Just how these prescriptions translate into strategies for teaching and learning and curriculum options is taken up in the chapter on Encounters.

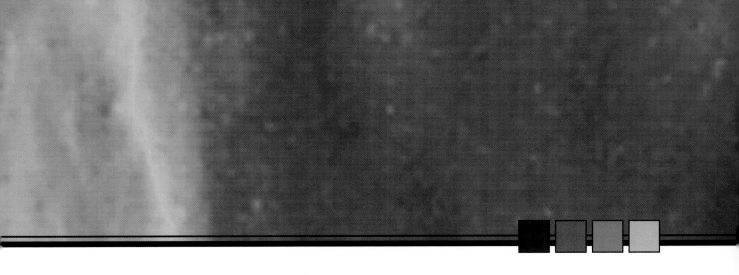

To achieve a closer convergence between the strengths of the liberal tradition and those of contemporary utilitarian/labour market orientations - common threads, as it were, linking the diverse elements in institutions, educational experience and the quest for knowledge - there is need for more rigorous conceptualising and analysis, more coherent curricula and designs for learning. They are to be found - for example in the incorporation of general education courses into professional programmes of study and the combining of work experience with degrees in science, social science and the humanities, in the continuance of liberal or general education and efforts to redefine a core curriculum in contemporary terms in the American college (pre-professional).

The issue is well phrased by Richard Sweet, in pointing to the *"social and economic importance of building a balanced national education and training system which complements the learning styles characteristically valued by higher education - conceptual analysis and synthesis, extended writing, learning by reading and investigation, and theoretical knowledge - with the wider range of cognitive, social and personal competences that are valued in the work place - learning from others, group rather than individual achievement, learning from experience, the achievement of specific outcomes and the practical application of competences. Ultimately the argument is one not so much for a balance between the sectors as for a balance between learning styles, for an integration of learning from others, from application and from experience with learning from abstraction and reflection"* (Sweet, 1992, p. 15).

The growth of private providers

Returning to the issue of institutional heterogeneity, we may observe the growth of private sector provision, described in the OECD report on alternatives to universities as an emerging third sector in many countries (OECD, 1991). Historically, the universities of Europe and several of the English-speaking countries have been and still largely are public institutions. Even if not any longer largely financed by direct public subventions, or regulated in detailed ways by ministries, the universities are public entities in respect of governance, control, use of assets, and accountability. They form part of the public domain displaying the broad cultural features of the public sector, attentive to governmental expectation and responsive to the varied requirements of broad public policy directions. This is true also of many private universities in the USA and Japan, so the distinction between 'public' and 'private' is by no means clearcut.

In some countries, notably among the OECD membership the USA, Japan, Korea and Mexico, and up to a point Italy and Portugal, there is a thriving and sometimes very large sector of private universities, under a great variety of forms of ownership and control. The combination of growing demand for access, an increasingly deregulated operational environment and opportunities for accessing public revenues or tax concessions has resulted in the emergence of a non-governmental sector in several European countries.

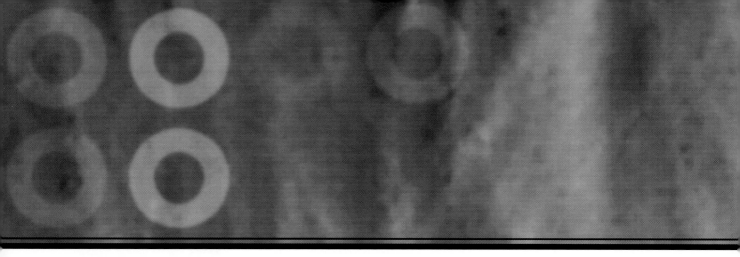

Still relatively small, this private sector, with the prospect of reducing costs of technology for course delivery and a readiness of students to pay fees for valued services, may grow into a complementary system of tertiary education. Its expansion is in part a response to growing and diversified demand, since these institutions are usually specialised in teaching and in subject areas such as computing and business, for which there are growing employment opportunities, or in 'alternative' studies such as para-psychology, religion and alternative health therapies- for which there are start-up business opportunities as well as personal fulfilment demands.

Outstanding questions

The existence of different, often overlapping, sectors, of study programmes and routes pose many questions for policy makers and institutions:

- Are the roles assigned to universities and non-university institutions as clearcut and stable as policy directions, resourcing and the different internal structures seem to suggest?
- Are the institutions able to define and maintain clear distinctions about their missions and the educational and research facilities and services they offer, given the overlapping and drifting that occur?
- Is research selectivity preferable to a policy that seeks to strengthen the capability of all institutions?
- Should the boundaries become more permeable, in respect of entry requirements, courses, qualifications, and areas of concentration?
- How do governments and regulatory authorities propose to maintain or change the boundaries as tertiary education becomes ever more widely available and flexible in delivery?
- Can a policy of 'equal but different' be sustained over time?
- What are the reasonable requirements of students and the community at large for information and advice about the kinds of provision, access to them, the standards and standing of the programme and awards on offer?
- How can better articulation be achieved such that students enrolling in one kind of programme or institution do not find themselves at a dead end on completion?
- Is there need to provide common or core curricular elements and to ensure that all key competences and learning strategies feature in all study programmes at least of initial degrees and other qualifications?
- Are synergies and other complementarities being pursued both horizontally within tertiary education and between the secondary and tertiary levels?

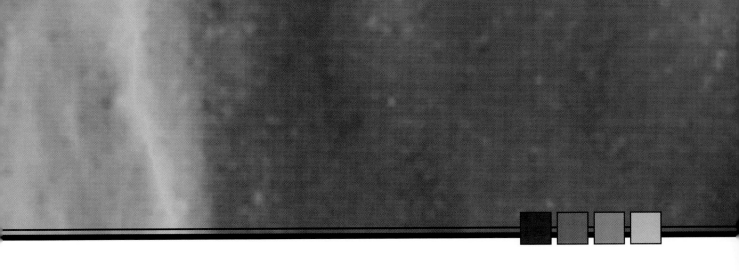

As witnessed in a 1997 OECD/Czech government seminar on diversification, there is a widespread view that greater variety is needed in higher education - in ways of gaining access to study, in course provision and curriculum, in teaching, in ways of studying and study settings, in length of study and requirements for awards, in financing and family support arrangements - and in institutional missions, profiles and ways of functioning (OECD, 1997b). There is a multiplicity of viewpoints on each of these elements and others in the literature and the policy environment. For example, some commentators have called for a relaxation of regulatory procedures in order to foster freedom of institutions to innovate (Birnbaum, 1983); others challenge the conventional wisdom that market-driven systems promote while government-led systems inhibit diversity (Huisman et al, 1998). Unless the established, public sector institutions are able to achieve greater openness and flexibility they will be challenged by a variety of alternatives: enterprise-provided education and training for those already in employment; education and training agencies including for-profit private universities taking advantage of more flexible arrangements for awards and recognition of learning; and the technology-driven 'virtual universities'.

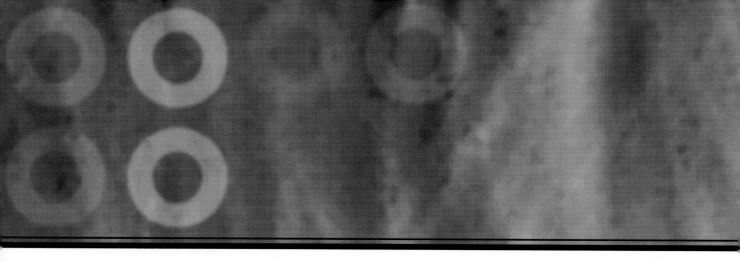

ENCOUNTERS: TEACHING - RESEARCH - SCHOLARSHIP - LEARNING

The four scholarships of academic life: discovery, interpretation, application, teaching (Boyer, 1990)

The image of 'encounters' aims to capture the interrelationships and interactions of teachers and researchers with students, and among teaching, study, learning, and research. Encounters occur in institutions and in the networks institutions are part of, and they are cast in different lights by such institutional processes as governance and management, strategic planning, resource allocation and utilisation and entrepreneurship. Abstracting teaching, study and research from these organisational and institutional processes misses their transactional nature and disguises the complexities in the academic workplace. which are at the heart of the contemporary university. It is just these complexities that need to be faced if sound judgements and decisions at to be made about future directions. They feature in several international studies recently reviewed (Altbach and Cheit (eds), 2001).

Looked at from another perspective, these encounters and the richness of experience that higher education should provide for students (staff as well) are in danger of being fractured and trivialised by the adverse effects of massification. *"One-to-one interaction between scholar and student has been replaced by the mass lecture and crowded tutorials. Leisurely reflection and scholarly contemplation has been replaced by rote learning. And market-like analysis has become common parlance."* (de Boer, Goedegebuure and Meek, 1998).

Paradoxical as it might seem, it is through the success of distance education in creating new designs for learning with technological applications that innovatory ways to rebuild teacher-student relationships have taken root in many universities, the more conventional as well as the dedicated distance providers. Well handled, the opportunities of on-line education could improve these relationships and foster a better quality of learning.

New and improved ways of teaching students is one of the challenges facing higher education staff. The status and prestige of research notwithstanding, according to the Carnegie Commission's international survey of the academic profession teaching students emerged very strongly as the principal defining characteristic of the academic (Boyer et al, 1994). This finding immediately raises questions about the relationship of teaching to what Boyer elsewhere describes as other major constituents of academic life: the discovery, interpretation and application of knowledge.

Then what of the students, often portrayed as being responsible for their own learning once in a university setting and also, often, at the more advanced levels, themselves contributing directly to the 'four scholarships'? Their perceptions, values and expectations do not always feature in the policy debates although, from time to time eg in 1968, they can have a decisive impact for which institutions and policy makers, to say nothing of governments, are unprepared.

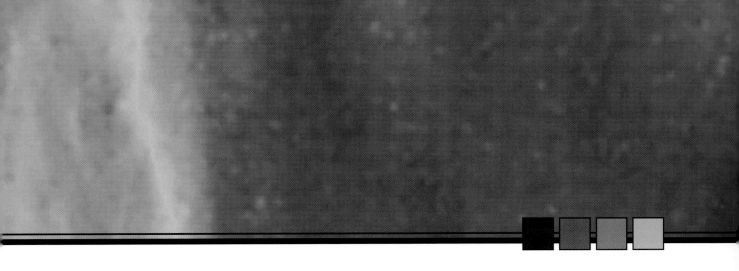

There are considerable uncertainties in the shifting patterns of relationships within institutions and among the various parties, the roles being performed and the processes of academic life. Three perspectives require consideration in considering the four scholarships: those of the student, of the academic and of the various constituencies being served.

But, first, what is meant by the four 'scholarships' and how do they help in understanding the functions performed by academics? 'Discovery' refers to the disciplined search for and verification of knowledge; 'interpretation' to the synthesis of knowledge, for example across disciplines or from diverse sources; 'application' to the uses of knowledge in addressing issues and practical problems in a rigorous way; 'teaching' to the communication and transformation of knowledge through the mutual engagement of teachers and students. The main value of this analytic device seems to have been its assistance in enabling institutions to shape their missions and academics to identify themselves as performing more one and less other of the roles connoted by the processes. Of course, some institutions and individuals will aspire to and claim excellence in all four of the scholarships, and it is obvious that students as well as academics engage in the scholarships, they are not merely their recipients. A practical use some universities have made of the instrument is to broaden the concept of research and to develop more liberal formats for the evaluation of academic performance.

Students to the fore

Generalisations about 'the student' perspective are difficult to make: there are many, diverse student perspectives. In the '60s, for example, highly publicised student action movements often had a very definite political purpose – to bring about a change in power relations both within the university and beyond (Frankel, 1968). Many changes resulted – to university governance and decision-making, curriculum content, resources for study, and teaching procedures. Did these and other developments have a major, enduring impact on the internal life of universities even when the more radical aspirations were not fulfiled? One observer, drawing on national surveys of undergraduates, visits and round tables, found in the American student scene in the 1970s disillusionment and apathy, a sense of powerlessness in an atmosphere dominated by Vietnam and Watergate (Levine, 1980). Yet the recognition of student needs as one central feature of institutional policy in the 1990s owes as much of its inspiration to the 1960s-inspired reforms, as it does to the growth of enrolments and the much greater diversity in the student population.

Students collectively have often been characterised in the aftermath of the oil shocks and recessions of the 1970s as quiescent, focused especially in the '80s and '90s on a narrow range of mainly vocational goals. Now they are sometimes accused of indifference to the major political, social and cultural issues of the day – a charge difficult to square with their involvement in environmental campaigns and protest movements, over economic globalisation. Students are reported in some Norwegian studies to be motivated by a combination of interests: future jobs, yes, but also by the intrinsic nature of

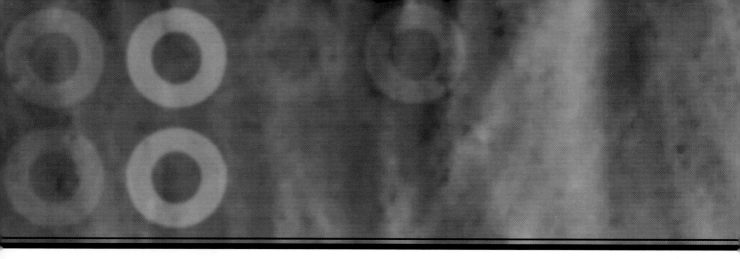

the subjects studied (Aamodt, 2000). In a series of UNESCO reports, representatives of international professional (subject-based) associations of students declared their support for a wide array of social, cultural and ethical positions, as well as expressing concern over graduate employment prospects (UNESCO, 1996). As against the assertion that students today are preoccupied by job preparation and labour market opportunities - there is evidence that this is grossly overstated. Few students have clear and definite ideas about their future careers; they make study choices not on narrow vocational lines but in the expectation of interesting careers and because of enjoyment or anticipated enjoyment of the subject matter (Pitcher and Purcell, 1998). Several of the UNESCO reports also support this view. The participation of organised student groups now in protest movements, such as those mentioned above and their support for various social and environmental issues, suggest that the focus of their critical energies has shifted from the inner life of the university to the wider environment. But here, too, there are counter tendencies, for example, forceful student protests in France over study conditions in universities and in Germany over proposed increases in fees.

The engagement of students with issues whether within the university or in the wider community is what attracts publicity. They constitute one kind of encounter. But for the vast majority of students and over time far more pervasive are their encounters with the academic demands and opportunities of formal study, and their participation in the life of the university as a centre of social and cultural life. Several issues arise: information and advice available to facilitate choice of type of institution and study lines; support and guidance in meeting study requirements; adequacy of facilities and resources; quality and relevance of curricula; standards of teaching, campus life and others. One concern of growing importance is the incidence of low performance, failure and dropout, to be taken up later. Another is graduate unemployment. A third issue, frequently overlooked, is how to develop a rich university experience for adults, part-time and off-campus students.

Why do students choose the courses they do? And what follows from what may be ill-informed choices? In a report for the Council for Industry and Higher Education, course preferences of students in UK universities were charted. Relationships between subjects chosen and employment opportunities were found to be uneven, strong for some subjects (such as medicine, veterinary science and law) and much weaker in others (such as mass communication, documentation and creative arts) (Smithers and Robinson, 1996a). Lacking data on the reasons students give for course preferences, it is impossible to say whether in fact enrolment in apparently employment-related courses is for precisely defined vocational reasons. Motives and interests are much more likely to be mixed and to relate to the overall lifestyle and opportunities promised by the institution as well as to future career avenues.

The European practice of enrolling university students directly in courses with a vocational orientation results in choices being made which may not relate closely to longer term career interests and aspirations. Some apparently professional courses are selected for a mixture of academic reasons and a belief that they provide entrèe to a wide range of occupations. Law is a notable example. The American efforts to sustain some kind of general education at least in the first two years of higher education are designed to maintain greater openness of decision-making and to keep alive the principle of breadth of study into adulthood. There are, however, conflicting reports on the educational value and quality of these programmes, with efforts constantly being made to revise and restructure content and teaching methods.

Whatever the content and form of the education, graduate labour market changes in the '80s and the development of whole new economic sectors have produced heightened expectations of and by students. These changes and developments were a mix of a relative decline in public sector job opportunities for graduates (OECD, 1993) and the growth of technology-intensive and service employment especially in the private sector. From being, typically, employees, graduates were beginning to be seen by more people as innovators, problem-solvers and job creators (Williams, 1994). Furthermore, and arising from the increases in participation and the so-called over-education thesis (graduate jobs not matching subjects studied and levels of attainment), some commentators have suggested that there is now an opportunity for the graduates themselves to be re-thinking occupational hierarchies and rigidities, i.e. acting as significant social change agents (Teichler and Kehm, 1995). To summarise, there is a multiplicity of sound reasons for students to be educated and to educate themselves as prospective innovators rather than as functionaries or conforming professionals.

What is the responsibility of the university toward students?

A primary obligation of universities is, through teaching, access to resources and assessment, to foster, facilitate and advance students' learning. But what is the nature of this learning? Being learned, in earlier times, meant specialisation (in prescribed subjects), concentration, focus and demonstrable performance (Seeley, 1867). This holds true today but with the vast increase in subjects studied at university and in the numbers and diversity of students - staff as well - 'learning' is often reduced to the mastery of content in modularised courses, the preparation of assignments and reports and the answering of examination questions. How well this connects with students' talents, interests, motivations, career interests and options and longer term needs as potential lifelong learners is often a matter of chance. Too often, the curriculum is defined as a set of courses and their assessment requirements whereas the curriculum as experienced is the whole life and culture of the institution, relations among students, the values they encounter, the lifestyles they explore and so on. These less tangible - or less controlled - aspects of university life are often what have lifelong impact. But do universities take them sufficiently into account in their planning and self-evaluations? Likewise, how often are interpretative and integrative

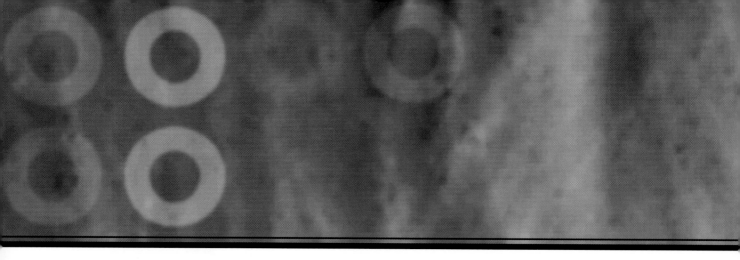

uses of knowledge, application to concerns and problems beyond the immediate realm of the specialised course, and multiple perspectives on issues fostered and facilitated?

How far are universities responsible for students' performance, as distinct from providing a structure for self-managed learning - in the form of a curriculum, lectures, tutorials (in diminishing quantity), demonstrations, assignments, tests and examinations - and resources such as libraries, computing facilities, laboratories and so on? Low levels of performance, dropout and failure rates were identified in the OECD multi-country review of the first years of tertiary education as a serious and growing problem (OECD 1998d). The OECD review commended efforts by institutions to identify students in need of special assistance, to provide special advisory and support services, to modify curricula and teaching in recognition of an increasingly diverse student population and generally to take direct responsibility for helping students to come to terms with the various pressures and demands that they daily encounter.

However, there is another viewpoint, that with diminishing resources per student and the shift toward universal access, universities should focus on providing courses and examining and not be held accountable for high failure and dropout rates (OECD/IMHE General Conference, 2000). Although this voice is heard, more common now is the expressed advice of academic leaders that teaching very broadly defined must be taken more seriously and that it is indeed important to identify and assist students whose study skills may be weak (Bok, 1982; Casper 1995; Tait and Entwhistle 1996; Mjoes, 2000).

Two schools of thought thus dominate the debate about responsibility towards students. The first is that the university provides opportunities, it is for the student to take them or not. Often, but not always this is associated with an *a la carte* approach whereby students are free to select from a very wide array of course modules, assembling their own curriculum in accordance with what may be very broad guidelines.

The other school takes a more prescriptive approach, whether it be in the form of the structured professional degree in which course requirements over several years are highly regulated, or the characteristically American view that there is some kind of core or framework of knowledge that all students should encounter in the pre-professional college programme. It is the belief that students should master a broad curriculum of general education that has provoked the widely publicised and perhaps fiercest debates about the responsibilities of academics, but also of students. In the wake of two very well known critiques in the late '80s (Bloom, 1987; Hirsch, 1988) many leading figures entered the fray in the early '90s (Cheney, 1989; Ratcliffe, 1990; Carnegie Commission for the Advancement of Teaching, 1992; Adelman, 1992b).

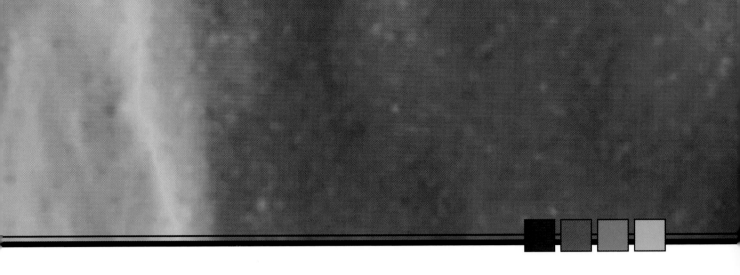

No comparable debate appears to have occurred elsewhere, but perhaps the nearest parallel is to be found in those systems, notably the UK, where 'graduate' attributes, competence and generic skills rather than curriculum content have been widely discussed.

Since the 1960s there have been many efforts to give greater prominence in institutional and system-wide policies to a broad range of clearly defined student needs. The quality of teaching and the standards attained by students is a recurring concern in the USA where special faculty development centres have been established and departments and individual academics made more accountable for student performance (Jones and Ewell, 1993; McGuinness, 1995). Various forms of assistance for students with special learning needs (e.g. physical impairment) have become commonplace in most countries, if still insufficient in some respects (Skilbeck, 2000). Universities have modified curricula, introducing whole new programmes and courses, including for emerging new vocations and in response to contemporary issues (environment, ethnicity, sexuality, alternative medical therapies, developing world needs, among others). Special student support centres have been developed by individual faculties. Guidance and counselling facilities and information services, although still far from adequate overall, have been improved (OECD, 1998d).

Nevertheless, as already mentioned, dropout rates are high and they may be increasing in some countries. From a large scale survey in the USA, Dey and Hurtado (1995) concluded that students are taking more time to graduate than in the 1960s or between 1972 and 1982: a norm of approximately six years (for four year degree programmes) has been established and is causing policy concern. Finance is seen as a major cause of non-completion, with increasing numbers of students taking part-time jobs to assist in meeting costs and keeping loans in check. Ireland is among the countries with a survival rate of almost 80% for initial degrees; there are several countries where it is 55% or less. On average about one third of all entrants to university level institutions do not graduate (OECD, 2000, C4). There are varied specific reasons that explain these rates, some positive such as finding employment. But failure is one explanation and the unavailability of suitable courses and poor teaching/learning opportunities and facilities are others.

In response to long standing concern over weaknesses in study opportunities, efforts have been made to establish principles of good practice in the education of undergraduates. In the USA, *Seven Principles of Good Practice in Undergraduate Education* have been enunciated:

- improved contact between staff and students;
- co-operation in learning among students;
- active learning;

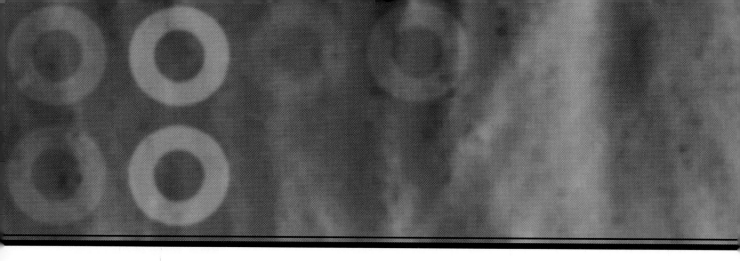

- prompt feedback;
- time on task;
- communicating high expectations;
- respecting diverse talents and ways of learning.

(Gamson, 1991).

That there should be need to enunciate such basic principles is indicative of problems in the performance of staff and students alike. Other initiatives in the USA are a consortium of 17 institutions, the Renaissance Group, which has been established for the purpose of improving undergraduate learning and teaching (Weidmer, 1993) and the programme of the Washington-based Fund for the Improvement of Post Secondary Education which has funded numerous projects in curriculum development, teaching and learning (Marcus 1993). In a number of countries - Australia, Denmark, France and the USA - interest has been taken in incentive-based funding whereby, for example, the level of grant to the institution is influenced by completion rates and student grants are affected by their success in study.

In Australia, the Commonwealth Government established a Committee for the Advancement of University Teaching, which for several years in the decade of the '90s provided grants to foster innovations aimed at improving teaching. This work continues under the Australian Universities Teaching Committee, with a modest level of funding. The fostering and support of innovation in teaching is strongly recommended in a recent large scale review of Norwegian higher education (Mjoes, 2000). With increasing use by universities of on-line teaching there will be an obligation to train staff in a range of pedagogical, technical and managerial matters. Necessary as this is, it should not result in a preoccupation with means of delivery and communication to the neglect of the wider curriculum issues outlined above.

Specialist journals have been established to facilitate communication and exchange of information and ideas on tertiary teaching and learning in science, philosophy, engineering and others. Fifty such journals were already in existence early in the '90s (Weiner, 1993). Various reforms and innovations are discussed in the literature: the uses of the new technologies; modularisation of courses; and replacement of traditional academic years and terms by a semester system with, as a result, more structured courses and feedback to students through more frequent assessments. This innovation, long established in the USA, Australia and the UK, has been more recent in France when it followed waves of protests and demonstration by students dissatisfied with the first cycle higher education programmes. Individual student records have been introduced in the United Kingdom, a step towards tracking student progress including transfer from one institution to another.

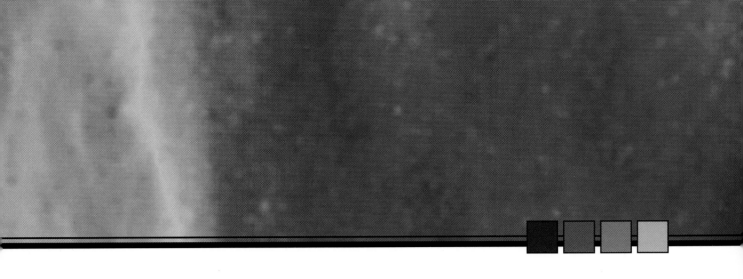

International competitiveness and other economic factors are frequently cited as a reason for improving the quality of student learning. 'Trained minds' are sought in increasing numbers (as long as the economy remains buoyant) For some, this line of reasoning leads to the idea of a national core curriculum for undergraduate education, with a common basis for assessing student performance (Woollard, 1996). In Australia, the Federal Minister of Education has recently announced a national trial of a test of general competence for graduates. These are among the signs of dissatisfaction with the unduly specialised, narrow, vocation-specific courses that have come to dominate many undergraduate programmes.

Work experience and recognition of prior learning

One of the most significant innovations of recent years in many university programmes is industry or work experience. As discussed in the previous chapter, credit is being granted in both undergraduate and graduate or advanced professional programmes. Providing students with on-the-job skills and pre-professional work experience have for long featured in professional disciplines and vocational programmes. They have now attracted support to ease transition from higher education to working life for all students (Thomas, 1995; Valo, 2000). Formal recognition of and credit for work-based learning was given very strong impetus in the United Kingdom through Enterprise in Higher Education (EHE), one of the largest research and development programmes of its kind anywhere (Hale and Pope, 1994; McNain, 1994; Whitely, 1995). Work-based learning has become important not only by virtue of its incorporation within degree and diploma programmes but also as a way of recognising and giving credit for prior learning, and for facilitating articulation of different levels and sectors of tertiary education. In some settings it is an important access route especially for mature age students. Its value in fostering relations between universities and industry has been widely attested. Now common in the USA and Australia and becoming more so in the UK, the accreditation of prior learning is still relatively rare in European higher education. Despite attempts, in Australia and the UK for example, to introduce national schemes of credit recognition, institutions and parts of institutions have declared a strong preference for individual approaches (Topley and Clinch 1992). This reflects the tradition of the academic autonomy of the university. There has been resistance - by New Zealand universities, for example - to what are regarded as intrusive and over-strenuous efforts to standardise and monitor degrees through the operations of national qualifications authorities which aim to articulate diverse forms and levels of competence.

...Are often linked to the competency model of learning

Schemes of work-based learning and credit for prior learning are often associated with the so-called competency movement, discussed in the previous chapter. Lists of such competences and strategies for their acquisition and

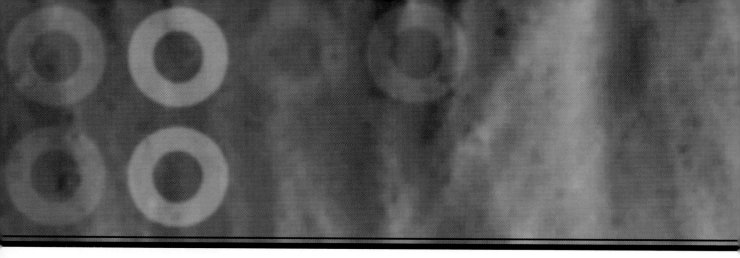

development are frequently found in the literature on vocational training and have begun to make an impact on higher education. Their advocates see this as a way of sharpening the focus on the purposes and outcomes of learning and specifically linking them to socio-economic needs. However, critics are uneasy about the implications for academic structures and widely used assessment practices.

There are other approaches as well. In the United States, competencies are associated with the affirmation of national goals for education. The goals movement has had a strong impact on schools thanks to the involvement of the President and State Governors. For undergraduate education, key requirements are 'an advanced ability to think critically, communicate effectively and solve problems' (Jones and Ewell, 1993). The goals call for a substantial increase in the proportion of college graduates able to demonstrate these attributes regardless of field of study or type of institution. Business and industry leaders have likewise called for improvements in undergraduate education including greater concentration by institutions on teaching, with more staff time in classroom. Calls such as these reflect the variability of standards of teaching and learning, and a tendency in many universities to give a low priority to undergraduate teaching. The Education Commission of the States, together with the National Center for Higher Education Management Systems, has enunciated an elaborate set of targets and means for improving teaching and learning, including cross-disciplinary knowledge and skills and closer attention to the diversity of the student population (Jones and Ewell, 1993).

The competency model, when detached from disciplines and settings, has met strong academic criticism, as neglecting learning processes, narrowing the range of desirable learnings, neglecting creativity and imagination, dualising theory and practice/knowledge and skill, placing enormous demands on teachers and leading to a dominance of remediation in university teaching (Taylor, 1996, pp. 69-70).

It seems unlikely that competency-based approaches will supersede more traditional ways of designing curricula and courses, setting learning requirements and structuring tests and examinations. The notion of generic competence not identified with disciplines or specific fields of study has been widely rejected by the academic community. Nevertheless, its close association with the impetus for reform to achieve greater relevance and better links with working life, together with moves in several countries to set up qualifications frameworks, will ensure that 'competency' remains on the agenda. Moreover, not all forms of 'competency' are presented as if they had no reference to disciplines and emphasis is often given to interdisciplinary learning, integration of education and experience and so on (Jones and Ewell, 1993).

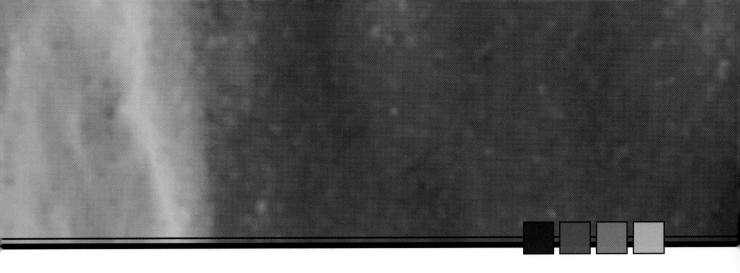

A further consideration respecting the competency model is that it is of practical service in environments where new and multiple providers aim to provide alternative forms of higher education which can be recognised and accredited in different ways. Qualifications frameworks, because they provide a means of recognising academic programmes and learning outcomes other than those passing through the traditional academic apparatus of established universities, are attractive to the emerging private, virtual universities. These institutions, when operating internationally like the private, for-profit University of Phoenix, or the Norfolk Island-based Greenwich University, need to achieve recognition for their awards and are often ready to take advantage of whatever flexibility in this regard is available to them.

Flexible, distance and open education, the virtual university movement and the expansion of on-line study aim to facilitate student learning ...

The main interest of the virtual university movement, however, is not the methods used to attain recognition but the potential use of communication and information technology to educate large numbers of students at an affordable cost and with the maximum flexibility ('time and space free'). Building on a century-long tradition in several countries of distance education by correspondence and low technology, the virtual university movement is another step towards the universalisation of tertiary education. The term 'virtual university' may be taken as shorthand for a considerable range of institutions, agencies and forms of education. But what is usually denoted is a single institution operating all its programmes and courses in such a way that students study off-campus by means of printed course materials, telephone hook-ups, on-line computing and other devices whereby they can complete degree and diploma requirements from home or work bases.

'Virtual' may also refer to the technological system whereby many conventional or on-campus universities are increasingly providing learning opportunities which do not require students to attend lectures, tutorials, laboratory classes and so forth, enabling electronic access to content and direct email exchanges, for example over assignments, interactive 'virtual' classrooms. The provision of professional up-dating programmes for staff of public or private enterprises while at their place of work in a major field of future electronic applications.

Another kind of 'virtual' university is a consortium of established institutions which provide courses and course materials to be used on-line or in other flexible ways, coordinated by a central agency. One example is the *American Western Governors' University*, an ambitious plan to establish a non-profit independent corporation drawing together not only existing higher education institutions but also business corporations that train their staff. The Canadian and Australian

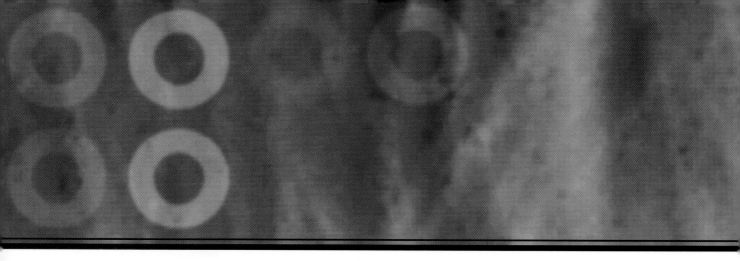

Open Learning Agencies are essentially mechanisms to facilitate ease of access by off-campus students to programmes offered by participating or sponsoring universities. Such bodies thrive on unmet demand and on student requirements for flexible, off-campus study.

Of growing significance is the mobilisation of the private sector, government departments and a variety of agencies in association with higher education institutions. Collaborative arrangements include, for example, the Queensland Open Learning Network, a public agency which defines its 'clients' as students, participating colleges and universities, government departments and business enterprises, for all of whom delivery and support services are provided through a sophisticated on-line technology and a network of regional study centres. The international consortium of universities – Universitas 21 – has been actively seeking a partner in the international media/communications industry for the development and global delivery of a wide array of courses and study programmes. Yet again there is the Vancouver-based Commonwealth of Learning, an intergovernmental agency working in close association with educational institutions, business, government and non-government agencies and international organisations to facilitate access to education including technology-based learning.

Alongside these innovatory institutions and consortia is the steady increase in use of on-line study opportunities by conventional universities. Still at an early stage in many systems and generally still concentrated in particular fields of study (computing, business studies for example) there is expected to be both a widening of the range of courses 'going on-line' and a blurring of traditional distinctions such as on- and off-campus, part- and full-time study, and a challenge to the identity of the university as the source and provider of advanced knowledge.

The question, then, for universities is how do they redefine their role in relation not only to new providers but to new ways of acquiring, developing, accessing and using their primary staple, advanced knowledge? The scale of the cultural changes required is formidable, as Renwick (1996) points out, calling for institutional self-renewal and leadership of the highest order. It is the introduction and spread of the new communication and information technologies (CIT) that has given impetus to a wide array of pedagogical innovations and institutional arrangements in higher education (Daniel, 1998; Trow, 1999b).

All of those structures and modes have as one of their principal objectives enhanced access by diverse groups of students to flexible learning systems. Increasingly they are building in electronic technology to supplement (but not displace) print-based and face-to-face learning. The terms distance, flexible and open education are often used interchangeably; it might

be better to think of distance education or the open university as means for achieving greater openness and flexibility, and the virtual and on-line university and the use of CIT as a mechanism and set of devices for achieving this. In the words of the Vice-Chancellor of the Open University, *"Open education is an end whereas distance education is a means"* (Daniel, 1992).

For long resisted, regarded as an inferior alternative, these more flexible approaches are becoming widely accepted (Middlehurst et al, 2000). The conventional view of inferior quality and lower standards of student attainment is not borne out by the evidence. Retention rates are, however, an issue, calling for closer attention to conditions of study, guidance, assessment practices and overall support (Benson, 1996; Long, 1994; McGivney, 1996; Roseman, 1996; St John et al, 1996). The perception by established, on-campus universities of the benefits (financial as well as educational) of the uses of technology in enrolling off-campus as well as on-campus students, has undoubtedly been a factor in the growing acceptance of these 'alternative' modes. Their value in facilitating partnerships with large private and public enterprises for the provision of professional staff training has been quickly recognised by some universities although disregarded by others.

In the western states of the USA, universities such as Stanford and other leading private institutions, the nine campuses of the University of California and the National Technological University are delivering an increasing number of courses and study programmes using CIT. The University of Phoenix, a private, for-profit institution, is developing as a major international provider alongside such established institutions as Britain's Open University. There are major distance or off-campus institutions in several Asian countries, Canada, Australia, South Africa, the Netherlands and others (Harley, 1992; Van Dam-Mieras, n.d. but 1998). In a growing number of traditional universities, there is a determination to reject old dichotomies between on- and off-campus and to transform face-to-face teaching through the use of the new technologies (Arnold, 1999). The more forward-looking institutions are not waiting for the 'ideal' technology at an 'affordable' price but are themselves pioneering uses and steadily upgrading their communication and information systems - as has happened throughout the history of distance education.

To what extent are these developments complementary to or an extension of what already exists? Do they foreshadow a radical alternative? There are those who argue that the traditional residential university will become redundant as structured learning materials of the highest quality, backed with tutorial support and guidance, available on-line both 'time and space free' become universally available. Institutions, it is claimed, have lost power to students: they will need to become much more flexible in response to student needs and demands. Specialised distance education institutions no longer command their niche now that delivery of courses through technology or with strong technology elements is becoming widespread in conventional universities (Kershaw and Safford, 1998).

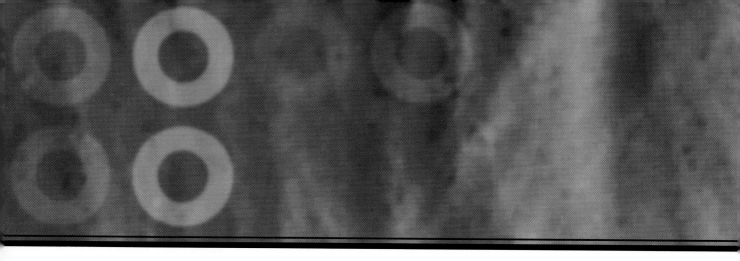

Advocates of the residential campus tradition point to the practical problem of effective access, the variable quality of materials and services, the positional advantage of on-campus study in many fields, the socio-cultural power and the enormous physical mass of high quality, face-to-face institutional provision. Whatever the outcome, it is already clear that the first stage of complementarity has been reached, that 'screen-based literacy' is already a requirement and that very large numbers of students are benefiting from distance and on-line education in one form or another. This is true not only of undergraduate but of post-graduates as well (James and Beattie, 1997).

Moreover, the technological challenge is really about ways of maximising student learning, not simply installing electronic systems. It will require institutions to abandon old rivalries and learn to work together. On-line developments are particularly worrying in this respect since only through more collaboration among universities and with media organisations can wasteful duplication and variable quality of courses and course materials and resources be avoided. This concern applies as much to on-campus programmes for full-time students as to the more traditional category of part-time adults studying off-campus.

...With growing opportunities for adults studying part-time

Now being vigorously marketed on both social-democratic and economic grounds as an effective 'second chance' system, part-time higher education of adults has in the past suffered in many countries as a result of institutional and staff preferences for the venerable full-time on-campus model. This has been particularly so in Europe by contrast with North America (OECD, 1987a, pp. 21-27). Yet, as Becher (1999) argues, universities *are missing an important market potential, if not a social obligation, in their relative failure to provide for the learning needs of professionals in mid-career*" (p. 157).

Part-time study provision in some countries is indeed a neglected aspect of higher education (Schuler et al, 1999) but in Australia and the United States, for example, both part-time (on- and off-campus) undergraduate as well as mid-career professional programmes form a very substantial part of the higher education system. There has been substantial growth in the number and proportion of older students in initial higher education in England, with a broader range of qualifications being accepted for admission (Parry, 1997). Participation in part-time adult education (higher education included) in the Nordic countries, with their social democratic roots, has burgeoned since the 1970s - but struggled to gain status (Rinne and Kivinen, 1993). For the UK, and particularly Northern Ireland, Pyper argued that if a comprehensive system of mass higher education is to develop, policy makers would have to base their decisions on part-time as well as full-time participation (Pyper, 1998).

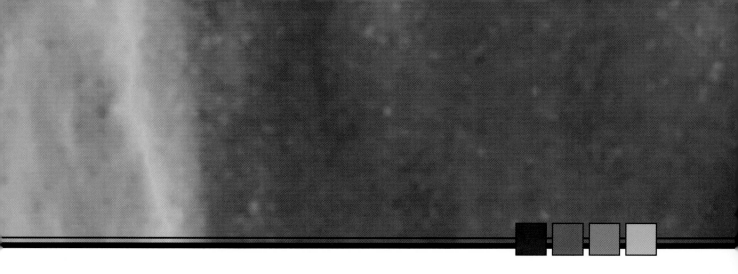

The issue of 'mainstreaming' adult, continuing, part-time education in Ireland was raised in 1994 in the *Report* of the National Education Convention and adopted as a policy direction in the 1995 White Paper, *Charting our Education Future*. It surfaced again in the IRDAC report *Quality and Relevance - The Challenge of European Education* and the *Report of the Steering Committee on the Future Development of Higher Education* in 1995 and in *The Report of the Review Committee on Post Secondary Education and Training Places* (1999). In 2000, more key documents have been issued: the report of a symposium on open and distance learning; *Learning for Life: White Paper on Adult Education*; and the proceedings of a national conference, *Higher Education. The Challenge of Lifelong Learning*.

Targets for Ireland are clearly set forth in the White Paper: to raise the figure of 2% of new entrants to higher education over 26 years of age to 15% by the year 2005, with an aim of further increases in subsequent years. The higher education institutions are challenged to meet these targets and to some extent have embraced them, at least in principle (Conference of Heads of Irish Universities, 1998). Government and the Higher Education Authority would need to put in place the financial and other arrangements to facilitate this rate and scale of progress (see also Part III).

Teichler has outlined the numerous and diverse roles higher education already plays in adult learning, through both advanced academic and professional programmes, short training courses, and others, among a mix of distance education, evening classes, sandwich and short courses (Teichler, 199 9b). Increasingly, as professional associations, large employers and governments introduce requirements or strong incentives for continuing professional development, conventional universities will have the opportunity to become major providers. They will not enjoy a monopoly, however, and those active in this field are already finding themselves in competition with private training firms, the training arms of the professional associations - and the virtual universities. The technological challenge to universities posed by commercial educational networks capable of offering a wide range of global products and the number and variety of providers of part-time, professional education growing in number and scale to meet expanding demand, cannot be disregarded. While some institutions have mobilised themselves to treat the challenge of competition as an opportunity, many others have not.

Post-graduate education

The growing perception among policy makers that research is a key driver of market economies, the basis of wealth creation and the quality of life, has raised the profile of research policy. Researchers are increasingly employed by the private sector - outside the universities. Advanced professional diplomas and post-graduate degrees are of growing importance in different fields of professional practice. Several countries, Ireland among them, are currently expanding

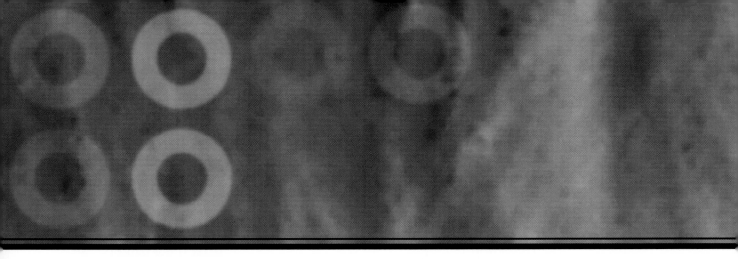

provision of places and support for post-graduate study. The nature and organisation of research and professional education in universities is under active scrutiny, and a number of significant structural and substantive changes are evident:

- Growth of taught post-graduate courses, particularly at the masters level, many with a strong professional orientation. Two distinct degree patterns are commonly found at master's level: professional masters, and research masters. Taught masters, especially, are increasingly seen as a source of university income;

- Considerable rethinking of doctoral programmes, especially those by research only is reflected in: alternative models (greater orientation towards the needs of varied research careers, especially those in industry); graduate school structures; reduced length of doctoral courses - focus on efficiency in research education;

- Placement of research students in industry and/or government at masters and doctoral levels has become an important element in universities' external networks;

- Inducements to post-graduate study are a mixture of: scholarships through universities, research institutes and industry; changes in fee and loan regimes; and vigorous marketing by institutions competing to strengthen their research profile;

- Increasing numbers of female students are enrolling in post-graduate study, although gender imbalance continues in certain fields of study.

(Henkel, 2000b; Slaughter et al, 2000; OECD/IMHE, 2000b; Skilbeck and Connell, 2000). Several of these themes are further addressed in the discussion of scholarship and research, later in this chapter.

The academic profession. Teaching...

It was the notable Irish economics professor, George O'Brien, who remarked that a professor *"is a teacher not a research worker in a laboratory. He should be an interesting teacher rather than a deep original scholar"* (cited in Meenan, 1980, p. 157). But such directness and absence of complexity in characterising the role of academics is rare today. Even when it is accepted that the primary responsibility is to teach and to teach well, there are structural features of universities and an assortment of demands on academics that stand in the way of an uncluttered role model. Teaching is embedded in a complex array of institutional functions and requirements and, despite its centrality, is often an uncertain factor in career advancement and recognition. Yet the values, attitudes, capabilities and interests of teachers - indeed of all staff - must weigh heavily on any decisions that are taken - or sought to be taken - about innovatory practice and future developments: *"almost everything in a university depends on the inner motivation of teachers - their sense of pride, their intellectual involvement with their subjects, their professional commitment to the role of the teacher, their love of students or of learning"* (Trow, 1989).

This observation was made in a criticism of growing policy interest in external assessments of teaching. It needs to be set alongside the roles of students as partners in the learning process, and of institutional leaders and managers to whom falls

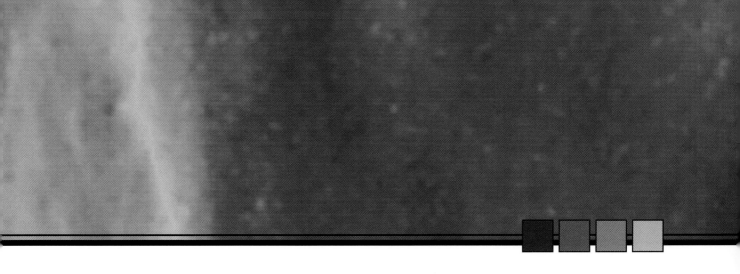

a responsibility for charting new directions while sustaining institutional health and vitality. While few would dispute that, even in the face of rapid technological advance, the teacher's role is vital, there are serious problems in the academic profession.

In a short secretariat memorandum, the Higher Education and Research Committee of the Council of Europe summarised conclusions of a number of studies which converge on a set of key concerns: internationally, teaching in universities is an ageing profession; conditions have deteriorated (staff-student ratios, salary relativities, career lines and standing in the community). There has been a very significant growth in the proportion of part-time and contract staff sometimes for the good reasons of importing outside expertise, new blood and mobility, but often also for reasons of economy or institutional flexibility that do not well serve staff career interests (Council of Europe, 1997). Halsey (1992) saw an emerging 'proletarianisation' and 'bureaucratisation' of the collegiate system (which in its ideal form consisted of a community of scholars enjoying recognition and status) as an outcome of the moves towards mass and universal participation. Kogan et al (1994) criticised the neglect of both demographic and qualitative aspects of policies on academic staffing in a period of continuing enrolment increases and the many expectations and changes to which they have given rise. Commenting on the paucity of data and systematic studies, Husbands (1998) called for improved data and policies attuned to the likely increasing demand for part-time teachers, in the UK (Continental Europe and North America, too).

Allied with these widely expressed concerns in the literature are the pressures of reporting and accountability requirements in relation to the use of resources, equity targets, and quality improvement and assurance requirements that fall on institutions, hence on staff. Changes to work practices consequent on the spread of new technologies and institutional reporting and management practices are additional sources of concern.

Philip Altbach envisaged one scenario for the future of the academic profession which, if it were to be realised, would greatly lower its status and possibly also its value to students and the community: 'The future professoriate will be different in a number of ways from the traditional academic model:
- Fewer faculty will hold full-time permanent positions
- More faculty will be part-time, responsible for teaching a limited number of courses, with little or no participation in the academic community and little contact with students
- More faculty will hold full-time non-permanent teaching positions. These faculty will constitute a kind of academic lumpen proletariat, going from one job to another with little prospect of a regular appointment
- The academic profession will be more diverse in terms of gender, race and ethnicity...

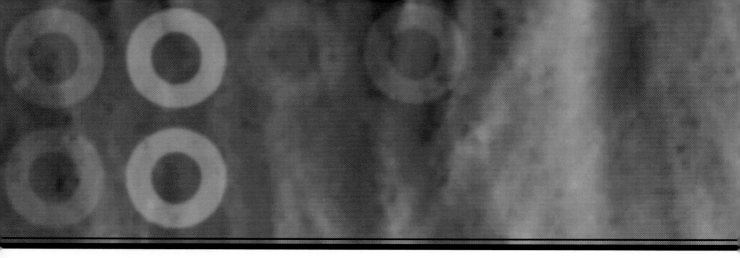

- The faculty will be less research-oriented. Fewer will have positions where research is possible
- The faculty will, on the whole, be less able academically - and the 'best and brightest' will be less frequently attracted to academic careers'

(Altbach, 1998, pp.351-352; Altbach and Chait, 2001).

...Is under considerable challenge but is the target of improvement measures

Encounters between students and teachers in such a scenario would often be problematic and could be de-motivating. But, there are counter tendencies, which suggest the need for at least a modified scenario. Altbach himself, reporting on the Carnegie survey of the international academic profession, said that despite evidence of declining morale and the numerous pressures, most academics found satisfaction in their work with opportunity to pursue their own ideas, professional autonomy and rewarding collegial relationships (Altbach, 1996). Universities have been putting in place a wide array of procedures for the better recognition and strengthening of teaching. They demand a wide range of positive attributes and achievements in both their recruitment and promotion policies, with teaching, research and service all heavily weighted. The growing incidence of part-time and temporary staff does raise problems, but part-time staff can bring university teaching very close to the external environment, including the professions, government and cultural institutions. Changes in employment conditions can be a spur to the development of stronger, not weaker staff. With the advent of technology-rich teaching on a large scale there are many new opportunities for creative and innovative teaching and new relationships both with students and the shifting world of knowledge. But are staff motivated and adequately prepared to take advantage of the opportunities?

It is very clear that strong initiatives in academic staff training and development are needed (OECD/IMHE, 1995). It is usually at the institutional level that this occurs and that is where its effects need to be felt to strengthen the insistence on practical credibility and demonstrable performance that have replaced the mystique of the ivory tower (Camlin and Steger, 2000). As one authority noted, by the mid nineties staff development programmes in higher education institutions had *"moved from cottage industry to institutional necessity"* (Webb, 1996, p. 2). But as he also pointed out, 'necessity' is not always recognised in institutional practice. Webb also contrasted the longer term career development assumptions of some staff development models with the increasing incidence of short term part-time contracts and other temporary arrangements.

Thus there are cross-currents: the structural destabilising of teaching as a long-term, satisfying, highly professional and well regarded career can be difficult to square with the drive to give it a central place in institutional missions and development

strategies. The ascendancy of research as a defining characteristic of a high status institution and the (relative) ease of assessing research performance have led to a perception that teaching is undervalued when, for example, academics seek 'relief' from teaching in order to do research or take on consultancies. On the other hand, and whether out of a genuine concern about threats to good teaching, or because of pressure (from students and from policy makers) universities have developed policies for evaluating teaching, staff training and the recognition of good performance (Boyer, 1990; Wright, 1995; Ramsden and Martin, 1996; Casey et al, 1997).

The use of incentives to recognise, acknowledge and reward quality teaching and strengthen motivation has slowly spread in the academic profession. Initially confined to and now well established in the ranks of senior institutional management, the idea of performance pay usually encounters academic and staff union resistance. The issue is not straightforward and becomes more complex in the team-work environment of technology-rich teaching. Some researchers have suggested that notwithstanding deteriorating salary relativities, and concern over generally worsening conditions, academic staff seek not performance pay but more time, better opportunities for core academic work and more definite recognition of their achievements in academic terms (Thompson, 1993; Kogan et al, 1994).

The academic profession, scholarship and research

As mentioned above 'core academic work' for the academic profession, worldwide, means teaching. Yet career advancement and 'recognition of achievements in academic terms' have been more often aligned to research and publications than teaching, Despite the introduction of schemes for appraising and evaluating teaching performance, there is much debate still about just what is being assessed and by whom. For example, is there a definite, agreed and well-founded expectation that teaching should be research-based? This could scarcely be the case, since it is difficult to find evidence of a close correlation between research activity and teaching performance. Some authors, nevertheless, insist on the mutual reinforcement of teaching and research - the arguments were summarised by Volkwein and Carbone (1994). Nevertheless, there are tensions in the relationship and in a large-scale survey Astin and Chang (1995) noted the difficulty of sustaining a balance in academic practice. Brew and Boud (1995) proposed that instead of attempting to find specific links between research and teaching, attention should be directed to what they have in common, namely the concern for learning.

Boyer's model of four 'scholarships', discussed in the first section of this chapter, is used by some institutions as a way of encouraging all academic staff to be active - if not in research, defined in a narrow way, then in integration or application of knowledge as well as teaching. Elements of the four scholarships are to be found in all universities, albeit in quite

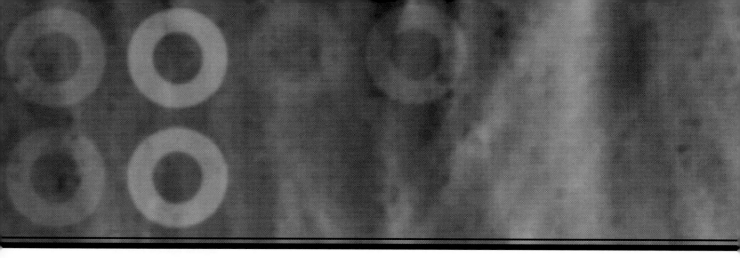

different degrees and balances. Similarly, public policy documents commonly link 'education' and 'research' in strategies to advance national interests. Many of these have been produced over the past decade: in France, Sweden, the UK, Ireland. A typical statement is: *"High quality education and the balanced development of both basic and applied research are prerequisites for successful innovation"* (Ministry of Education, Finland, 1995, p. 13).

Yet there is an older view that questions the high degree of specialisation entailed by research as the term is now commonly understood, or at least seeks to locate it in the borderland or 'outlying camps' of the university (Ortega y Gasset, 1946, p. 75). y Gasset would have at the centre a cultural core, achieved through a 'systematic, synthetic and complete pedagogy'. This view is at odds with the arguments frequently advanced for undergraduate as well as post-graduate teaching being research-grounded (see below) and with the specialisation and atomisation of undergraduate degrees.

Unlike teaching, for research there are widely accepted criteria for assessing performance. Built on the principle of peer review, they entail a domain of public knowledge - research findings and the designs and methods used in reaching them. But it cannot be assumed that the research environment in higher education is stable. With greater interest in partnerships, networks and applications, assessment of research quality has become quite complex. The funding environment has become highly volatile and even leading research universities are having to reposition (and diversify) themselves, including through new alliances and partnerships, in order to remain viable (Elton, 1986; Gellert et al, 1990; Barnett, 1992a; Ramsden and Moses, 1992; Clark, 1995; Taylor, 1996; OECD, 1998a).

As Clark says, *"in the United States and elsewhere, the relationship of research to teaching and learning has grown increasingly complex, ambiguous and controversial"* (Clark, 1995, p. 3). It has not been established invariably that either research enhances teaching, or that teaching/supervision is a significant stimulus to research. The weight of evidence does not support a strong, complex interplay of research-teaching across the whole field of higher education subjects and levels. Of course there are particular relationships according to level of study - for example between supervision of PhD students and the productivity of research of supervisors (Kyvik and Smeby, 1994) but do they justify a belief in necessary and inextricable relationships across the board? Ben David (1972) in an influential study for the Carnegie Commission argued that not all good teaching in universities depends on the active, current engagement of the teacher in research. He added that while every university teacher should be required to do *"some investigation of his own ... to expect from all of them original contributions to knowledge, that is to publish in their field writings that are worth being quoted, is completely utopian"* (ibid, p. 113). Ahead of his time, Ben David called for a new kind of higher degree preparing the 'non quotable' scholars to teach effectively in higher education. This would indicate at least two parallel lines of preparation - the established PhD route with research training a key

component and a professional doctorate route including research training, but of a more varied kind and combined with appropriate professional preparation whether for academic teaching or some other knowledge-intensive career. These two lines would be related in various ways to the four scholarships model discussed above.

The trend, however, since the '70s has been toward a great concentration and specialisation of research with, on the one hand, the setting of higher standards and selective individual/department/institution funding and, on the other, a common (if unrealistic) career expectation that everyone seeking academic career advancement will be trained to a high level and perform as an active researcher. As growth of the sector continues, the argument for selective funding of institutions and departments for research gathers momentum. Arguments from different quarters are advanced in favour of a greater concentration of research funding in a small number of institutions.

In the United States, the category of 'research universities' is well understood and broadly accepted; in the United Kingdom and Australia among other countries, concentration is both strongly advocated and is occurring. Yet there is still no general acceptance in these countries of a categorisation of research-intensive/and essentially non-research universities. Those that are less favoured in competitive tendering do not accept a 'non-research' categorisation. The policy of concentration in Australia, up to the present, has been based on the principle that all universities will have research excellence but not necessarily in all fields. Universities most favoured in research funding have grouped themselves and are arguing for special status (and funds).

Although it would be possible in principle sharply to demarcate research and teaching functions and to distribute staff duties accordingly this is not the practice, even where there may be a tilting of the balance strongly one way or the other: many research posts may entail no teaching or even supervision, and there are teaching-only posts. However, the intimacy of the link is frequently affirmed (Volkwein and Carbone, 1994) and the university traditions and culture (in the spirit of von Humboldt) are inimical to sharp separation.

In this context it is necessary to raise again the question of those forms of postgraduate education and supervision where the lines differentiating teaching and research are often meaningless. Several studies find a relative neglect in development and reform measures of the requirements of postgraduate education and research training - a lack of balance in policy. Clark made this point strongly in his efforts to resuscitate the Humboldtian concept of the university as a centre of knowledge-based inquiry (Clark, 1995). As for provision for postgraduate education, through interviews and a literature

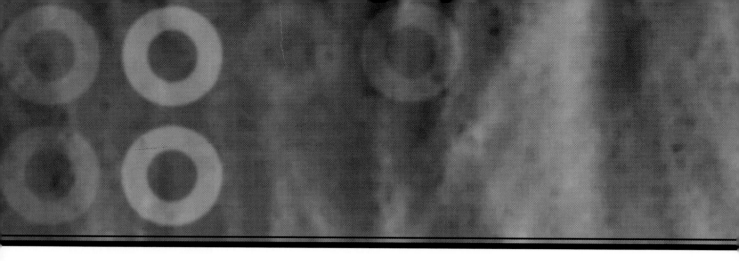

review Holdaway (1996) identified many substantial weaknesses. These included lack of facilities, support mechanisms, weak supervision, neglect of intellectual property rights, high dropout and protracted completion rates. While such problems are widespread, they have not been adequately addressed in policy initiatives directed at university research.

Research is the focus of new partnerships and alliances ...

The old (Humboldtian) idea of university research, largely contained within and advanced through the disciplines and academic departments, has come under increasing strain through the emergence of so-called mode 2 or network/ partnership research (Gibbons, 1995; Gibbons et al, 2000) and issues over knowledge ownership and intellectual property rights. These have come to the fore in mode 2 type partnerships and alliances - defined as productive working relations between university researchers, those in specialist research institutes and industry and commerce - and between this networked research community and the entrepreneurial commercialisation of the products of research.

The tradition of the open currency of knowledge communication and exchange came under heavy pressure in the Cold War period through military research contracts which contained secrecy clauses. These gave rise to a great deal of criticism especially on American campuses in the 1960s. But there is no less secrecy and perhaps a much greater complexity of control and ownership in regard to the fruits of commercially sponsored research and even more so when academics and industry colleagues are in close working partnerships rather than in arms length contract relationships. Put very simply academic researchers may not be at liberty to integrate their teaching with their current, possibly major research interests. Critics of the increasing commercialisation of universities - through the sale of services, contracts, the charging of fees, industry partnerships, control of intellectual property, ownership of and investment in private companies and so on - are concerned not only with course content but also with the principles of free inquiry and exchange of knowledge.

One issue is how to develop a new balance between the firmly and still widely held values of intellectual freedom in both teaching and research, and the benefits of closer working relationships with a wide range of social and economic actors. Another concern, particularly at the level of institutional management, is that institutional policies, ethical and legal requirements are often poorly understood or knowingly by-passed by more entrepreneurial members of staff. A third issue is how to define and develop new, convergent pathways that draw together the processes and results of research, the motives and interests of students, the expertise and experience of industry and the professions, and the skills and commitments of teachers. Such pathways would constitute a major, much needed contribution of higher education to national and regional innovation policies. While some examples exist they do not sit comfortably with academic structures or with funding procedures and they require an enormous effort to plan and implement.

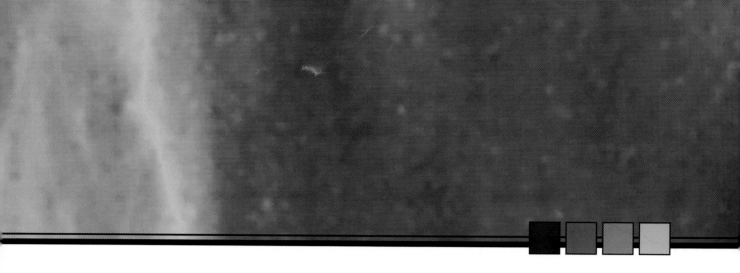

For Ireland, the Technology Foresight project of the Council for Science, Technology and Innovation, envisages a re-positioning towards a knowledge-based economy with complex interrelationships and partnerships among industry, government, higher education and various social actors. The government has accepted the case for research excellence in establishing the Technology Foresight Fund (taken up again in Part III).

The funding of research on the scale of the Foresight Fund and with these intentions raises many of the above issues which will have to be addressed. Much needed as the additional resources are for research, there is no less need for imaginative efforts to develop innovation strategies incorporating the kind of pathways mentioned above.

Geiger (2000) notes important difference in patterns of interaction between universities with large and with small firms. Most academic staff have but limited industry experience and the history of technology parks and start-up companies in many universities in other countries does not present a picture of consistent success. There are also issues, alluded to above, of the very unequal access within institutions to research funds, industry links, consultancies and commercial opportunities. The paths to be followed by universities in building the knowledge-based society and economy will be difficult. Study of experience in those countries where universities are endeavouring the follow these paths would be of great benefit in the new Irish funding environment.

...And a research/inquiry/scholarly culture must permeate the university

The encounters among teaching, research and learning, or Boyer's four scholarships, are numerous and varied. Efforts to interrelate them are apparent in the institutional mission statements and strategic plans that are increasingly favoured as instruments for direction-setting and action. If the aim is not the unification of knowledge, sought for in the classical canon, then at least it is a coherent set of connected and mutually supportive activities. Good teaching cannot be shown to be dependent upon or underpinned by research in all cases but there is a widely shared view that a vigorous, broadly defined research culture should pervade all parts of the university and that there should be a constant endeavour to engage students at all levels in critical, systematic inquiry – which is the essence of research. For this, teachers need to be scholarly, up-to-date and, for preference, active in the pursuit of knowledge. The concept of a pervasive research culture for all universities has a bearing on funding strategies. Such a culture would not be achieved or could not be sustained if highly targeted funding only of pockets of 'excellence' were to become the norm.

Research is still held to be of value in the university environment in its own right, and better when not constrained by extraneous considerations. There is no overall diminution of the arguments that have long been advanced in support of

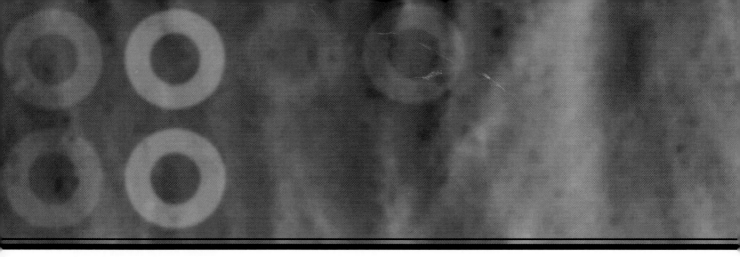

this view or of its acceptance by policy makers and research funding agencies. But it is expected that the value of research be demonstrated, not necessarily through immediate direct applications or the solution of practical problems, but in open discourse about the nature and uses of knowledge. In other words, the image of the ivory tower has largely been discarded. While there is great reluctance to accept constraints of secrecy for either national security or commercial reasons, pressures to reduce openness and transparency continue and may be growing.

The ideals of a unity of different modes and forms of knowledge and shared discourse, bringing together the disparate elements - of subjects, fields and levels of study, teachers, researchers, students and users of knowledge - remain unrealised except in pockets here and there. But there can be renewed efforts to find coherence and complementarity in processes and structures so often seen as separate and unrelated. That indeed would seem to be a necessary condition for the functioning of the knowledge-based society and economy. Moreover, as ideals they serve as a kind of beacon in debates about the purposes, values and directions of universities and a belief in them can continue to enrich the encounters which have been the subject of this chapter.

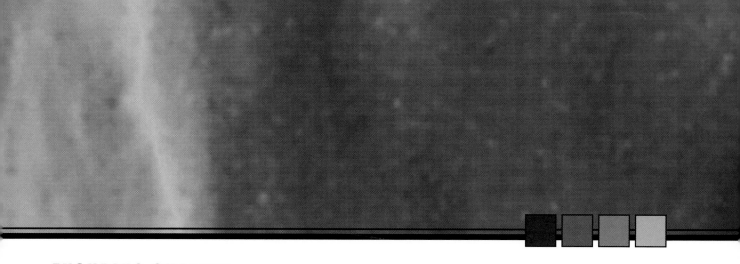

ENSURING QUALITY

'Everyone supports quality, its improvement, its assessment but everyone has a specific idea, different objectives and methods… and they relate directly to questions of power and influence' (Lamoure, 1999, p. 278).

In one sense, it seems paradoxical that sustaining, reporting on, evaluating and auditing 'quality' should have become one of the dominant concerns in higher education policy during the past two decades. After all, education is itself an evaluative, critical, qualitative process: a quality of experience, of learning, an outcome of sustained study and reflective inquiry. 'Higher' education should mean a higher quality, a standard or benchmark against which experience of many kinds, learning at all levels and of all types, study and reflective inquiry are to be appraised. This somewhat abstract approach is given substance when distinguished university leaders raise objections to imposed external requirements and certain procedures for quality assurance which they regard as, at best, tangential and at worst a destructive intrusion into the processes of higher education.

On the other hand, there is nothing new in appraisals of the quality of higher education. Until recent times, these appraisals were generally the prerogative of committees or commissions, or individual critics. Thus Abraham Flexner, anticipating contemporary critics of the college curriculum, early last century found the American College wanting in that it was *"deficient, and unnecessarily deficient, alike in earnestness and pedagogical intelligence … in consequence our college students are, and for the most part, emerge, flighty, superficial and immature, lacking, as a class, concentration, seriousness and thoroughness"* (Flexner, 1908, p. 11). Nowadays, while the judgment might be as severe in substance, it is likely to be far less direct in expression, to be based on much more systematic methods, and to have all the apparatus of carefully recorded and evaluated evidence. It is, however, the requirement of a careful, objective procedure, with the construction of manuals, pro forma, the gathering of evidence, self-evaluation by institutions, faculties and departments and external audit, the preparation of reports and so forth that is leading to a lot of the criticism of the whole idea of system-wide quality assurance.

An international quality assurance movement has emerged …

Despite the objections, steps are now being taken in ever more countries to identify, evaluate and publicly report on higher education processes and outcomes. These involve quite elaborate schemes which commonly combine structured institution/faculty/department self-appraisal with external audit; they entail detailed reporting and administrative procedures; and they are costly.

Two key terms in the contemporary quality lexicon are quality *assurance* and quality *audit*, reflecting a concern for evidence that matters are as they are said to be, and should be, in higher education. For this purpose, there are legislation, regulations,

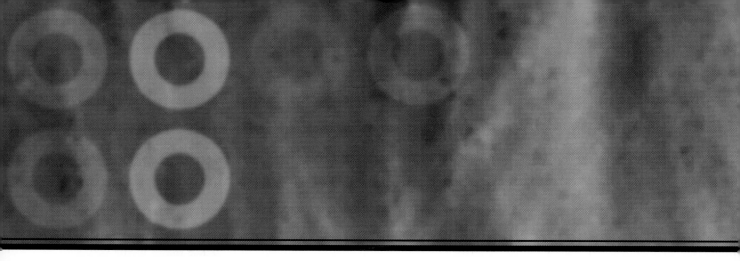

the setting up of specialist agencies, associations and conferences of 'quality professionals', training programmes and a growing literature. While, as yet, funding has not commonly been related directly to the results of quality evaluation, connections are being made. Despite frequently expressed misgivings, it seems unlikely that, as quality indicators are developed alongside the quantity indicators (which at present influence when they do not determine levels of funding), direct links can be avoided.

What reasons are there for national systems of higher education to be seeking from universities greater clarity and explicitness? Why the demand for well documented evaluation reports and for public audits of the procedures universities have in place for self-evaluation? The Higher Education Quality Council in the United Kingdom gives several answers, among them:

- To achieve greater consistency in requirements for the award of degrees and diplomas;
- To assist in clarifying the aims of higher education and standards of performance;
- To clarify and elaborate the attributes expected of graduates;
- To better inform the public and policy makers.

The Quality Council also took the view that academic staff need to improve their ability, individually, to assess standards and, collectively, to achieve more consistency in their assessment decisions (Higher Education Quality Council, 1997). Hence, behind 'assurance' and 'audit' is an expectation of 'improvement' and, by implication, a belief that all is not as it should be.

Not surprisingly, the literature on the quality movement largely sidesteps the issue of just what quality is in higher education. Although there is a generic language of 'fitness for' and 'fitness of' purpose, it is for all practical purposes impossible to specify the immensely varied contents and processes of higher education. Analyses by vast numbers of specialists reviewing and reporting on their own domains would be required. Since this is quite unfeasible, except on a selective and occasional basis, broad strategies have been developed to provide information and facilitate judgements about general and specific features of academic performance. There is some risk of a fashion emerging, whereby points are scored (or lost) according to a convention comprising desiderata for results, outcomes and procedures.

National agencies have been established in a number of countries in the name of assuring quality of higher education. They include: in France in 1987, the Prudential *Comite National d'Evaluation*; in the Netherlands in 1988, the committee of the Association of Dutch Universities; in England, Wales and Scotland, the committees of the Higher Education Funding Council and the Committee of Vice Chancellors and Principals early in the 1990s, and now the single national Quality

Assurance Agency; in Denmark in 1992, the National Centre for Quality Assurance and Evaluation of Higher Education (now titled the Danish Evaluation Institute); in Sweden in 1993, the National Agency for Higher Education; in New Zealand in 1994, the New Zealand Universities Academic Audit Unit; in Australia, in 2000/2001, the Australian Universities Quality Agency.

Although the purposes and working methods of these and other like bodies differ, what they share is an authority, which is often vested through legislation, to appraise and report on performance of higher education institutions, either directly or indirectly. When themselves conducting evaluations, as for example in the Netherlands (and by agreement Flanders), Denmark or Sweden, the method is direct, with teams appointed by the agency reporting on what they judge to be the standard of teaching, research, resource management, strategic planning or other aspects of the institution/ faculty/ department in question. There is, however, a growing realisation that the complexity, cost and intrusiveness of direct external evaluation might better be avoided, and that institutions, faculties/ departments are themselves in the best position to undertake direct evaluations. The role of the agency, then, is (*inter alia*) to carry out a kind of meta-evaluation, or audit, a check that internal evaluations are being conducted and their results acted upon. Regardless of approach, a measure of public reporting is usually entailed.

As Brennan says, *"The growth of external assessment of higher education quality has been one of the most marked international trends in higher education in recent years"* (Brennan, 1997, p. 23). But what remains at issue is whether the most appropriate and cost-effective role for the external agency is audit – to ensure that evaluation procedures are in place – or the carrying out of the evaluation processes themselves. Even where external evaluation is the norm, less prescriptive approaches are being adopted, with greater encouragement to diversity and innovation (Nilsson and Wahlen, 1999).

Whatever the position taken on this issue, since recommendations are normally made and important decisions may be taken in the light of findings, it is important that there is sound evidence and that impartiality and fairness are maintained. Rigour, reliability, validity and sufficiency of evidence are seen as necessary in achieving confidence in the process (QAPHE, 1999). One might add sensitivity, insight and depth of understanding of academic culture. Much of the criticism of external reviews centres on these points.

Yet a common consequence of reviews, noted in a Swedish study among others, is greater attention to decision-making procedures within the institution and to the quality of leadership (Nilsson and Wahlen, 1999). Well conducted assessments, combining internal and external viewpoints, can have very beneficial outcomes. While these cannot be guaranteed there

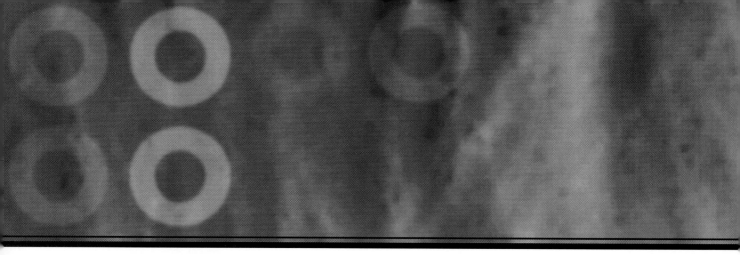

should be a reasonable assurance that reviews whether internal or external will have ascertainable results of benefit to the institution if not the system of which it is part.

A National Committee in France provides an interesting example of arms' length evaluation

The French system of national evaluation of universities is of interest, internationally, because of several distinctive features:

- A National Evaluation Committee, reporting directly to the President and quite independent of the Ministry of Education and of the universities, with no funding responsibility;
- With a remit to evaluate the 'public service missions of higher education in France';
- It evaluates both the governance of institutions and the quality of their public service missions (it does not evaluate teachers, a function of the *Conseil National des Universites* performed through peer review; management audit is carried out by the *Cour de Comtes*, the central audit office);
- It operates on the principles of institutional self-assessment, governed by common rules and external assessment by peers, with a published report to follow;
- More credence is given to qualitative judgements than to quantitative measures;
- The Committee regards evaluation as integral to the increased autonomy of French universities

(Staropoli, 1994).

Despite the Committee's belief that its focus is a dialogue with institutions, this has been disputed by some institutions which also have taken exception to certain decisions that have followed the reviews.

Evaluation can result in power shifts both within institutions and between them and the state. Awareness of this is shown in the different national approaches. *"If quality assessment has enjoyed a certain international dynamic, the evaluation systems thus set up in different countries are, for their part, embedded in the national context, in the fabric, economic, social and political, not to mention the history of higher education and its ties with the State"* (Lamoure, 1999, p. 278).

The national context sets the direction for procedures in Ireland that, as specified in the University Act, 1997, lay the onus very much on the universities to conduct their own evaluations and to report the outcomes. Prior to this, the Conference of Heads of Irish Universities in 1994 sponsored a seminar which resulted in 1995 in the establishment of the Irish Universities Quality Steering Committee (IUQSC). In consultation with the Higher Education Authority a pilot programme based largely on the European Pilot Project was launched (Conference of Heads of Irish Universities, 1999). A variety of reviews has been conducted or is planned and the HEA is seeking information on procedures and results.

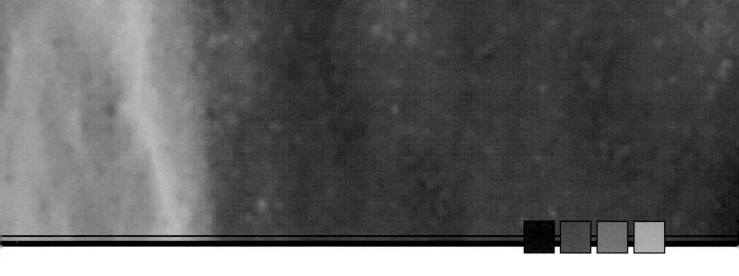

But what are the evaluation objectives, what are the effects?

The different legal statutes, mandates, working methods and reporting procedures of the several national agencies and other arrangements now in existence are reasonably well understood and discussed in the literature (Brennan and Shah, 2000). What is less well documented and discussed are the effects and results of the quality movement. Since one of the objectives is to ensure that quality, however defined, is being sustained, or improved, where that is judged to be necessary, an important consideration is a systematic body of knowledge of just how well higher education is performing. This consideration is apposite to the system as a whole, not only individual institutions and units within them.

At present, knowledge about the results and effects of the quality assurance movement in respect of learning, teaching, administrative and financial procedures, institutional management and so on is far from adequate: it is diffuse, scattered in reports (many unpublished) of the institutions and the agencies and not in a form that might lead to valid and reliable judgements on the overall performance of the sector either within countries or internationally.

This lacuna is partly a consequence of the diversity of the approaches adopted and of the data, partly a reflection of this still relatively early stage in the development of the whole movement. For comparative purposes, while it would be of interest to a national government to reach an overall judgement, none of the international or intergovernmental agencies has as yet established the means for significant cross-country analysis of this kind. Nor is there a sufficiency of knowledge or incisiveness of informed debate about core concepts, notably 'quality' itself. As a result, while a trend to establish procedures and agencies can be plotted and reports (many unpublished) have proliferated, it is scarcely possible to reach conclusions about effects other than in a rather piecemeal way. Much of any such appraisal would have to be based on the reports of the agencies themselves and they have a definite interest in a positive account of their own work.

...And why is so much evaluation thought to be necessary?

There is a climate of review and evaluation in contemporary society extending far beyond higher education. The specific reasons for establishing national evaluation procedures in higher education - as distinct from a long standing practice by many institutions of both internal and external reviews, external examining and so forth, are intimately related to the expansion of the sector and the massive enrolment increases, the adequacy of preparation students have received in order to undertake higher education, and to mounting costs (Thune et al, 1995, p. 25). There are in addition special reasons that justify reviews: reported management inefficiency or malpractice in some institutions; the sectoral impact of structural changes such as amalgamations or the closing of small institutions; the introduction of whole new study areas or the incorporation into universities of professional training previously the responsibility of specialist vocational colleges; public sector management and efficiency reviews; and so on.

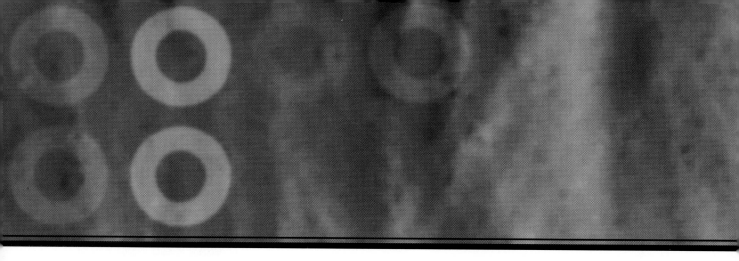

None of these special reasons, by themselves, would require a permanent, single purpose national agency and indeed many reviews are carried out as normal administrative practice by special committees or existing bodies as well as by the institutions themselves. But they all contribute to a general mood or expectation that more rigorous and systematic procedures are needed to ensure that standards are being maintaineand formal requirements met. At the least, national criteria, agreed procedures and a public reporting mechanism would seem to be required, where they do not already exist. A significant contribution to the debate about the goals, values and changing nature of university education might also seem to be a reasonable outcome of all this activity.

For higher education, among the several main driving forces in the establishment of more regular evaluation procedures, mentioned above, is growth of the sector and the associated pressures. These are significant issues of public interest. Are the needs of new cohorts of students being met? What has happened to failure, dropout and stopout rates? Are students taking more or less time to complete? Is financial pressure having a deleterious effect on study? Are curricula educationally sound, well planned, up-to-date, relevant, of good standard? Are standards consistent across the sector? What uses are being made of the new technologies in teaching? How adequate, and well-used are libraries, computer and other services? Is management efficiency being maintained? Are resources being put to good effect in support of worthwhile purposes? And what are these purposes? 'Quality' is also used as a surrogate for 'relevance', meaning that what universities do in their teaching and research may be judged to have merit in its own terms but not be sufficiently related to external expectations and needs. This sense of the term is to some extent captured in the concept of 'fitness for purpose' and is a source of wider debate about the role of the university in society.

Questions of this nature are of much interest to institutions in their self-evaluation; students and governments have further concerns. For students, including prospective students, and for their sponsors and funders, reports on institutions are a valuable source of information. Quality assurance measures may be instituted as *quid pro quo* for greater management autonomy, as a way to improve community understanding, out of a national competitiveness fear of 'falling behind', or in a belief that the costs of a quality higher education are too high, and that quality at a lower price is achievable (Goedegebuure and Van Vught, 1994; Taylor, 1996). Similarly, as McGuinness (1994) observed, governments are as interested in whether higher education 'is doing the right things' as in 'doing things right'. This distinction corresponds to that enshrined in the approach now adopted by the UK Quality Assurance Agency: 'fitness of purpose' and 'fitness for purpose'. As Ball (1996) remarked, whose purpose is to count? Who are the clients? In an age of mass or universal tertiary education, these are public interest questions that cannot be adequately addressed only through internal, self-evaluation. But it is questionable whether, as yet, the quality assurance movement is bringing them to the fore.

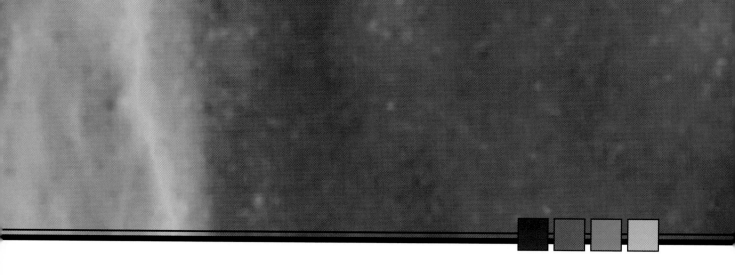

Does emergence of the 'evaluative state' imply a crisis of trust?

There are widely divergent views on the increasing involvement of the state and its agencies in evaluating higher education processes, structures and outcomes. As early as the late '80s Neave (1988) had in some consternation identified an emerging 'evaluative state' in Europe. The Commission of the European Communities (1993b) traced growing concern in many of Europe's higher education systems about quality of facilities and educational provision. Moreover, the increased mobility of students and academics and the internationalisation of the European labour market meant that there was a cross-national interest to be served (see below). While accepting the need for some kind of external evaluation procedure, and being willing to participate in pan-European projects, representatives of European member countries and institutions have tended to resist the idea of evaluative procedures leading to a greater standardisation.

It is not only the spectre of an over-intrusive state seeking standardised approaches that raises academic hackles over ownership and control of quality assurance. The cross-border globalisation flows of technology and innovation, investments in and proprietary rights over knowledge, labour flows and internationally competitive markets are also generating concern over a new kind of dominance, the global product. This might be in the form of tangible goods, ideas or processes. The internationalisation of higher education, through research networks and partnerships, the marketing of intellectual property, cross-border movements of students and so on raises issues of international standards of quality and the standardisation of academic products and processes. The Sorbonne and Bologna declarations of the European ministers of education are an example of national leaders seeking a greater harmonisation - but in this instance on the basis of a declared respect for the distinctive culture and traditions of each country. The increasing internationalisation of higher education has led institutions to share their experience of evaluating their international work but also to reflect on the possibility of internationalising the quality assurance procedures themselves (OECD/IMHE, 1999a). Global movements are raising numerous issues transcending those in national systems.

Trow has written about an emerging 'new industry': *"The assessment and evaluation of academic programs in colleges and universities has become a major industry in Europe and the United States"* (Trow, 1994b, p. 17). Like Thune, van Vught and others, Trow attributed its emergence to mass higher education, a sea change in the context and in the trust placed in universities. But since universities differ so markedly one from the other, and since 'quality' is in many respects ineffable, Trow questioned whether externally imposed measures in common use are appropriate: *"Essentially we want to assess the quality of an institution's intellectual life - the process of education - rather than its outcomes, which are long delayed, difficult to recognise, difficult if not impossible to measure, and mixed with many other forces and factors outside the institution"* (ib.,pp. 37-8).

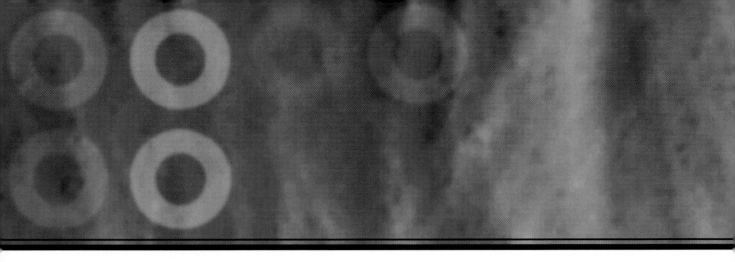

Lack of clarity in the array of terms that are used: accreditation; quality assurance; control; assessment; improvement; and others has been noted by critics. More serious perhaps than terminological confusion and misguided confidence in certain evaluative procedures was what Trow perceived to be a breakdown in fundamental relations between the state and the university. Externally imposed evaluations, he said, are *"a substitute for a relationship of trust between government and the universities, trust in the ability of institutions of higher education to broadly govern themselves"* (Trow, 1994a). Trow was referring to evaluation in the hard sense of external assessments of teaching and research carried out in Britain by Funding Council committees and individuals appointed by the Council and linked directly to funding.

For the Funding Council, Clark made a response, pointing out that the appointees were themselves mainly academics. But this did not touch on Trow's basic point about trust. Trust, however, is contingent on mutual understanding and confidence that things are as they should be. It is precisely the uncertainty over this point in periods of rapid change and growth, with huge demands on public resources, that has led to calls for transparency. If universities were believed not to be sufficiently transparent, it was argued, measures were needed to bring this about.

In 1999, the Higher Education Division of the Australian Department of Education, Training and Youth Affairs published the first in what was said to be an annual series of reports on the quality assurance and improvement plans of Australian higher education institutions. In introducing the report, the Division declared that the Australian approach *"is one that values the autonomy of our universities while insisting on accountability and 'value for money"* (DETYA, 1999b, p. 2). Reference to the latter consideration indicates a qualified regard for autonomy but is consistent with what has become a feature of appraisal of education and research performance: efficiency in use of financial resources. With the recent establishment of the Australian Universities Quality Agency – funded by the federal government and with the active involvement of the Australian states and territories, through the Ministerial Council for Employment, Education, Training and Youth Affairs (MCEETYA) – more comprehensive and detailed appraisals of the quality of university performance can be expected in future. These are likely to entail a systematic, national approach combining target-setting against university goals, and institutional self-evaluation, according to common criteria, with a standardised and public reporting procedure.

There remain divergent views on the value of quality assurance

Despite the assurances that are being given on preserving the independence and autonomy of universities, and the emphasis being given to audit and peer review, concerns voiced in the early days of the quality movement have not been allayed. In a review of national evaluation systems, Kells (1999) deplored the 'patronising, expensive and often quite political activities, in the name of accountability' (p.209), whereby the state and its agents have gained the initiative and

control the universities themselves should have taken. The thoughtless transfer of models across national borders, Kells argued, flies in the face of cultural differences.

However, the Liaison Committee of the European Rectors Conference has been active, through the Committee for Higher Education of the European Communities, in prompting methods and mechanisms for European-wide quality assessment (Van Vught and Westerheijden, 1993; Thune, Kristoffersen and Wied, 1995). Work of the Committee has included the development of a European pilot project in which some forty-six institutions participated in 1994-1995 (Ottenwaelter, 1996). One ambition of this project was to develop an 'evaluation culture' for Europe, building on steps taken at the national level and with the involvement and support of the institutions through the Association of European Universities. Four principles common to the national systems in place at the time (those of Denmark, France, the Netherlands and the United Kingdom) underpinned the design of this project (see above) (van Vught and Westerheijden, 1993; Brennan and Shah, 2000).

In the official report of this project, countries and institutions were emphatic that they did not wish it to be seen as leading to standardisation of degrees or greater central and bureaucratic control of universities (European Pilot Project for Evaluating Quality in Higher Education 1995, pp. 9-10). The project was positively received for enhancing awareness of a need, facilitating cross-border exchange, enhancing national practice and for its collegial approach. Thus, although many commentators have been concerned about risks of intrusiveness and thoughtless cross-national borrowings, this project has helped pave the way toward both a more balanced appraisal of the control procedures and international collaboration.

Sharp criticism of quality assurance procedures occurs wherever external procedures with a strong hint or actual use of imposed compliance measures are adopted or proposed. Objections - in addition to Trow's point about trust - are that they encourage non-disclosure and conformity without actually improving quality and are not cost-effective (since they usually identify more that is good than bad) and are episodic (Newby, 1999). There are, inevitably, undercurrents of dissatisfaction when decisions are taken to close departments or programmes rather than strengthen them. This is perceived to be a mainstream disciplinary stance taking precedence over distinctive local features and needs. Whether quality is perceived as a threshold, or standard, to be attained or a process susceptible of continuing improvement (Barnett, 1992a) is also an issue requiring clarification.

Speaking at a national conference which preceded the establishment of the Australian Universities Quality Agency, van Vught questioned whether it is feasible to combine, in a single review framework, the purposes of assurance (thresholds)

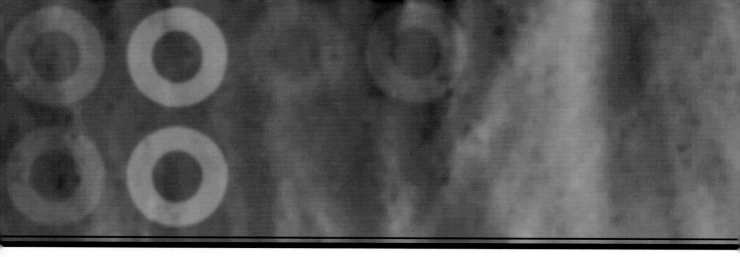

and improvement (Skilbeck and Connell, in press). An issue that inevitably arises for national systems of evaluation is whether judgements relate to the system as a whole or only to the institution in its local setting. The closing of a department, for example, might be based on a low national ranking in a situation where there is an 'over-supply' of graduates in a particular field, or because the institution's own priorities in a tight budgetary situation give the department a low ranking.

The emergence in the course of the 1990s of an international quality assurance movement heralds a new phase in the evolution of institutional evaluation. National level agencies operating on broadly common principles and using a repertoire of methods variously classified as quality assurance and quality audit are becoming more popular with governments. Their procedures and findings are having an impact which is likely to increase in the first decade of this century. Important as this movement is, it should not deflect attention from other approaches that have been adopted for higher education evaluation: performance indicators; accreditation; benchmarking; peer review; research assessment and so on.

Other evaluative approaches are also being taken

Performance indicators have been introduced in several national systems but with variable success. As yet they provide relatively little information about teaching and learning processes and outcomes. As defined by Cave et al (1991) a performance indicator is 'an authoritative measure - usually in a quantitative form - of an attribute of the activity of a higher education institution. The message may be ordinal or cardinal, absolute or comparative. It thus includes both mechanical applications of formulae (when the latter is imbued with value or interpretative judgments) and such informal and subjective procedures as peer evaluations or reputational rankings.'

There is considerable disagreement about the validity and usefulness of performance indicators for system-wide comparisons - although they are deployed in this way. A wider measure of agreement exists about their usefulness for institutional managers and as part of benchmarking exercises which take account of the specific context of operations and the distinctive orientations of individual institutions.

In her review of the uses of performance indicators in Commonwealth countries, David (1996) supported the widely held opinion that, in their present form, higher education indicators are of relatively little use for system-wide purposes or for international comparisons. A key problem is lack of standardisation but even if this were achieved, the indicators would be of limited value unless combined with a variety of other appraisal and evaluative measures. Moreover, even the major

OECD development work on education indicators carried out since the late '80s has, as yet, yielded only a relatively small number of process and output - as distinct from input - indicators for higher education.

Benchmarking, as an institutional device has attracted growing interest, in part due to dissatisfaction with the approach through performance indicators. Institutional benchmarking is a procedure for improvement, and equates well with the idea of a self-managing learning organisation (Commonwealth Higher Education Management Service, 1998). An Australian study, with a high level of institutional involvement, has resulted in a large and comprehensive set of benchmarks, for use primarily by institutional managers, although capable of wider applications (McKinnon et al, 2000). The set incorporates a core of 25 out of a total of 67 benchmarks. There are criterion-referenced items, for purposes of setting standards, and quantitative (competitive) items. The benchmarks are designed to embrace 'the most important aspects of contemporary university life'. It is instructive, therefore, to note their coverage:
- Governance, planning, management;
- External impact (e.g. reputation, competitiveness, strategic community service);
- Financial and physical infrastructure;
- Learning and teaching;
- Student support;
- Research;
- Library and information services;
- Internationalisation;
- Staff.

The benchmarks (some or all) are designed for use by senior staff to assess and improve performance, and by groups of universities, for mutual comparison. They would be capable of being used for a whole higher education system seeking international comparison. As mentioned above, Australia has recently established a national quality assurance agency, but there is no indication as yet of the procedures it will be adopting.

Not all systems have taken the route of establishing a national agency for quality assurance - Germany for example and the United States, to name two of the very large systems which include many of the world's most highly regarded universities. Although lacking a formal national agency, there is indeed quality evaluation in Germany, both internally in the procedures universities have in place for assessing learning, awarding diplomas and assessing their own performance, and externally through evaluations that are intrinsic to research funding procedures (Muller, 1994). In the United States,

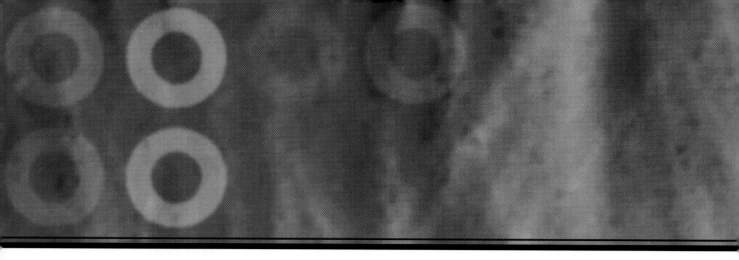

some states have their own procedures including links between attested performance and funding. Colleges and universities in receipt of public funds in some form or other must be accredited and there are several projects under way to give them the accrediting bodies a stronger role in continuing quality appraisal as distinct from periodic (and sometimes rather perfunctory) formal re-accreditation of member institutions. Accreditation by institutionally-owned bodies in the United States has been questioned for a perceived lack of independence and for procedures which over time have become rather mechanistic. Evaluative projects have been undertaken to develop more searching and continuing processes for assuring quality. A general weakness of most systems, American or European, is the lack of systematic follow-through and international comparability of findings (Amara, 1997).

A project of considerable interest and already mentioned, was launched several years ago by the UK Higher Education Quality Council. It aimed at establishing a widely shared, explicit set of standards for defining 'graduateness'. The intellectual underpinning of this project owes much to earlier work on competences and generic or core skills, much of it in the vocational sector and to theories of cognitive development which dwell on strategies of learning that cross disciplinary areas.

The UK project hoped to achieve wide agreement on the generic qualities to be expected of any graduate. These generic qualities are often implicit in teaching, assessment and other aspects of academic practice but sometimes explicit as well. Terms like 'general cognitive skills', 'core skills' or 'personal transferable skills' are used in describing the qualities. A common definition of graduateness was held to be of value, if not in raising standards then in overcoming much of the unevenness of practice for example in assessment, and the ambiguities surrounding degree classifications. It could also be of value to employers more interested in a range of capabilities than in specific subject content (Higher Education Quality Council, 1997).

Launched through the separate agencies of the Committee of Vice Chancellors and Principals and the Funding Councils, further work on 'graduateness', should it proceed, will be the future responsibility of the Quality Assurance Agency.

It is necessary to make separate mention of procedures for determining the quality of research. Although there is a firmly grounded tradition of both national and international peer review in the form of the refereed journal article or monograph/book, and the vetting of applications for research grants, these have been questioned. Essentially, they aim at or attest to the quality of individual or team efforts; they do not of themselves provide a measure of the overall research performance either of an institution or a state/national system. For institutional purposes, a prominent place for research in annual reports, strategic plans etc and the appointment of research managers at a senior level are now commonplace. For system-wide purposes, some countries have introduced research assessments. The most reviewed form of retrospective assessment of research (with implications for forward funding) is the English Research Assessment Exercise (Bourke, 1997; McNally, 1997). Discipline-based and incorporating the principle of 'research active' staff, this exercise relies on traditional methods such as peer review of publication; it also draws on the more recent devices of performance indicators and productivity measures. Widespread publicity given to the results in the media has helped generate a 'league table' mentality which raises as many questions as it answers.

There is an unanswered question as to whether a certain standard and quantum of research performance should feature in judgments about the overall quality of an institution. Were current research performance to be agreed as a defining feature of the institution or a significant element in its mission, the question would scarcely arise. However, with the abandonment of essentialist definitions of 'the university' and a great variation in institutional profiles, in quality audits it is not only the goals and methods but also the status of appraisals of research that may differ quite markedly from those of teaching.

Internal and external approaches

The different approaches and perspectives on evaluation procedures and the methods that are used have been categorised in many studies. Brennan (1999), in a review of how quality assessments are actually proceeding, identified four approaches:

- Academic - the culture of academic disciplines (or 'tribes' as Becher (1989) described them)
- Managerial - procedures and mechanisms used to ensure quality
- Pedagogic - technical and teaching proficiency
- Consumerist - related to employment and practical uses of learning.

Dill (1999b) and Woodhouse (1999) distinguished three approaches identified in the quality assurance literature:

- Audit - which verifies whether or not an institution is doing what it says it is;
- Assessment or quality assurance - which determines 'how good' an institution is;
- Accreditation - which determines whether an institution is 'good enough'.

Accreditation and assessment, both of long standing in higher education, are closely associated with self-regulation and autonomy. Audit, the more recent approach, might, according to Woodhouse, deal with the appropriateness of an institution's objectives (fitness of purpose), the suitability of its plans to achieve them, conformity of action to plans, effectiveness of its actions in achieving the objectives. Peer assessment is usually part of all three approaches. An important difference between types of reviews is whether they are 'whole institution' (as was the case with the three year national

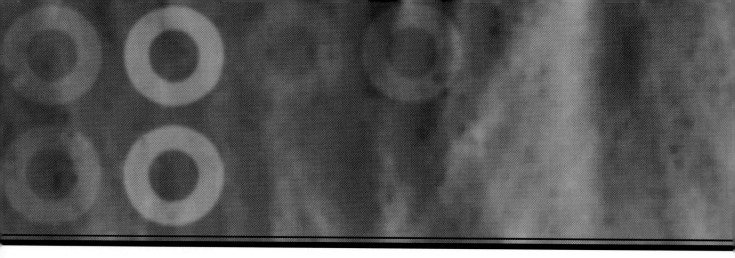

project in Australia in the mid-nineties and as in New Zealand, and as common with institutional self-review) or discipline/department/based (as in the Netherlands and Flanders, for example).

In order to understand the main lines in the contemporary international debate about quality assurance, just two fundamental categories are needed: (1) those ways of evaluating which are carried out by and within the institution for its own purposes; (2) those ways of evaluating the performance of an institution conducted by groups and agencies external to the institution and with a strong systemic flavour. For each there are rationales (and counter arguments) and procedural matters to consider (the efficacy of different methods and approaches). Despite oversimplification (for example, when an institution seeks advice and invites external examiners, is the evaluation 'internal or 'external'?) these two categories help to clarify the main points in the debate and to identify the position taken by different actors. Institutions aim to maintain independence and control, while seeking to improve their work, by internal means. They prefer not to have funding tied directly to the results of the evaluations but to use them in planning future development. Governments and other external actors (e.g. employer groups, professional bodies) aim to find out more about the outcomes of institutional behaviour and how they are being achieved; they are also interested in ways of relating funding to performance although only modest steps have been taken thus far.

Bodies like the European Rectors Conference and many of the national agencies are seeking to demonstrate that these two broadly defined approaches can be complementary, rather than mutually exclusive, in sensitively designed evaluation work. Peer review is universally regarded as one essential requirement, as is transparency. Procedures should be negotiated and agreed by the partners.

Large investments both financial and human are being made in the continuing development of procedures for quality assurance/audit. With the passage of time and accumulating experience, in some systems - the UK for example - very detailed, carefully worked through procedures are resulting in quite elaborate schemes. In others, such as Sweden, there are reports of greater flexibility, and recognition of the need for evaluative procedures themselves to foster diversity and innovativeness (Stenslake, 1999; Nilsson and Wahlen, 1999).

The next decade will determine whether sufficient attention is being paid to follow-through, systematic comparisons, and clearly ascertainable benefits to demonstrate that this investment in quality assurance/audit is yielding commensurate returns. Whether the concerns so strongly voiced in the '90s remain will also be an important consideration since acceptance and positive action by the higher education community are needed for successful implementation.

Common to all procedures for quality review, performance evaluation, benchmarking and so on is an underlying condition of success, namely that the people using them will do so competently, fairly and in a manner calculated to produce positive, productive outcomes. Openness, simplicity of procedures (consistent with depth and incisiveness) are virtues, not always apparent in practice. The knowledge and insights to be gained through intelligently conceived, searching and well managed quality evaluation are needed by both institutions and higher education systems. They are of direct interest to government, students, families and the community at large.

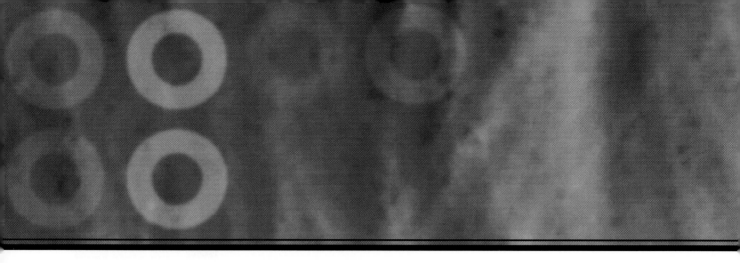

GOVERNING, MANAGING, RESOURCING

Many universities and many whole university systems have been administered by people who look inward into their institutions rather than outwards to society as a whole, by people who lack the confidence to make strategic alliances with external bodies or the flexibility that recognises that such partnerships only succeed if their universities can adapt themselves to new ways of working; and by people and committees which cannot balance opportunities with long term planning and cannot take decisions quickly but only after a convoluted and circumlocutory process has been gone through (Shattock, 1997).

There is a growing convergence, internationally, regarding state–university relations

Among the major transformations of the contemporary university not least is the changing pattern of relationships with the state. Each country has its own distinctive mix of relationships, reflecting national cultures, regulatory, legal and constitutional arrangements, methods of funding and so forth. The combining of a steering/funding role for the state with self-government and increasing independence in decision-making by the institutions to balance academic autonomy, has emerged as the common basic pattern. Autonomy in academic matters remains largely intact, although it can be affected by resourcing priorities and management styles. Transparency and accountability also form part of the mix. There is now something resembling an emerging international convergence both in steering by the state and trends in governance and management. This applies to public systems; steering is more variable where there is a large private sector, but resource and management issues are broadly similar. Burton Clark, surveying international practice of the early '80s from an American standpoint, considered systems of governance as:

- Collegial, or
- Political, or
- Bureaucratic, or
- Market.

(Clark, 1983).

From a British perspective, Becher (1994) proposed three ways of looking at the changes underway:

- The command model (exemplified by pre-1989 Eastern/Central Europe and, to a lesser extent, France);
- The autonomous model (UK universities prior to the 1980s);
- The exchange model (whereby governments provide resources in exchange for services).

Maassen and van Vught (1994) taking a Continental view, distinguished between state control and state supervision. The former, a state-created and –financed system combining state bureaucracy with faculty guilds, results in the state controlling access conditions, the curriculum, degree requirements, the examination system and the appointment of academic and

some other staff. Historically, this has been the standard Continental approach, although when academics are state officials and when there are academics in key posts in ministries, 'control' by the state may not be what appears on the surface. In the model of state supervision, found in the US and in the UK ('pre-Thatcher'), universities are chartered corporations, with a high degree of self-determination over matters controlled on the Continent by the state, and governed by trustees, faculty guilds and administrators. A recent trend, in the UK, is an interest by some university leaders in more definite steps towards full privatisation. This reflects disquiet over a combination of state regulations and highly constrained budgets on the one hand and, on the other, a sense of opportunities to gain from greater entrepreneurship.

Changes to governance of institutions is an inevitable concomitant of the developments outlined in the previous chapters of this study. The rate of change has often been slow and there are many unresolved tensions even though it has long been recognised that improvements are much needed. Embling (1974), in his 'Europeanisation' of the findings of the massive array of Carnegie studies of higher education, listed achievement of more effective governance and the assurance of more effective use of resources as two of the six major areas of the Commission's work of greatest relevance to Europe's higher education system. Nearly thirty years on and in an era marked by economic liberalism, expanding international horizons, fiscal restraint, moves to reduce public debt, structural adjustment, public accountability and increased transparency of all public operations, it is obvious that universities - heavily dependent on public funds and performing public roles - need to rethink all aspects of governance, management and resources. This requirement has been raised in Ireland through a searching report undertaken by Deloitte and Touche on commission from the Higher Education Authority (Deloitte and Touche, 1997) (see Part III below).

Most systems are now experiencing forms of de-regulation with framework laws and policy 'steering' replacing detailed regulation, block rather than earmarked funding and incentives to foster flexibility and innovativeness. Such moves as these are captured by Becher's term 'exchange', which also broadly corresponds to Clark's 'market' model.

In a study of seventy-five countries, states and provinces, using nineteen indicators, McDaniel (1996) challenged the conventional sharp contrast, drawn between Continental and so-called 'Anglo-Saxon' patterns of state-institution relationships: 'hands on' for the former, 'hands off' for the latter. McDaniel's analysis showed greater convergence; differences lie mainly in the area of policies affecting personnel and students (greater power for institutions in the USA) and education programmes (greater authority for the European institutions).

It is a move toward the exchange or market model that many governments are coming to favour: New Zealand, for example, as part of an overall redefinition of state services following passage of radical national finance legislation in 1988

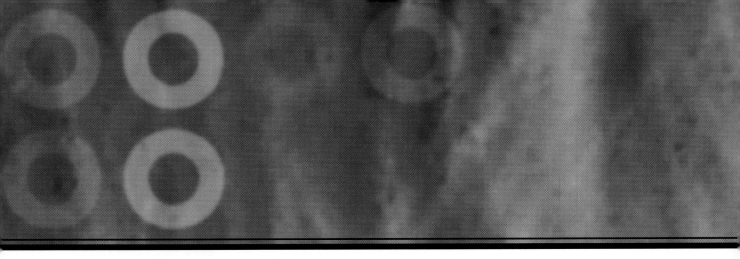

(now under review); France following the adoption of State-institution contracts as an element of resource allocation; and most governments in respect of research contracts and, increasingly, funding according to specific enrolment and equity targets and teaching priorities. It is doubtful whether the implications of the above changes for all members of staff of universities have been thought through. When, as is becoming common, the budgets of public universities draw on a wide variety of sources, with formula-based core funding a diminishing proportion and income-earning a growing necessity, staff must become much more cost-conscious and entrepreneurial in spirit. This does not make the university a commercial business, but it does mean that commercial understanding and skill must be developed and incorporated more thoroughly into academic culture (Elliott, 2000).

While heterogeneity of institutional types and variety of study programmes are actively fostered, there are growing similarities in policies affecting university governance, management and resource allocation and use. Common features stand out and this is so despite the impression of 'bewildering variety' that a leading German higher education researcher observed in an overview of trends in higher education in Western Europe (OECD, 1997b). A feature, often debated, is a greater consolidation of the decision-making apparatus within institutions and a greater concentration of power both at the institution and the system/state levels.

As mentioned above, the systemic term 'steering at a distance' has been used, in the Netherlands and Scandinavia, to denote a combination of greater devolution of authority to institutions (the 'distance' element) with a strengthening of the strategic role and hence the ultimate power of government (the 'steering' element). 'Steering at a distance' also puts the onus on institutions to strengthen their own strategic capability. This need not mean centralisation within the university but clear definition and articulation of numerous decision sites across the institution.

Collegial steering and decision-making has not disappeared, but is being reshaped through the more decisive roles required of senior members of staff in coordinated strategic planning and resource management, the greater participation of external people in governing bodies, links with industry, government and the community and the need for a greater degree of self-financing by all parts of the university. The key point is a strengthening of the quality of decision-making and academic management, regardless of site and level of responsibility.

...For a complex set of reasons

The reasons for these developments are complex, not easily disentangled. They relate to:

- the closer interfaces between higher education, the society and the economy;
- the very substantial resources deployed by institutions which include large public subventions;

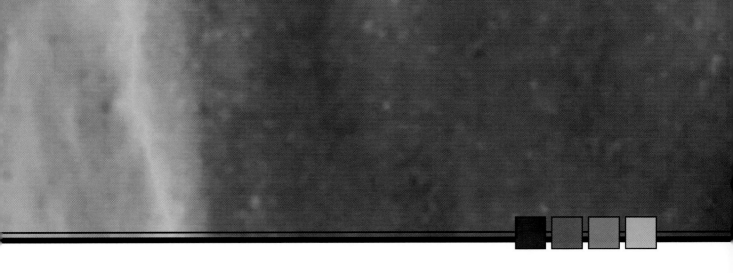

- the increased visibility and transparency of public sector institutions in the aftermath of consumer rights movements;
- the scale of the higher education enterprise system-wide and in the form of very large, powerful institutions; and
- the diverse financial and legal as well as academic consequences of poor decision-making.

In a study of trends in six European countries, Kogan (1998) drew out implications of changing state-university relations in a set of developments that are having a major impact on the functioning and management of higher education institutions. For Kogan, accountability, efficiency, devolution of financial and administrative decision-making, and quality assurance measures are reshaping the relationship.

Devolution of authority from the centre to institutions and within them leads to calls for its effective and transparent use; and the scale of resource available to universities means that there must be adequate accountability. Calls for greater efficiency naturally arise in these circumstances. The demand for quality assurance, as discussed in the previous chapter, arises out of increased expectations of performance in terms of economic competitiveness and social development, which are now apparent for all levels of education not only in OECD countries but, increasingly, worldwide.

Behind these and other moves in the changing state-institution balance is the realisation by governments of the strategic policy uses to be made of higher education institutions as the development of knowledge and its applications come to underpin economic performance and all major domains of social policy. It is to be expected, therefore, that achieving a high standard of institutional performance will be a focus of concern and that this will be assessed at the level of the system and with reference to systemic criteria. This includes university leadership and management.

The universities are being mobilised as national (and transnational) assets. In the words of a leading American authority on the (triangular) relationship between States-Federal jurisdictions and institutions, there is 'a new and more penetrating questioning about the underlying purposes and effectiveness of colleges and universities' (McGuinness, 1995, p. 265.) For the institutions, working in an environment characterised by relative resource scarcity from traditional sources, increased visibility, and competitiveness, there are considerable incentives for demonstrating enhanced performance, not just of single institutions but the system as a whole.

That Ireland is coming to adopt this strategic view of the universities is apparent in the succession of reports and strategic studies from the early '90s onwards. It was in the '60s that the far-sighted Investment in Education report (OECD, 1966) was produced by the Irish authorities as the background to the first of the OECD education policy reviews. But only in

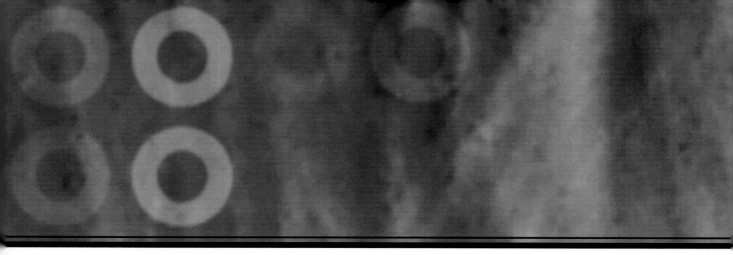

more recent years have resources to universities begun to flow on the scale needed and been focused so closely on national economic and social development.

The terms 'managerialism', or the 'management' or 'industrial' model, have been applied to procedures adopted by institutions to strengthen their decision-making procedures. By critics, this is nostalgically (and often inaccurately) contrasted with the collegial style whereby decision-making was, or was believed to be, widely dispersed across the whole academic community. A more balanced, but in some respects qualified, view of the complementarity of at least elements of the 'managerial' and 'collegial' approaches was expressed by the UK Committee of Standards in Public Life (1996): *"The strength of the older universities lies in the representative nature of their councils and their commitment to collegiate government and consultation, given expression by the powers of the academic led senate. The smaller governing bodies and less autonomous academic boards of the new universities and further education colleges offer the potential for swifter and more responsive decision-making. But may encourage an 'us and them' division between staff and management"* (p. 31).

Recent changes in governance and management are contested and resisted

It is often said that 'managerialism' reflects the increasing adoption by academic institutions of business practice. The historian Raymond Callahan argued that over more than a century American education absorbed the essentially business goals of efficiency and accountability, resulting in the progressive displacement of centres of inquiry by agencies for absorption of young people into business enterprises (Callahan, 1962). Over several decades higher education analysts and commentators have documented – and frequently castigated – what they discern as the growing dominance of market forces and the emergence of a credentialised, professionalised society in which treasured liberal academic values are lost or distanced (Hutchins, 1936; Aronowitz, 1985; Bloom 1987; Anderson 1992; Lutz and Field 1998).

There is substantial evidence of this business impact – it would be surprising if there were not, given the growing number and diversity of industry-education linkages and the prominence of industry, commerce and finance in contemporary culture. But critics of this trend tend to take a rather one-sided view, ignoring the continuance of powerful academic structures and processes. They may also overlook changes in the business community itself, some in response to the same socio-economic forces and public policies that impact upon higher education. The structures and patterns of decision-making which continue to provide for an open academic dialogue and collective decision-making are being blended with insights and procedures from business, government and other organisations. It is not a case of universities simply aping business management.

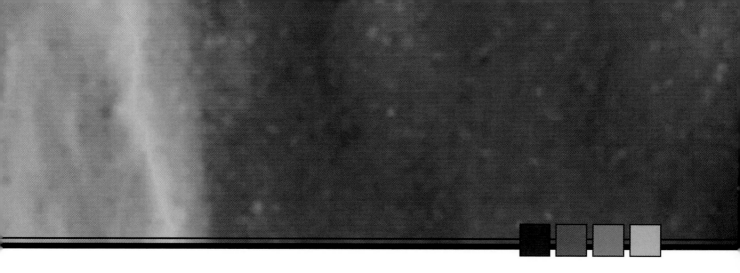

These are important features of the collegial style which, however moderated, should continue to permeate higher education institutions. Reasons include the need for fundamental respect for expert, specialised knowledge in the distinctive kinds of decisions an academic institution makes, concern for the interests and motivations of staff members, and the value of maintaining cultural solidarity of the university community.

Collegiality has itself evolved, broadening from its elite origins into a much more inclusive process. Prior to the reforms of the 1960s and '70s, it was uncommon for junior academics to be treated as full college members. Likewise, students, technical and support staff were often largely or totally excluded from governing and senior decision-making bodies. The 'democracy of intellect' was founded on a rather narrow constituency. This has been successfully challenged even though attention has now shifted from representativeness as such to the power actually exercised by the more representative governing and academic councils and the quality of their judgements and decisions.

The first major impetus for change in the modern era and challenge to the then restricted collegial system came from the actions mainly of students, junior (and some senior) academics who sought, in the reform drive of the 60s, to open out the university and broaden the base of decision-making. This was followed relatively soon thereafter by the 'managerial' shift, in response not to radically-minded students and staff, but to the socio-economic challenges and new relationships with government. More and more varied external demands, larger student enrolments, increased scale of operation, larger and more varied staffs, greatly increased budgets, pressure on resources, and greater competition all resulted in the rapid development of new hierarchical structures.

It is these structures which, in the opinion of the authors of the Carnegie Foundation international study of the academic profession, appear now to have an unfortunately divisive effect within the institutions: 'as higher education dramatically expanded to accommodate increasing numbers of students, universities developed a hierarchical 'industrial model' of governance. Layers of administrators were created to handle everything from personnel policies to facilities to financial aid. Faculty, organized administratively into academic divisions and departments, became more and more removed from issues affecting the institution as a whole. Decisions emanating from afar often seemed at odds with daily realities, creating within the institution a climate of confusion and sometimes distrust' (Boyer et al, 1994 pp. 15-16). This kind of analysis fuelled the dissatisfaction that is a continuing feature of university life.

Changes in management and governance, actual and needed, featured in a series of articles in the journal Higher Education Policy (11, 1998) in reports about institutions in several countries experiencing moves towards a greater concentration of

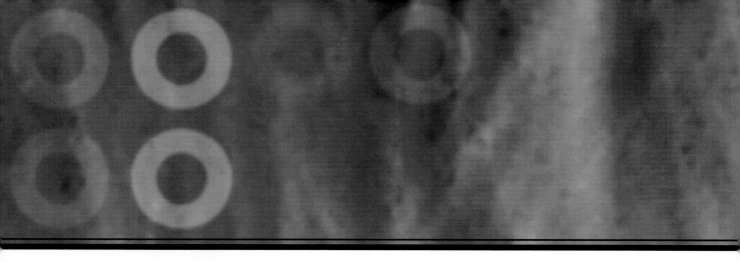

formal authority and more corporate forms of decision-making: Australia, Austria, Denmark, the Netherlands, Norway, the United Kingdom. These affect both academic and administrative leadership (although one element in the corporate or managerial model, namely appointment rather than election to posts such as rector, dean and department head, remains relatively rare in Continental Europe and is variable in other countries). One interesting conclusion is that segments of the older models (Humboldtian academic oligarchy; '60s-'70s democratisation) remain rather like tilted sedimentary layers. They are not wholly displaced by new practices, but relate to them in new and different formations of authority and power.

The value and effectiveness of the newer practices continue to be widely debated. 'Managerialism' is an unfortunate term, which by some academic critics is used like a weapon to attack a style of governance and decision-making which they believe excludes them from major institutional decisions. On the one hand, governance procedures have often been changed, leading to a greater concentration of power at the top - whether of the whole institution or faculties, departments or other operational units. On the other hand, decision-making procedures have been streamlined, often to meet external reporting requirements, manage project funds and achieve efficiencies. Many academics hold fundamental beliefs about their responsibilities to the scholarly community, to truth and knowledge rather than to the apparatus of an institution – even the one to which they are contractually bound and on which they depend financially. The changes which have been introduced to make universities more responsive, efficient, effective, accountable, transparent and to link them better with their communities are lumped together with examples of excessive use of power and incompetent leadership in a general condemnation of 'managerialism.

What is now needed is a more open, reflective analysis and discussion of just what kinds of changes, governance and management would best suit the large, modern, more open and more entrepreneurial university. Too many issues can be entangled, as the language of the following passage indicates: *"Universities are locations for research and teaching by academics who think of themselves as professionals with rights to organise and manage their own labour and govern themselves on the basis of a light collegiality... Academic work and academics both serve to defy the easy reach of managerial control. It is hard to reconcile the logic of bottom heavy professional authority that is rooted in disciplines and departments with the kind of top down bureaucratic authority that is rooted in a formal position that is geared to the management of the whole university"* (Dearlove, 1998, pp. 118-119). If a statement such as this points up internal tensions, it also suggests the need to distinguish good governance and sound management from 'managerialism'. No project of this nature can be expected to succeed independently of an appraisal of the academic values, goals, mission and culture of the institution.

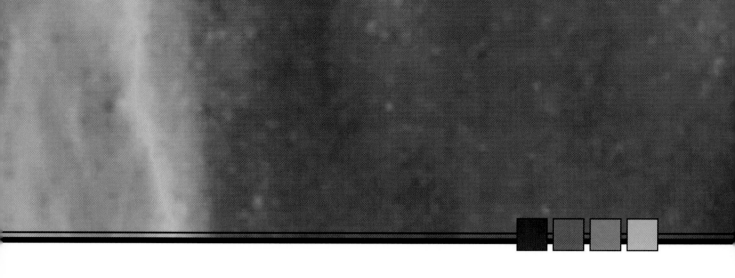

There are also difficulties arising from what is often treated by academics as unwelcome and unnecessary intrusion by government. Reflecting on changes in governance and university- state relations and public funding in Australia since the 1970s, Pechar and Pellert (1998) conclude that, now, there is a 'poisonous atmosphere between universities and government' (p. 150). At the extreme end of a widespread dissatisfaction in the academic community, this comment is nevertheless indicative of unresolved issues in the lines of authority and responsibility that have been progressively redrawn. The rate and scale of change have exceeded the ability or the readiness of either the institutions or the state bodies to establish an adequate pattern of new, constructive relationships.

Part of the problem is deeply entrenched attitudes and patterns of behaviour within both ministries and institutions. The steps taken since the 1980s in France to institute formal contractual relationships with universities through agreed strategic projects in research, education and documentation (libraries, etc) have 'helped to transform fundamentally the landscape of French higher education' (Abecassis, 1994) by establishing the universities as independent institutions (instead of merely arms of the bureaucracy) and as cohesive entities (not just collections of disparate elements). But the changes have *"had to contend with longstanding and deeply rooted habits of bureaucratic centralism"* (art cit, p. 13). In addition to aiming to give a more prominent place to teaching in the institutions, the projects envisage a stronger role for the university president and aim to strengthen the role played by universities in forming higher education policy. The projects require a great deal of change within the universities since, first, they cannot proceed except on the basis of a well structured internal evaluation and, second, they are a form of long term strategic planning responsibility which has hitherto in France lain with the officials rather than the academic community.

Clearly, for the contemporary university and higher education system, new administrative systems are required with an increasing reliance on data for management and decision-making and the use of strategic planning and resource-planning models. Facility with data sets has enormously increased as a result of computerisation. Higher education institutions have adopted in succession the well-known techniques of Programme Planning and Budgeting Systems; Project Evaluation and Review Techniques; Zero-Based Budgeting; and Total Quality Management and Re-engineering. It is the readiness to adopt such technical apparatus, much of it developed in private enterprises and by management and financial consultants, that lends force to the charge that universities have sometimes been too ready to adopt business management procedures which are not well integrated into the academic culture. Concern is being expressed that the cost structures in universities have grown beyond the comprehension - or interest - of many academics who nevertheless make financial decisions. Diversification of funding sources and of university operations will require new skills and changed attitudes in the academic community (Elliott, 2000; Karmel, 2000).

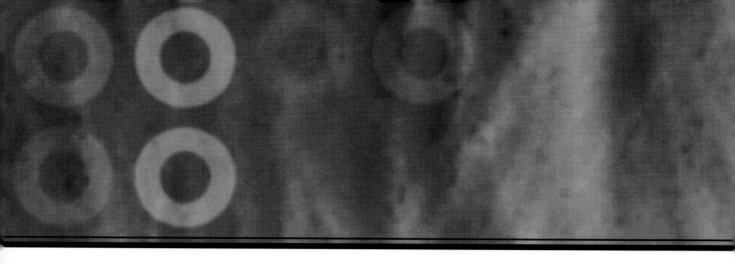

Where they are not being attacked (usually from within their own ranks) over 'managerialism', universities are liable to be criticised (also usually from within) for succumbing to bureaucratisation. Gortnitzk et al (1998) define bureaucratisation in simple but telling terms as the process whereby an increasing percentage of resources flows to administration instead of teaching and research, a trend they observed in data from Scandinavian countries and the USA. (Similarly, 'managerialism' might be briefly defined as a disproportionate flow of power from the academic community to the executive team surrounding the president/rector/vice-chancellor, increasingly driven by fiscal constraints and accountability requirements). Is this trend the price to be paid for adoption of the steering model and its accountability requirements, but also for bringing the universities into the mainstream of economic and social policy?

Expansion of the system and the formalisation by the state of strategic policies for or involving the universities inevitably lead to the enlargement and greater systematisation of administrative procedures. These relate to a very wide range of activities: records on students and course progression; personnel management; academic decision making; governance; finance and resource allocation; contracts and sale of services; international relations and many others which require specialised attention and expert systems. Extension of the statutory and regulatory environment of social policy has had a measurable impact on institutional procedures.

In these circumstances 'bureaucratisation' and 'managerialism' often seem to be a shorthand pejorative rather than analytically useful terms. Where does collective (or corporate) decision-making, planning and deliberation to achieve necessary and desired results end and 'bureaucratisation' begin? When functions (or whole departments, faculties and institutions), for example, are consolidated or merged, a long, sustained set of management processes must be instituted to ensure success – and that established values are sustained. The steps that are needed to develop institutional capacity and capability in face of growth and to respond to external forces often require a shift from departmental differentiation and inwardness to a more integrated, institution-wide strategy (Dill, 1996 and 1998a). Shifts of this nature, now common in universities in several countries, entail complex administrative and management action again extending over long periods of time. An Irish example is the seven year long process of review at the University of Ulster (Taylor, 2000). Nevertheless, restlessness in the academic world over contemporary directions in decision-making indicate that the price being paid may be too high. Very broadly defined, academic 'governance and management' would benefit from a critical appraisal in the framework of academic values and the internal and external communities they are designed to serve.

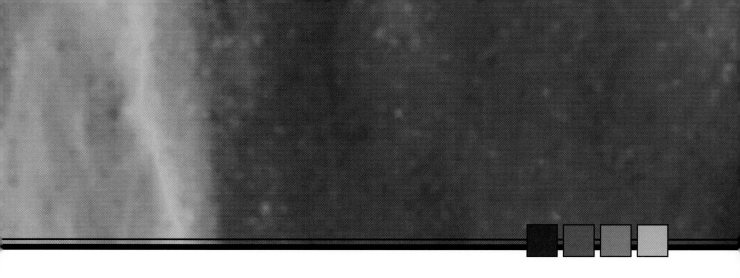

Ways of improving governance and management are now widely canvassed

A number of proposals have been forthcoming to help develop the more forward looking, adaptive, and institution-wide cultures that policy makers and analysts are calling for:

- Smaller, more expert, representative governing bodies
- More technically advanced record systems
- Greater strategic and management use of the large data sets that are being built up
- Staff appraisal and training in human and resource management
- Staff exchanges with industry, professions and government
- Development of methods for systematic, evaluated knowledge of the institution and its behaviour (the institution as a learning organisation)
- Better monitoring of student performance
- Total quality management, performance indicators, benchmarking and other procedures to enable institutions better to position themselves comparatively - regionally, nationally and internationally
- Increased professionalism of managers, better understanding of personnel, management and resource issues across the whole institution.

(Davis 1996; Dill 1999a; McKinnon et al, 2000; Williams, 1997).

However, the invoking of systems and techniques can stand in the way of a sensitive understanding of both the distinctiveness of academic culture and of the vital human factor. Large-scale changes including the development and implementation of strategic plans for institutional futures and the institution-wide assimilation of communication and information technologies inevitably call for rearrangements in roles and responsibilities and the introduction of new procedures for decision-making, monitoring and evaluation of results. Inevitably relationships are affected and new group interactions are called forth. Understanding of organisational change processes as human and social, not just technical, is essential. In general, disruptions occur; changes in perceptions, attitudes, and perhaps values are sought; the active interest and commitment of large numbers of people are likely to be required.

It is not only the growth of institutional strategic planning and the impact of the new technologies that entail these organisational and behavioural changes. The huge enrolment increases with declining staff-student ratios, reduction or abandonment of tutorials, enlargement of seminar groups and so on have changed patterns of relationships between students and staff. The greatly increased use of communication and information technologies, where attention tends to be directed at the technology, including training for its use, have implications for relations between teachers and learners, and among staff. The regulatory environment - health and safety, equal opportunity, ethics and various extra-institution administrative requirements are among the forces that are changing relations within the institution.

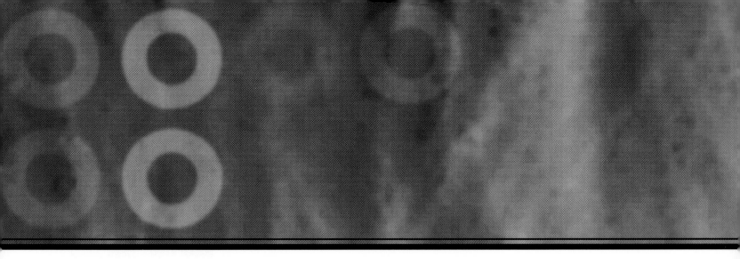

Closer attention is needed to interpersonal qualities and leadership roles and responsibilities

Although the changing environment of higher education requires enhanced management and leadership skills across the whole institution (and system), much of the literature on leadership concentrates on senior staff - heads of institutions and their immediate colleagues, deans and department heads, heads of research teams and so forth. The frequency of reports of low motivation and staff dissatisfaction are indicative of widespread problems, which cannot be addressed unless a wider purview is taken to embrace staff at all levels in a diffused model of leadership.

The reasons for concentrating so closely on the 'powerful actors' of leadership theory (Middlehurst and Gordon, 1995) at this time are perhaps understandable. There is great pressure on people in positions of formal authority to demonstrate tangible outcomes in accordance with system-wide and institutional priorities. A culture of competitiveness and results is impinging more and more on the beliefs (and myths) of the academy.

Is leadership along the lines of business management by holders of these positions really possible in universities, even if it were agreed to be desirable? Reponer (1999) is one of the sceptics. Universities are knowledge-intensive, expert organisations producing knowledge services which are in some critical respects intangible, difficult or impossible to standardise and measure. Heads of institutions and other leaders don't really know what's going on in highly specialised, largely self-governing departments and project and research teams. This of course may be true also of large private sector business and government departments so it is not universities alone that need to grapple with the issue of well-informed, effective leadership and decision-making. Each can learn from the other.

Itemising the difficulties of certain approaches to governance, management and leadership in higher education institutions is one thing; it is not, however, equivalent to demonstrating the impossibility of action. The leadership literature in higher education (as in other spheres) once the difficulties and challenges have been adumbrated, mostly addresses those directions that are thought to hold promise of success. The highly influential management theorist, Drucker (1992) has said that whereas managers maintain, leaders change.

Both qualities are in great demand in contemporary higher education. University heads, faculty deans, department heads, heads of libraries, computer and other centres, major administrative units all need skills in motivating, building agreements, networking, exercising non-jurisdictional power, planning, monitoring, evaluating, institution building - intelligence in action.

Policy-making and other forms of leadership are also required at the system-level, more so with the gathering interest in (1) a broader 'steering' rather than (sometimes as well as) (2) a narrower 'regulating'. Legislation provides a basis or foundation but policy initiatives such as fostering high quality performance, achieving equity goals, anticipating national needs for expertise and knowledge require leadership of a very high order. Yet this is found to be in short supply in the policy arena. McGuinness (1995), in commenting on a lack of policy leadership and sense of clear direction, painted a bleak picture of aspects of higher education in the United States: *"Except for a few bright spots, the overall picture of state coordination and governance across the United States is one of uncertainty and stagnation"* (p. 275).

Despite the critical tone of much of the international commentary on university governance and management and on system-wide policy making, McGuinness's appraisal is very much at the sharp edge of the continuum. Ireland can count itself fortunate that, the battles notwithstanding, relations between the universities, government and the Higher Education Authority appear to be very good. There is also a high degree of respect for the coordination and leadership provided by the HEA and its Chairman.

The extent of the contemporary leadership challenge facing universities was brought out in a review of diverse data sources by Hoff (1999). Higher education leaders in America are faced with multiple challenges: *"In most cases they are multidimensional, broad in scope and require complex assessment, planning, implementation, and evaluation. And many … are not new… societal, technological, economic, and political factors are altering the way in which they must be viewed … foremost in the minds of educational leaders today are the changing demographics of our student and faculty populations, alliance building with community and global organizations, changing and diminishing financial resource bases, fund raising and development activities, rapid technological advancement, diversity, continuing professional and leadership development activities for all constituencies on campus, community building both on-campus and with the surrounding community, gender equity, curriculum reform, and ethical considerations in relation to all services and programs offered"* (pp. 311-312).

The topics discussed in previous chapters underline the necessity for the university of the future to develop better leadership, management and decision-making capabilities. The art of successful change will be to move effectively in this way while maintaining and strengthening the qualities and virtues of academic life. To do this with multiple-sourced, varied and often constrained resources requires the setting of clear targets and priorities within a framework of values as well as of strategic planning. Closely monitored implementation and evaluation of performance are not extraneous requirements, alien to an academic culture but consistent with the fundamental values of inquiry, criticism and the growth of knowledge. What is required is an extension of these values and processes from the subjects of academic specialisation

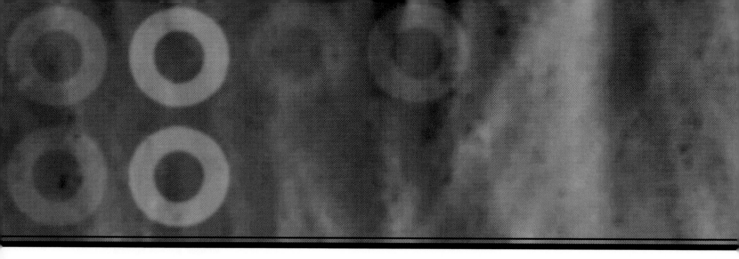

into institutional governance and management and all aspects of organisational life. Rapprochement instead of a nagging confrontation. With challenges of the scale and complexity addressed in this report, in an increasingly competitive environment, there are serious threats to weaker, less effective institutions and to poorly led and managed parts even of strong universities. Amalgamations on a large scale have occurred in several countries, thus far seeing the disappearance of non-university rather than university institutions. But many universities have been radically changed as a result of joining with and assimilating other institutions and individual departments within universities have either closed altogether or been merged, when demand for places declines or the overall quality of teaching and research falters. Leadership effectiveness and sound management in universities increasingly requires a readiness and aptitude to deal decisively and sensitively with such complex issues. Academic staff need more sensitising to these issues and more opportunities to improve their management and decision-making skills. The stability or continued existence of (all) existing institutions cannot be taken for granted.

Financing pressures: there is an imperative need internationally for new sources of funding and greater efficiency

As in all other aspects of higher education, funding sources and procedures and management of finance are in an increasingly fluid state. A report from the Netherlands indicates five successive stages over time in the funding of higher education in that country:

- Earmarked input funding;
- Input funding (using a model) on the basis of norms, with limited spending freedom;
- Introduction of some output measures (e.g. student success rates); increase in spending freedom;
- Mix of input-output norms; maximal spending freedom;
- Moves towards funding-based largely or solely on outputs and bi-lateral agreements; longer-term funding horizons.

(Koelman, 1998).

These changes might seem to suggest a continuing, expanding source of state funds, but this would be a mis-reading. The state interest is in increases to be achieved by diversifying funding sources (Meek and Wood, 1998). Hence the emerging concept of the tightly managed, 'entrepreneurial' (the earning as well as the spending) university, when funding, whatever its source, becomes dependent on outputs, quality of performance, and the sale of services.

In reviewing a large volume of national and regional reports from Member countries and expert papers on higher education resources and finance, prepared for the 1998 UNESCO World Conference on Higher Education, Skilbeck

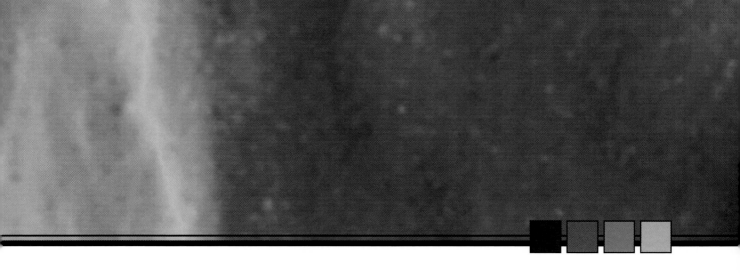

(1998) established two central global preoccupations. The first is how to mobilise new or additional sources of funds in face of stagnant or declining funding from traditional sources, principally national and state governments. The second is how to achieve efficiency and productivity gains without loss of academic values and quality or abridgement of access and equity commitments.

While a multitude of sources can be cited to demonstrate the salience of these concerns across the world, there is no clear agreement in the international community about how best to address them. In the report of the Dearing Committee in the UK three primary sources of (existing and possibly additional) funding were acknowledged:

- The state;
- The student;
- The employer or other purchaser of services.

The Communique and Report of the 1998 UNESCO World Conference indicated acceptance of the first and the third of the 3 'Dearing sources', but only oblique references were made to the second even though, in the Conference Commission on Management and Finance, there was little dissent from the proposition that additional resources would need to be sought from the student (Skilbeck and Connell, 1998). This, however, is a politically sensitive issue in many countries, Ireland included. The World Bank is clear that students, as major beneficiaries of private rates of return on the (highly subsidised) investments in higher education, should pay more. It has been estimated that tuition charges and fees account for more than 10% of recurrent expenses for higher education in only 20 countries throughout the world (Wassen and Picken, 1998).

Student-centred funding does not mean the same thing as a policy of no fees for tuition falling on students. What it refers to is a shift of funding from the institution to the student who is thereby enabled to purchase a service of choice. In Australia, the 1998 Review of Higher Education Financing and Policy by the West Committee was quite unequivocal in seeking a shift in government funding from institutions to the student, through a life-long earning entitlement, in wanting to enable institutions to set their own fee levels for all students, and income-contingent government loans (a variant of the present Higher Education Contribution Scheme which permits income-contingent deferred payment of tuition fees).

These funding recommendations are consistent with an overall re-orientation toward enabling the student to make choices and allocate resources. The targeted funding of research, contracting for delivery of services and other shifts in resourcing which present new challenges and opportunities to institutions are part of the same mentality. However, even were this

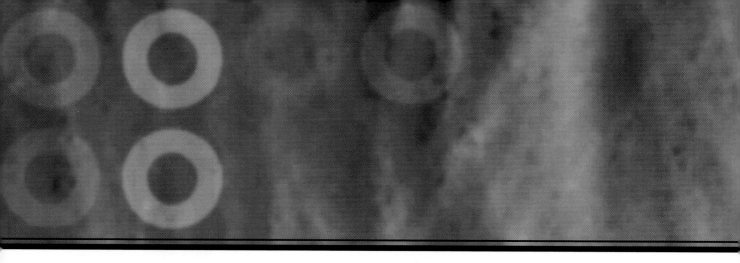

array of radical changes acceptable to the minister, the political environment would militate against their adoption. They might be seen as a form of frontier setting for future policy debates.

There is an increasing number of schemes with government backing or on direct government initiative to encourage, facilitate or (more often) require student contributions to tuition costs and/or reduction in such direct subsidies as maintenance, housing, travel and other services. Assistance in meeting these requirements includes loans, usually government backed and at minimal rates of interest, deferred payment schemes with discount incentives for 'upfront' payment, and direct aid concentrated on the most needy students or on target groups to meet economic needs e.g. systems analysts or bio-technologists. Some schemes provide support directly to institutions, for example in support of equity groups; others aim to focus government funding on the students rather than the institution (West Committee). It is important to have well-functioning, effective schemes to support low income students since cost (along with aspiration and academic preparation) has been posited as one of the main barriers to higher education participation (Choy, 1999). Where private rates of return to higher education are low relative to social rates (Scandinavia), student fees are not favoured (Aamodt, 2000). But the issues are always complex whether tuition fees are charged or not: exemptions: variable fee levels; targeted groups; repayment of loans; the role of private providers; rates of return debates; and so on. As access to and participation in tertiary education becomes more nearly universal - a right and an entitlement rather than a privilege - the overall relative rate of private return is likely to continue to decline and the public good argument may become stronger, with interesting implications for cost sharing.

Public returns to the state in the form of tax revenues generated by individuals' higher productive contribution and other less tangible measure are often argued as justifying continuing subsidy, notwithstanding higher private rates of return. The complexities of this issue are beyond the scope of this report. It is sometimes argued that there are better education investments for the state than high cost university programmes and, if subsidies are available, there are more needy groups than undergraduates with high income-earning potential. The World Bank has in the past sought a much greater concentration of resources in developing countries on primary education than universities. More recently, the Bank, without abandoning this view, has focused on the plight of under-resourced universities. Notwithstanding the global debates, the argument for high levels of public investment in higher education and research is widely accepted by governments in all OECD countries.

It is also accepted that, 'other things being equal, policies designed to widen access need to incorporate the financial means to support some groups through their studies' (Hogarth et al, 1997; Skilbeck and Connell, 2000). But, despite decades of

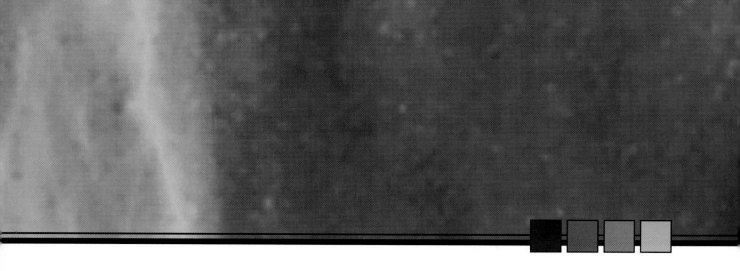

study since the time human capital theories were being developed, there is at present no agreement over the kinds and levels of charges for example for different subjects studied or the proportions of costs to be attributed to the different parties or indeed, in some countries, whether students should make direct payments at all.

In the judgment of two critics of those regimes where costs to students are considerable, the United Kingdom has a higher education system subsidised by student debt (McCarthy and Humphrey, 1995). This is too glib since there are many variables to consider: capacity to pay; equity; role of the state; taxation regimes; subsidies; rates of return; mechanisms of cost recovery and so forth. Moreover, resistance to direct charges and fee increases for students for tuition is mostly confined to initial degrees and for full-time students. It is common practice to charge for higher degrees, advanced diplomas, many short courses and part-time students. Tuition charges imposed on postgraduate students can have a negative impact, for example by limiting occupational choice (Anderson et al, in press); charges falling on part-time (but not full-time) students can be inequitable and demotivating and have been strongly criticised, for example in Ireland. Differential charging, although widely practised, entails many arbitrary elements.

As for attribution to employers, the Business and Industry Advisory Committee at the OECD, in line with human capital theorist Becker, conceded the case for employer contributions to the cost of continuing, occupation-specific training and professional development, but not for more general education and training at initial degree and diploma levels. Industry contribution to university research OECD-wide sits on average at 5-6% of university research funding (OECD, 1998e) and even if this figure were increased, and employers paid more for continuing education, the contributions from this source would still form a relatively small part of the whole. The funding of research as well as teaching in most countries thus remains heavily dependent on public sources and, as in Ireland, is seen by government as vital for the development of infrastructure of the 'knowledge-based economy'.

External research funding bodies have, in recent years, sought to increase their control over how their funds are spent. They have used a variety of mechanisms, and approaches leading to a more competitive r&d environment with reduced availability of non-competitive public funds. Also new types of funding agencies have been created, with considerable restructuring of existing bodies (OECD, 1998e; OECD/IMHE, 2000b). Universities have, in this new climate, become more focused on generating revenue through exploiting their intellectual property, for example through different types of patents, licencing agreements, royalties, first mover advantage. Complex legal disputes have begun to emerge over ownership of intellectual property, particularly in the United States, not only between the university and commercial organisations, but also between university staff and graduate students (OECD/IMHE, 2000b; Slaughter, 2000).

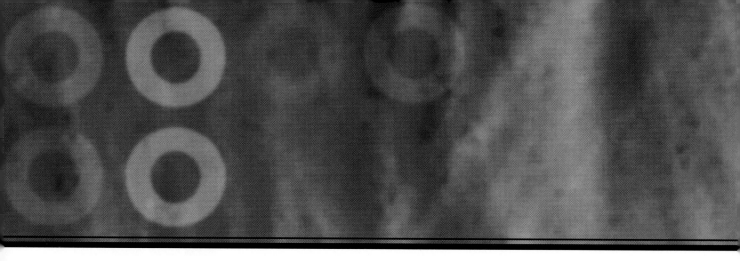

There are variable patterns of charging in different sectors of tertiary or post-secondary education. Efforts by government to increase revenue contributions by students are mostly concentrated on the university sector, with negligible or low charges being more characteristic of other sectors. This is partly for historic reasons, partly a measure of public priorities. It may also reflect awareness that, typically, lower socio-economic groups in society are disproportionately represented in the non-university by comparison with the university sector. More varied participation, as enrolments in higher education increase, means that there will be more students/graduates in 'at risk' situations, financially.

Although other sources of finance than government funding and student contributions are canvassed – and most actively pursued especially in North America through the traditions of alumni support, private philanthropy and fund raising, for most systems it appears that the only realistic option for a significant increase in resources available to higher education – failing regularly increasing public subsidies – is fees for students. Increasingly, public universities in several national systems are taking advantage of arrangements that enable them to charge at full cost rates for international students whilst being held in check regarding home-based students. The USA has long held the world's leading position in recruiting foreign students (although many are not charged at full rates). In others, such as Australia, Japan and New Zealand, public policy has encouraged institutions to develop new markets for fee paying students (Joint Council, 2000). Whether for home-based or international students there is an issue of equity: changes should not have adverse equity effects. Specifically for students, whether home-based or international, payment of high fees is raising delicate issues of the quality of the service provided and the temptation to adjust standards to ensure high pass rates for high payers.

It is not necessary to go further into the intricacies of higher education funding to appreciate that the rapid growth in demand and huge volume increases in participation, when coupled with continuing pressures on public finances, have produced a global crisis to which, thus far, only relatively short term and mainly expedient solutions have been found. There are numerous anomalies, such as charges to part-time but not full-time students and neglect of special conditions affecting certain minority groups (refugees, travelling people, etc). Weaknesses include defaulting on loan repayments, and disagreements over the rate of return calculations that have been a factor in the moves toward user pays. Institutions, most seriously in the poorer regions of the world, are grossly underfunded but in even the wealthiest regions there is a great concern over the continuing ability to finance expansion while maintaining quality.

With this background, it is obvious why the attention of policy makers has spread from funding mechanisms, formulae and procedures to include efficiency measures, more productive management of assets and alternatives to full-time, campus-based, labour intensive higher education. The challenge is to demonstrate that all possible steps are being taken to contain costs, increase productivity and maximise returns from all the assets, human and material, that universities have at their disposal.

With the objective of developing the best possible management and strengthening accountability for resources, the then Australian Minister for Employment, Education and Training, Simon Crean established a review of higher education in 1995. This review addressed a wide variety of issues: governance, strategic management, workplace reforms and financial and asset management. Accepting that many changes had been made, the Committee argued for a much more dynamic approach. To achieve 'truly contemporary approaches' and 'to exploit the opportunities as they became available', universities were recommended themselves to internalise continuous management improvement processes. This was an unequivocal statement on the need for Australian universities to develop new styles of resource utilisation and decision-making (Committee of Inquiry, 1995).

Cost containment, from the perspective of governments, has taken a variety of forms, all of them constituting challenges to - and opportunities for - institutional management:

- Reducing the individual unit of resource;
- Requiring public institutions to fund salary increases from their own resources and jointly fund capital/research projects;
- Tying resources (e.g. formula funding) to performance and penalising when agreed targets are not met, i.e. incentives for efficiency and quality;
- Stimulating private funding initiatives including institutional borrowing in the money market and facilitating financially rewarding partnerships with industry (e.g. though the tax system);
- Imposing or increasing the student share in meeting costs (maintenance as well as tuition);
- Encouraging or requiring mergers of institutions and internal management-led restructuring;
- Steering university profiles (and costs) by the use of criteria of national/regional need and appraisal of quality of teaching and research;
- Fostering an 'entrepreneurial university' mentality.

Universities have in fact demonstrated a remarkable capacity to respond to these and other challenges but are under increasing pressure to find a course between what is financially advantageous and educationally worthwhile. For example, should low demand/low enrolment courses be cross-subsidised or run down and how are decisions best made on such issues; should the rewards of entrepreneurial activity be shared (wholly or in part) across the whole institution or confined to the earning departments and staff; should fee-paying post-graduate programmes and research contracts be given precedence over more intensive undergraduate teaching? And so on.

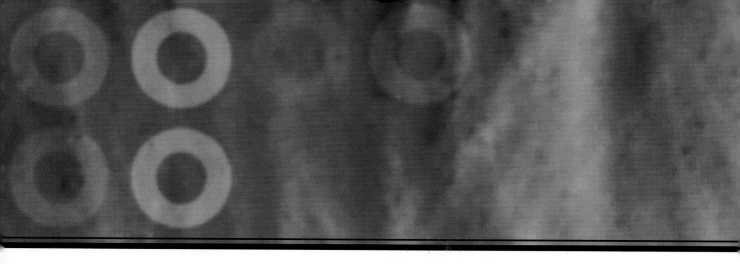

As already mentioned, policy interest is moving in several countries towards the concept of the entrepreneurial university – which not only increases its earnings and diversifies its revenue sources, but displays the full apparatus of cost control and efficiency gains in all its operations (Shattock, 1997). Institutions, in addition to being encouraged to be entrepreneurial, have been stimulated (or pressurised) to form alliances, share resources, amalgamate for economies of scale and take advantage of potential savings through investment in technology, for both educational and administrative purposes. Financial penalties have been imposed for failure to meet course completion targets and such techniques as marginal funding to meet new growth targets are deployed.

National policy targets in countries where the dominant or exclusive model has been the public university now also include permitting or encouraging private sector initiatives. Williams (1996) identified six forms of semi or full privatisation in higher education:

- Universities run as completely commercial organisations (e.g. Asia, South America, USA, Australia)
- Universities run as non-profit making trusts and receiving the bulk of their funds from either the public or private sector (e.g. by religious bodies in Europe and USA)
- Publicly-owned universities receiving a significant part of their income from student fees (e.g. Australia, the Netherlands, Portugal, South Africa, Spain, UK, US)
- Publicly-owned universities receiving a significant part of their income through other private sources – such as consultancy and letting out facilities for private sector use
- Publicly-owned universities or universities with trust status contracting out the provision of subsidised services for private sector use
- Publicly-owned and financed universities receiving and allocating their resources on the basis of market criteria.

While not all of these forms of privatisation signify efficiency gains, they reflect a trend in government to create environments for higher education most conducive to tapping multiple sources of funds. They all are perceived as alleviating pressure on public budgets while addressing different aspects of demand.

Efficient use of funds and assets is a management responsibility which raises difficult issues for universities – collegial roles, transparency, ethical concerns and sometimes uncertainty over ownership and degrees of freedom in decision-making. Participation in decision making is essential, but academic training in and of itself does not equip people for these management tasks although there is a long history of successful financial management by certain distinguished academics including, it is reported, John Maynard Keynes. The shifting, highly complex field of institutional finance – when many universities are managing annual budgets in the range of hundreds of millions of dollars and more and with huge capital

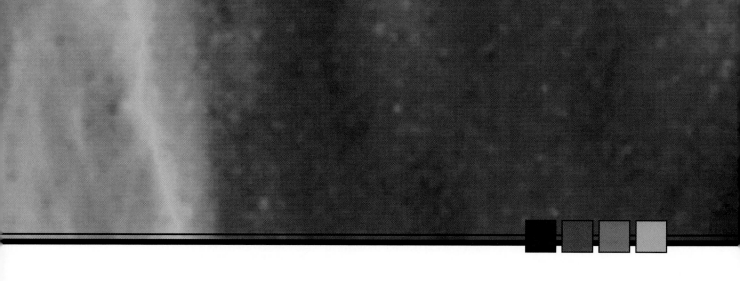

assets – is a heavy responsibility which calls for high levels of expertise. This is another factor in the shift towards the 'managerial model'. As demands for sound and effective management of these very large resource bases gather momentum, the need for this expertise will increase, not diminish. Not all of these management tasks can - or should - be performed by professional administrators alone. But how are academics to be best equipped to engage with these matters?

There is need also for the debate over sources of funding for higher education to move beyond the fixed positions which have been adopted in some quarters and the rather rigid measures still in place regarding allocation and utilisation. At the same time, commentators have drawn attention to serious risks in the relentless pursuit of the so-called free market philosophy in higher education including the importation of dubious money - management procedures, and the challenge to social values and institutions (Colclough and Manor, 1991; Tilak, 1998). The loosening of tight regulatory frameworks will of course require a wider diffusion of resource and other management responsibilities. The effective exercise of university autonomy in the age of the entrepreneurial, globalising university depends on a broadening of skills and shifts in attitudes of the university academic as much as it does on the leadership and management capabilities of administration specialists and those in the most senior positions of authority.

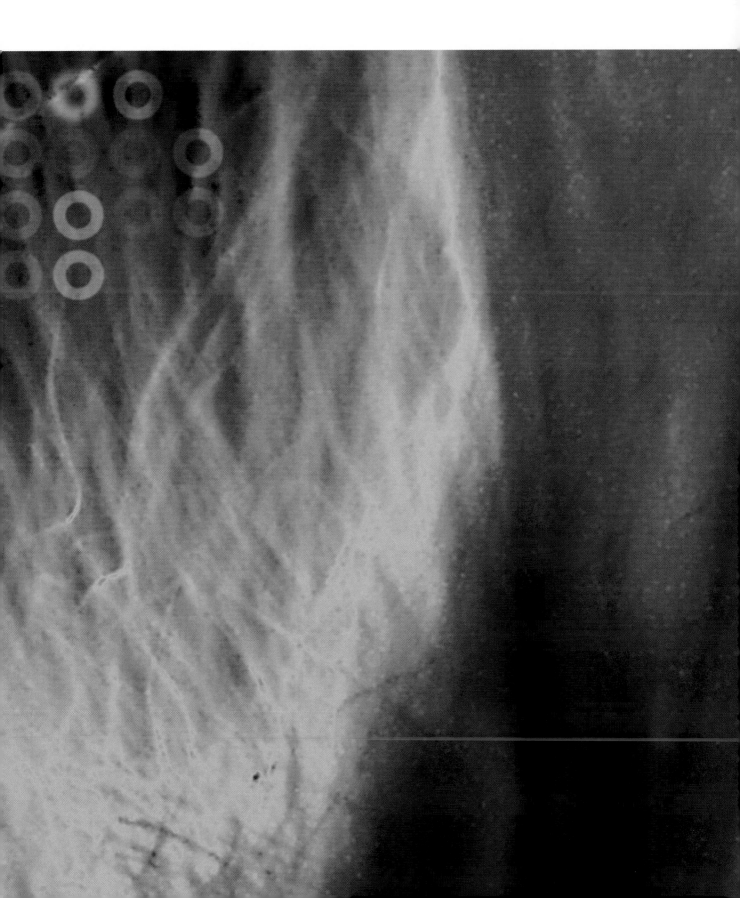

part III | Focusing the Challenge:
The Universities of Ireland

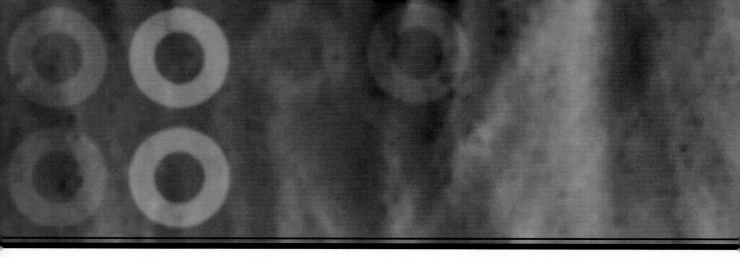

Will the word [university] in future always have to be qualified by an adjective, if it is to signify anything? **Research** *university;* **teaching** *university;* **entrepreneurial** *university;* **technological** *university;* **corporate** *university,* **virtual** *university? Does it matter?* (Williams, 1999, p. 5)

It would be presumptuous to infer from the foregoing overview of international trends and issues specific implications for individual universities, but there are challenges for the institutions collectively and for the university system of Ireland. And, whatever picture may be drawn of the changing world of higher education, the lineaments of challenges and opportunities can be drawn by any university for itself. There is no need to dwell further on either parallel movements across the industrially advanced countries or the uniqueness of each system (and institution) to accept that there are common trends and issues and an international dialogue on them. The extension of this dialogue in the Irish context is the aim of this concluding chapter. To achieve it, a marriage is required of the international environment of policies, trends and issues, and conditions within Ireland.

The reports, policy initiatives and legislation relating to higher education that have been issued or enacted in recent years indicate both a need and a readiness to embark on far-reaching changes and reforms. Flushed with a decade of substantial economic growth, successful membership of the European Community and a strong international profile, Ireland is clearly seeking to position itself among the leading OECD countries. The National Competitiveness Council aims to place Ireland in the top 25% of OECD countries investing in human capital. But for the university presidents, this is too modest: 'The aim should be to be at the leading edge in the development of human capital.'

The universities, in respect of research, should be enabled through the National Plan to deliver *"world class expertise and research capabilities' in the two designated priority areas of information and communication technology and biotechnology"* (Conference of the Heads of Irish Universities, 2000a, p. 5). To achieve this, the presidents continued, *"a quantum leap is required in planning for, and investment in, access to universities and in third level teaching, learning and research"* (p. 10). Accordingly the presidents outlined an ambitious set of development targets (pp. 46-49) which balance the advancement of research with goals of equity, opportunities for adult and part-time study and lifelong learning.

The strength of the Irish economy and wide - ranging changes in society make possible developments in higher education which could scarcely have been contemplated even a decade ago. At the same time, they give some urgency and a sense of direction to the contributions higher education can make. In addressing this challenge, the universities must have convincing answers to any questions that might arise concerning their readiness in practice to meet the development

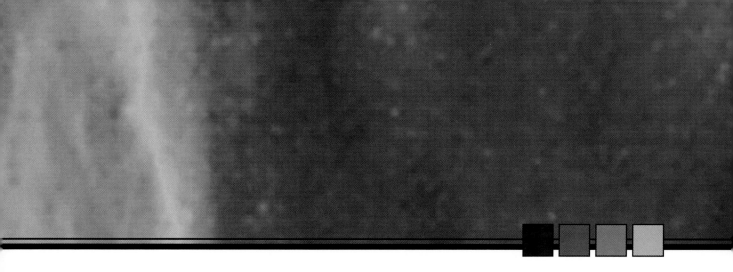

targets that the presidents have outlined, even supposing they gain the increased funding that they are seeking. It is evident that there would have to be a sea change in several aspects of current practice and substantial infrastructure developments.

The matter can be put more starkly. In common with universities in many other countries, the Irish universities are facing a series of decision points, with choices to be made sooner rather than later. Essentially these choices revolve around shaping and managing the future, acting ahead of events, maintaining control of agenda, seizing opportunities on the basis of well-prepared strategies and reviewing and reforming procedures for taking decisions and carrying them through to satisfactory conclusions. The alternative for universities to positive action on all of these fronts is not the maintenance of the *status quo*, but a steady and inexorable decline and loss of authority, influence and resources. In their reports on *Guaranteeing Future Growth* (CHIU, 2000a) and *Technology Foresight* (CHIU, 2000b) and in that on *Future Needs* (CHIU, 1998), the university presidents have staked out very prominent positions on the high ground.

Although not formally committed by these documents, the institutions would of course be mindful of the challenges posed by them, as well as those set forth in the 1997 Deloitte Touche report on governance and management and the 1999 Report of the *Review Committee on Post Secondary Education and Training Places*, among others.

These challenges facing universities should be seen in a context where there are already - or on the horizon - different ways of addressing higher education and research roles than by simply augmenting and concentrating resources in universities. Alternatives already exist, internationally, for carrying out each and every one of the main functions traditionally performed by universities. They have been discussed in the preceding chapters, but several bear repeating:

- Teaching is increasingly being delivered on-line and by correspondence internationally by private providers and consortia of prominent universities; private, off-and on-campus universities are demonstrating a capacity to sectionalise the market and provide courses at lower costs than public providers;
- Research, including basic research, is being and can be carried out by specialised research institutes, both independently and from government and industry bases;
- Information from traditional repositories and sources, notably libraries is becoming available on-line and there will be, as a result, access by students and staff to a much larger array than any single institution can provide;
- Private firms and consultancy groups, including teams of academics, are providing services on a contractual basis comparable to those available through units within universities (e.g. course units, programme evaluation, installing specialist systems etc) and on a competitive cost basis.

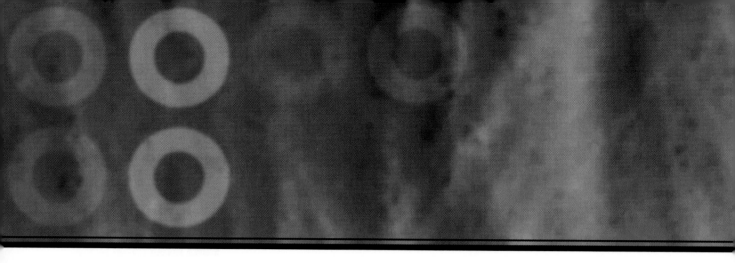

The synergies which can be achieved within and among universities, the benefits of cross-subsidisation and of large concentrations of varied resources should not be underestimated. Against this, however, are the high costs entailed and the inflexibilities of traditional structures and procedures. Universities in Ireland, as elsewhere, continue to enjoy public esteem and network-based power and influence. They also have other relative advantages which can induce a sense of security, in the face of emerging threats and challenges from a changing environment. The issue is not the advantages and strengths, which are real enough, but whether they are to be used in the full in order to scan the environment, determine capabilities - and weaknesses - map out desirable and attainable futures, and plan and implement change strategies. No Irish university faces the prospect of collapse - far from it - but for several the alternative to wholeheartedly taking on the challenges and seeking opportunities could be relative decline and marginalisation.

Laying the groundwork for future development of Irish universities

There is in Ireland today a window of opportunity which, if availed of, can strengthen the higher education system, enhance its status internationally, and enable it to demonstrate its central role in meeting national development priorities. The presidents have clearly set this as their collective aspiration, in the documents referred to above. However, action will necessarily be at the level of each institution. Every university, under the Universities Act, is obliged to prepare a strategic plan and this is an important task not to be undertaken lightly. Such plans need to be well balanced, to embody the full range of values, purposes and missions of universities which are social, cultural and moral as well as intellectual, professional and vocational. The national development agenda tends to highlight economic competitiveness and links with industry and commerce focus on employment and profitable returns from investment. Important as these are, they do not address the full scope of university responsibilities and roles in society. How far advanced are the universities' plans, what is their scope, and what steps are envisaged to implement them?

In the succession of studies, reports, policies and legislation there are numerous proposals and possibilities for institutional planning. From this body of material, while there is no single analysis of strategic directions for consideration by the universities, a question arises. Do the universities see this as an opportunity to review potential roles in line with an agreed national development agenda? Have they determined that they should systematically represent their collective capabilities, expectations and perspectives on the future to government, industry, the voluntary or non-government sector and through the media, to the public at large? This kind of action, which requires full cooperation, coordination and a mutual investment of resources, is increasingly being taken by peak bodies, such as the heads of universities and, internationally, by associations such as the European CRE. It reflects a growing competition everywhere for public resources but also for occupancy of the public space - space where influence is exercised on national - and international - policy. The

traditional networks and amateurishness no longer suffice for these purposes when the arenas are being occupied by highly professional lobby groups and media specialists well versed in strategies for effective change.

While directions have been indicated by CHIU, it is not evident that the Irish universities have as yet, and on the basis of carefully prepared strategies and plans, sufficiently mobilised themselves either individually or collectively to achieve maximum impact. For example, great concern has been expressed at the prospect of the recently announced, significant augmentation of research funding by-passing the universities through the establishment or enhancement of dedicated research centres. If, as the universities believe, this could lead to a wasteful duplication of infrastructure and, with destructive competition for scarce human resources, be harmful not only to the universities but to the national research endeavour, has a system-wide, collaborative strategy for the future of research been initiated by the universities acting in unison? If so, has it been prepared and presented in full recognition of the professional standards now required in the public policy arena? This is essentially an exercise in positioning to gain a result for which there is a thoroughly researched case, demonstrating national and not only sectional interest.

It is worth recalling the succession of documents and initiatives which have brought higher education in Ireland to a position from which there can be a powerful drive forward along the lines envisaged in CHIU reports. Leaving aside earlier documents, of which the report for the OECD *Investment in Education* (1967) is a landmark, the starting point for the recent reform programme is *Charting Our Education Future*, the 1995 White Paper, which itself acknowledges the role played by the National Education Convention (1993) in setting in motion a major national education debate.

The main interest for higher education in the 1995 *White Paper* is chapter 5, but this is preceded by a declaration of principles which underlie both that chapter and many later initiatives. The principles address the role of education in advancing social and economic well-being: rights, quality, equality, pluralism, partnership, accountability - and the importance of knowledge and skills for national competitiveness and development. The twin pillars of the 'OECD model' are firmly in place: educational expenditure as investment in economic growth and social cohesion. The universities themselves can be expected to develop the arguments for the third pillar: the advancement of knowledge in a culture of disinterested study; the dissemination of intellectual values; and providing a voice for critical and creative moral concerns. The latter has become of vital importance as the growth of knowledge engenders ethical and social issues of fundamental importance for all people.

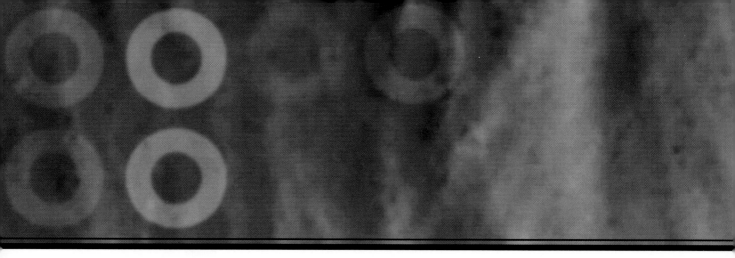

Higher education, in this context, is charged with 'a responsibility to respond to the changing needs of society and the legitimate interests of the state.' Conversely, there is a societal responsibility 'to safeguard the traditional aims of higher education, including the full development of the individual, independent inquiry and the pursuit of knowledge.' Both the education of students and research and its applications underpin the mission of higher education, to be achieved through a diversity of institutions sharing a common philosophy of education. This said, which directions were set in the 1995 document?

The White Paper enumerated a number of challenges, all of them, in one way or another, picked up in subsequent policies and action programmes:
- Enrolment growth;
- A more diverse student body;
- Achieving and maintaining high standards of teaching and research;
- Effectiveness in addressing social and economic expectations and efficiency in meeting them;
- Greater accountability and transparency;
- Improved equity (grounded in 'persistent, targeted and regularly evaluated policies').

The directions set and challenges posed in the White Paper are rather general; they are also familiar elements in the agenda of contemporary education policies in many countries, finding echos in the trends and issues discussed throughout this report. Three features of both the National Convention and the White Paper deserve special mention:
- The future development of higher education is not treated as a separate topic but is integral to a framework of lifelong education. (Few universities, anywhere, have taken the measure of this challenge which goes far beyond adult and continuing education programmes being a kind of add-on);
- There is an affirmation that national education policy must be set firmly in an international context. (Some universities are far ahead of others in seizing the opportunities: for Ireland, 'international' should not mean simply Western Europe and USA plus a few projects in developing countries; a global perspective is required);
- A wide array of reform measures and strategies is foreshadowed and many of these have been carried through or are in active preparation. (But there is a great deal of unfinished business).

These three features in themselves constitute a powerful agenda for change, and are supported by an array of social, cultural, moral as well as economic arguments. Subsequent reports and pronouncements have sharpened the focus.

In June 1995, the Steering Committee on the Future Development of Higher Education (chaired by the then Chairman of the Higher Education Authority) issued its report: 'future' referred to the twenty year period to 2015. This report

envisaged continuing growth for all sectors of tertiary education, based on increased levels of participation by school leavers and mature age students, with no diminution of quality. The Steering Committee endorsed retention of the binary system and the orientation of its parts respectively towards 'academic knowledge' and 'practical applications'. Support was also given to a distinction drawn by the Science, Technology and Innovation Advisory Council (STIAC, 1995) between more applied and basic research: close coordination across all sectors including credit accumulation and transfer was advocated. The role of higher education in economic and social development would be expressed through improved technology transfer, campus companies, contract research and joint efforts with industry in job creation and through increased participation by under-represented groups.

The pertinence of the recommendations in this report is shown by subsequent action taken on several fronts, including those documented by CHIU in *Technology Foresight and the University Sector* (CHIU, 2000b). However, there are some interesting omissions from the Steering Committee analysis. Unlike the White Paper, the Steering Committee report made little acknowledgement of the challenges from the changing international environment: there is still the sense of a largely self-contained system of Irish higher education even though the reality was in fact different. A second point is that there was no attempt to reflect on ways of broadening the resource base of higher education through sources additional to state revenues. However, reference to industry partnerships, campus companies, etc. did open an avenue in this direction. Fees from overseas students would be another but was not explored. Third, the report did not raise issues of institutional governance, leadership and management. Not part of the terms of reference, changes there would seem to be necessary to achieve some of the report's recommendations, for example regarding liaison with industry and regional development priorities. These were, however, taken up by the report prepared for the Higher Education Authority by Deloitte Touche (1997).

Of the three points made in the previous paragraph, the resource issue was and remains crucial for the longer-term planning and strategic perspectives the universities need to develop. In his minority report, the Department of Finance representative set out the over-riding public expenditure control approach which the Committee could not ignore in order to reach recommendations acceptable to government. However, longer term horizons are needed if the investment approach, first outlined for Ireland in 1967 in Investment in Education, is really to take hold. Debates over private benefits and annual budgeting should not cloud the fundamental point that human capital - *"an intangible asset with the capacity to enhance or support productivity, innovation and employability"* (OECD, 1998c, p. 9; Becker, 1975) - requires long term public and private investment strategies and continuing enhancement over the lifetime of individuals. The investment, from a university perspective, must be in fundamental and applied research, innovation and knowledge-based start-up enterprises,

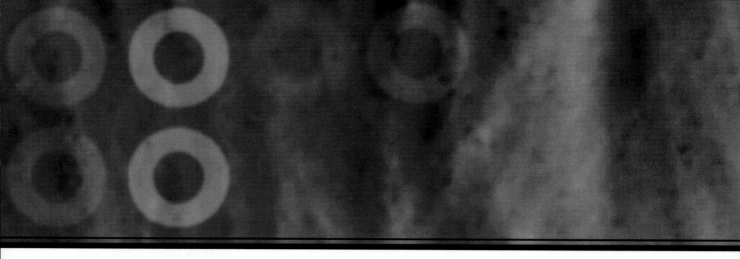

staff training and development, broadening the base of access; strengthening the capacity to train post-graduate students; undertaking advanced professional training; and developing international networks (CHIU, 2000a, 2000b).

Several of the reports and policy initiatives since the publication of the Education White Paper have carried forward the momentum. Although there has been a considerable number and variety of initiatives, including several in cognate fields with messages for higher education, the following are quite central to higher education policy and practice:

- The Report of the Commission on the Points System (1999);
- The enhancement of research and development set out in the National Development Plan, including the Programme for Research in Third-level Institutions (1999);
- The Report of the Review Committee on Post-Secondary Education and Training Places (1999);
- The programme of studies and reports on Equity and Access and the forthcoming Equality Review of Universities (1999-2001) (Clancy and Wall, 2000; Osborne and Leith, 2000; Skilbeck, 2000);
- *Learning for Life: White Paper on Adult Education* (2000);
- The reports of the Expert Group on Future Skills Needs;
- Two major pieces of legislation: the Irish Universities Act 1997 and the Qualifications (Education and Training) Act 1999;
- The two CHIU reports published in 2000 (*Technology Foresight and the University Sector; Guaranteeing Future Growth*).

These sources are indicative of a ferment of ideas and proposals for moving the country as rapidly as possible towards an advanced knowledge-based society/economy. In addition to the above items, mention should be made of a number of others, *inter alia*: the Business, Education and Training Partnership Forum, the report of the Business, Education and Training Partnership Forum and the funding of additional places through partnerships, the Technology Foresight reports, the issues raised in the Deloitte and Touche report on governance and management of universities, the Value for Money Report of the Comptroller and Auditor-General on Procurement in Universities, and the targeted initiative scheme of the Higher Education Authority (Targeted Funding for Special Initiatives and Related Issues). There are also numerous international programmes and projects to which the universities and the HEA contribute and from which they gain further expertise.

With such a wealth of material and activity, there is no shortage of ideas. There is a constant sharpening of the focus on cross-sectoral, cohesive public policies and areas of strategic importance. The universities are in a good position to take from all this whatever they are able to put to best advantage: conducting internal audits; evaluating their strengths and weaknesses; developing and implementing their own strategic plans.

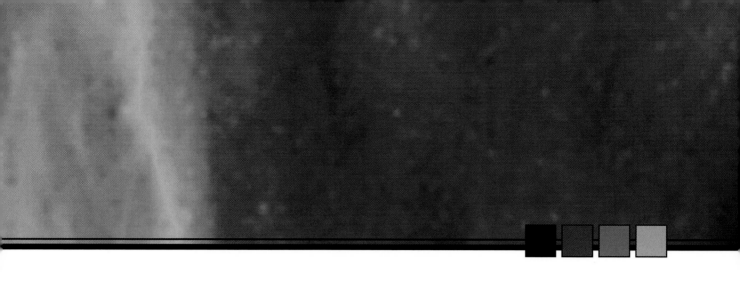

Few of the (above) reports address what in the international experience of educational reform has proved decisive: the mobilisation of people to implement plans and carry them through successfully to meet the targets set, to institutionalise them and maintain momentum. This usually entails long term commitment, sustained effort to overcome the barriers that inevitably arise, and serious investment in staff development. Implementing and sustaining reform require different skills and procedures from policy analysis, planning and start-up. It appears that there is insufficient attention to the human, social and institutional requirement of implementing policies and long-term follow-through, in the succession of Irish policy and reviews and proposals. That is an area of particular importance for universities, with their traditions, deeply embedded values and structures - and the reluctance by many members of the academic community to become footsoldiers to the cavaliers of government and economic policy.

Although each of the documents and programmes enumerated above warrants separate, extended treatment in any attempt to map the Irish higher education reform agenda. For the purposes of this chapter it suffices to make the following points:

- Until quite recently the Irish universities have been by international standards, seriously underfunded. They have lacked the capacity to meet to the full rising individual and social demand for access and for advanced knowledge and skills. They have not been able to contribute as comprehensively as they might to the great drive forward of the Irish economy in the '90s - although they have provided flows of skilled personnel mainly from first degree programmes. Irish higher education policy has been constrained and has only recently been able to begin to make the full range of connections that are needed with the overall national policy environment. Despite all the limitations, however, the educational standards attained by Irish graduates compare well internationally and well educated Irish people are in demand in the international labour market.

- Ireland's relatively low ranking among OECD countries in respect of mature age participation in higher education has been identified as a significant weakness on both economic and equity grounds. This is now a more pressing concern with shortages in the labour market of highly trained personnel and the need for continual upgrading of knowledge and expertise. Targets have been set, which include substantial enrolment increases, and a variety of support measures including finance. There is need for greater openness, flexibility and innovativeness if suitable conditions are to be established to attract mature age, part-time students and suitable programmes of study provided. Marketing strategies will be required, related to university strengths and to national needs. There are clear, definite challenges here for partnerships involving all tertiary level institutions as well as for government, the Higher Education Authority, employers, the adult education agencies and indeed the wider community, to recognise and support stronger moves towards continued study for adults.

- A greater measure of openness and flexibility regarding routes and access into higher education for school leavers has been identified as a reform target, in recognition of the characteristics and needs of diverse groups of students including those under-represented in higher education. This implies both system-wide changes and action by individual universities on their selection and admission policies and procedures, curricula and teaching. Such changes would be in line with the numerous initiatives internationally to broaden access, increase flexibility of study routes and establish more student-centred programmes to facilitate educational opportunity. Equity issues apply as much to the adult as to the youth population and to staff as well as students.

- The 1999 National Development Plan for research, technology development and innovation sets out ways to enhance research and development in higher education through a major investment programme. The Plan includes provision of IR£ 560 million for the Technology Foresight Initiative, which has commenced with the establishment of the Science Foundation of Ireland under the aegis of Forfás. There are four pillars of support for research and development: the existing unified teaching and research budget allocated by the Higher Education Authority to the universities as a block grant; the funding of individual research proposals and projects following competitive application processes and peer review assessments; the funding of institutional research strategies on a basis of competitive peer-reviewed evaluation; 'mission oriented' research where institutions and researchers respond to invitations for research proposals in priority areas identified by government. Described by Dr Don Thornhill, Chairman of HEA, as 'the most important and exciting development that has ever taken place in the history of research in Ireland.' (*The Irish Scientist Yearbook 1999*, p. 28), with further funds from other sources, this dramatic augmentation of the research capability of the tertiary institutions is a challenge to demonstrate world quality, the capacity to develop longer term strategies for R&D and ability to liaise, cooperate and share resources nationally and internationally. While there is also an expectation that research will contribute to innovation in ways that yield economic pay-offs, the programme is open to basic research in the sciences and to the humanities and social sciences where results and applications, albeit of intellectual and social significance, would not, or not necessarily, be judged by economic criteria. That these considerations are being taken into account is reflected in the wide variety of allocations made in the first round. This policy is consistent with the arguments considered in earlier parts of this report for maintaining in universities a breadth of studies at the frontiers of knowledge. However, the programme does raise major challenges for the universities. The first, discussed above, is the need for the universities to demonstrate quite convincingly that an entirely separate system of research institutions independent of universities is not necessary and would be a waste of resources. Several further issues need addressing: concentration in already strong areas or the development of a very broad research base; the development of infrastructure, and management strategies; connecting research with teaching including the much-needed expansion of post-graduate programmes and student numbers; industry-community-partnerships; cross-institutional/cross-national collaboration; attracting researchers of the necessary calibre and providing career routes for them.

- The universities have responded positively and promptly to the reports of the Skills Group on labour market needs and economic development, not least because of the availability of state capital funding to expand enrolments and provide much needed new buildings and equipment. This is a recent demonstration of their readiness to take up

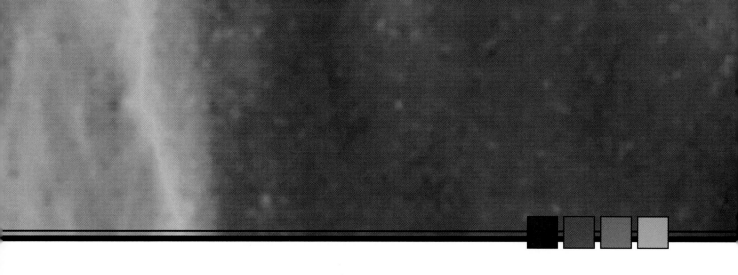

challenges quickly and comprehensively within a policy framework that is supported by targeted funding. It is important, however, both for government and the universities, to avoid two of the worst features of targeted funding: over confident judgements about research priorities including 'pay dirt' research; and structural inability to maintain follow-though when it is needed to sustain worthwhile initiatives over the longer term.

- Legislation affecting universities: The Irish Universities Act 1997 and the Qualifications (Education and Training) Act 1992 have a number of ramifications, the details of which it is not necessary to enter into here. A general point is highly pertinent: the establishment of a broad legal and regulatory framework which clarifies roles, functions and obligations, many of which while already in existence gave rise to ambiguity and uncertainty. Of special note are the relations between the Higher Education Authority as both a funding and steering body and the universities, and the creation of a framework which recognises a multiplicity of routes into higher education both formal institutional and more informal. While the universities retain their traditional control over the award of degrees, and a large measure of self-determination, greater flexibility concerning forms and routes of study, some leading ultimately into the university sector, has been formally acknowledged and recognised for purposes of recognised credentials. The HEA has a responsibility to ensure that major policy determinations are implemented and monitored - equity and quality requirements, for example; it also has a responsibility for the well-being and effectiveness of the system overall. But it is for the institutions to take the action and to monitor and evaluate their own performance. The Qualifications Authority has scope to foster significant innovation which will provide for a much wider range of opportunities, higher education included. Arising from both pieces of legislation is a challenge to universities to demonstrate that they are taking the initiative and acting in line with best international practice.

- The changes in governance, decision-making and management detailed in the 1997 Deloitte Touche report provide a comprehensive set of targets. To these might be added the emerging management challenges of the new technologies, of the international partnerships, the new research environment, and unrelenting funding pressure. Forward-looking leadership including an agenda of reform for internal governance and management is widely accepted internationally as necessary if universities are to take full advantage of the opportunities and responsibilities facing them.

Future Directions: A Resumé

The Irish universities may be seen to confront challenges in two spheres. The first is **internal** where there is need to demonstrate greater innovativeness and resourcefulness in meeting higher education and knowledge needs of a flourishing economy which is experiencing increasing labour market pressure, and a rapidly evolving, fragmenting unequal society. The second is **external**: here, the universities need to better position themselves to meet the challenge of an increasingly

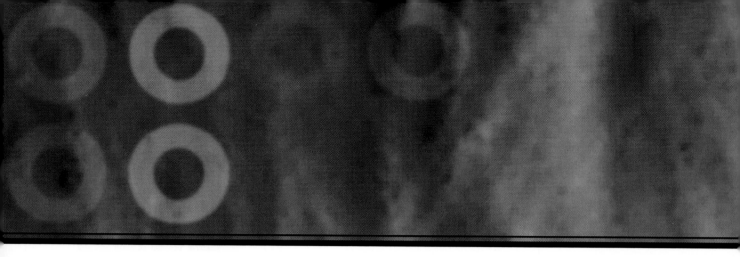

competitive and expansionist international academic environment. How might these challenges be met? Many observations and suggestions have already been made and of course the universities have in train measures for their continuing growth and development. Outlined in these concluding pages are what appear to an external observer to be the most feasible of the needed directions to follow:

1. Systematically extending the range of opportunities for higher education to all sectors of the Irish community able to benefit from them.

This will mean more positive, system-wide and institution-specific policies and strategies with clear, attainable, funded targets. It will be necessary to make more flexible provision to accommodate (a) substantial increases in mature age entry, and (b) equity groups of whom those from the lowest socio-economic categories are the prime, but not the only, target. The national policy framework is largely in place, with planning and research in place or under way. More work, however, is required notably on strategies for universities to pursue in a framework of lifelong learning and in relation to the roles of other institutions in the tertiary sector. The challenge now is for the universities, in a variety of partnerships with government, the HEA and community bodies to demonstrate their commitment and readiness to implement existing policies, to monitor and evaluate effects and to contribute to ongoing policy formation.

2. Achieving variety, extending choice and targeting under-used talent within a more balanced system of higher education.
Since there are several structural features in the system which tend towards homogeneity not to say conformity in a hierarchy of institutions and study programmes (e.g. the Leaving Certificate Examinations, the Points System, traditional views about what constitutes 'a university', funding formulae, community perceptions, etc.), questions naturally arise as to why changes are needed and, if so, how are they to be achieved. Several of the reports cited above provide very direct answers to these questions. The key point is that existing structures and provision are not providing sufficient opportunity for all who could benefit from higher education to do so. There are still some broad unresolved policy issues to address, such as reform of the Leaving Certificate and ways to introduce and strengthen alternative routes; these and others are on the current national agenda.

The anticipated drop of 36% (74,000 to 47,000) in school leaver numbers from 1998 to 2012 poses an immediate challenge to the overall provision of tertiary education. It should not become a battle among institutions for a diminished supply but is instead a definite opportunity to: increase the proportion of school leavers entering tertiary education end-on, but not necessarily as full-time students; diversify study routes into tertiary education; increase opportunities for open and

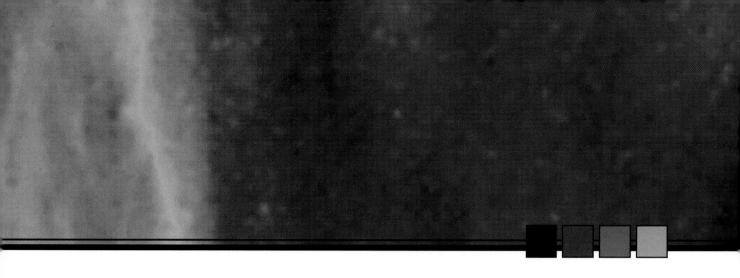

flexible learning for adults; increase the recruitment of fee-paying overseas students; achieve a better internal balance of numbers and resources within institutions, e.g. by increasing the numbers of post-graduate students and those on post-experience professional programmes. For the universities the challenge now is to show a readiness to work collectively as a system, in tandem with the institute of technology sector, and the secondary schools. Targets should include the introduction of procedures for more systematic recognition of prior learning; credit transfer; joint (cross-sectoral) study programmes; part-time study including work and home-based study by distance education; and further diversifying curricula, teaching and assessment procedures; and developing on-line learning on a national, co-operative basis. Reducing failure and non-completion rates (although not unduly high by international standards) should be a target for equity and efficiency reasons.

3. Strengthening partnerships with industry and community organisations.

Building on existing partnerships and other outreach arrangements, including those for financing mature age study, there is need for universities to demonstrate a greater responsiveness to the rapidly changing economic environment through outreach schemes in all subjects and fields of study – and not only those with obvious business/employment links. These could include work and community experience as a normal component of all degree programmes, closer integration of university career guidance and community liaison programmes into academic work, business-university fora, sponsorship by industry of an even wider range of study programmes and studentships including those in humanities and social sciences; joint research projects to include those on the operation of partnerships; and further progress in the areas of start-up companies; training in the establishment and operation of small businesses; and more prominence in reporting and public communication to these socio-economic dimensions of university activities. To avoid excessive pressure on the already high concentration of resources and expertise in the Dublin region, opportunities for a better regional balance should be sought, including R&D partnerships with regional Institutes of Technology.

4. Improving procedures for self-evaluation, quality assurance and public accountability.

The Universities Act sets forth procedures for quality assurance which place the onus on the universities to undertake self-evaluation. There is a well-established practice of such evaluations, usually on a discipline/department/faculty basis. These commonly involved university-selected external experts; reports have been primarily for internal use, and have not been considered collectively as a form of system-wide monitoring and evaluation. They have not in the main been seen as public documents aimed at contributing to a wider public understanding of the contribution of the universities to Irish society. Such reports are of value to the institution and will doubtless continue to play an important role in institutional development and strategic planning. A more comprehensive, systematic approach covering the whole sector and resulting

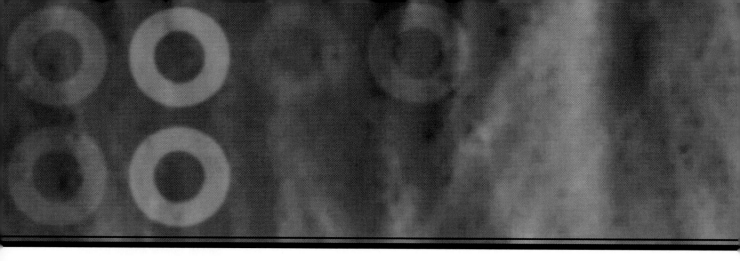

in published and widely available overall evaluative reports would be of great value. The purpose would not be to set one university off against another (avoiding the unfortunate 'league table' mentality favoured by the media) but to assess the overall quality of higher education, to identify specific weaknesses and targets for improvement, to mobilise resources, and to gain a wider, more informed understanding in the community of the roles being performed by the universities. For these purposes it seems that there would best be further joint efforts by the institutional heads and the HEA in the design of such a national quality assurance system. But the universities should not wait. It is for them to take the initiative to ensure that a national system is introduced over a reasonable time-scale and that it meets the best international standards. A question for consideration is whether it would be preferable to develop a single system for the tertiary sector of the Institutes of Technology and universities, or whether, as at present, there should be separate arrangements. But systems for quality assurance are one thing. There is need to foster innovation and to reward achievement in improving the quality of both the educational experience and the way the institutions operate. There are examples of good practice in this regard – in Australia, Sweden and the USA among others - which are worthy of study as quality review procedures in Ireland are further developed.

5. Preparing and supporting the academic profession for the challenges of growth, diversity, technology-based learning, applied scholarship and international competition.

In the succession of Irish reports on future directions for higher education, little is said about the attributes, capabilities, motivation, working conditions and professional development needs of the academics or any other categories of staff. Yet, in common with most other comparable countries, Ireland faces the prospect of the 'greying' of the academic staff and a future shortage of well qualified new entrants to the academic profession (El-Khawas, 2000). Amongst other requirements is an increase in post-graduate places and a greater readiness to draw in part-time and contract staff from industry, the professions and the public sector. Concern has been expressed about effects of part-time academics on programme continuity, staff-student interaction and advice, and research capability. Those concerns are all quite capable of being addressed in an overall staffing strategy and the accruing benefits will outweigh any remaining disadvantages.

There are very serious challenges to appoint new staff with aptitude for a broad range of entrepreneurial as well as academic roles and to provide professional development opportunities for the present staffs of the institutions. There is need for studies of the demography of the staff as well as the new cohorts of students referred to above. Growth of student numbers, greater diversity including equity groups and mature age students with whose educational needs many teachers may have little experience, and the spread of technology-based learning, pose considerable challenges that will all have to be met in positive ways. Good teaching needs encouragement and appreciation including fuller recognition in recruitment

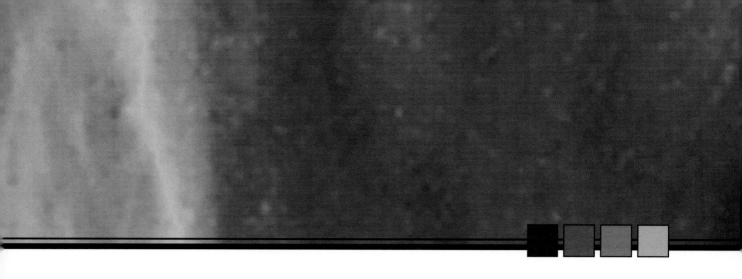

and promotion procedures. The examination-bound conventions of the 'right answer' and the fostering thereby of rote learning have long been signaled as potential weaknesses. They become all the greater in a modern society where emphasis is given to problem-solving, team work, oral communication, the search for information from multiple sources and self- and group-directed initiative. University teaching does not always respond to these requirements whose focus is 'learning how to learn, to know and to do'. There is often in educational practice a weak linkage among declared goals, assessment practices and the content and processes of teaching. Staff development should focus more on improving each of these and their inter-relationships and not only on teaching methods and the uses of technology.

Systematic, comprehensive staff development is a crucial requirement of the contemporary learning organisation and there are many different ways of providing for it other than conventional courses and workshops (usually attended by a small minority of enthusiasts and lacking high institutional profile). Since there does not appear to be an established policy framework in Ireland to address these and related needs, a first step might be to initiate at the national level some studies of good practice, which would lead to a policy debate. But should the universities wait for this or should they not, rather, themselves initiate a collective inquiry to pool experience, pinpoint gaps and indicate what they perceive to be needs? A process of this nature, a practical demonstration in cross-institutional cooperation, would be an immediate contribution to the more lengthy procedures required for national level policies. It would be unusual and probably counterproductive to establish a national programme given a long history of resistance to formal training of university teachers and the existence of a multiplicity of internal institutional arrangements. Ireland, however, could play a valuable role in this regard - setting a range of closely coupled improvement targets and treating staff development as the key strategy to achieve them.

Staff development focused on the educational (teaching-learning) role of the university is one aspect, the other is the continuing effort required to meet the immediate challenge of the new research funding and the emerging challenge of intensified international competition. On the first aspect, it is obvious that a research culture cannot be greatly expanded and enriched unless there are researchers of high quality. Their selection, training, conditions of employment and career expectations and needs would have to be a major feature of a national R&D strategy. Since there is a very strong emphasis in the Irish policy literature on both economically applicable and socially and culturally relevant research, there are opportunities for the universities to treat the future development of a research community as a partnership embracing a wide range of economic and social actors. Such a move would be a very large step toward dispelling the notion of academic research as secluded, inward-looking and detached from the main currents of contemporary life. But, in addition to all this, staff of universities will need to better equip themselves to take on the more responsive, entrepreneurial and innovatory roles that are now needed.

6. Resources.

For the universities to play the part of which they are capable and if increasingly expected of them, the resources issue needs to be squarely faced. Research funding has been dramatically increased but core funding, for the essential tasks of educating the Irish population to an advanced level, has not. Politically sensitive as it may be the 'free tuition' policy is regressive; it results in a much lower private contribution to costs and a deflection of public funds which are badly needed to improve infrastructure and to sustain the country's policy agenda for development. The universities need to demonstrate maximum efficiency, ability to generate resources and a readiness to reform; government in turn needs to adopt more progressive funding policies.

7. Ways of recreating the university.

A defining characteristic of the modern learning organisation is the readiness to recreate itself through a close understanding of its environment and the opportunities provided by that environment for both adaptive change, and novel ways of growing and developing. This observation should not be taken to mean that the universities are moribund. This is far from the truth and the evidence is in their rapid, substantial growth, and the quality of their product. 'Re-create' is a positive act by a dynamic institution to embrace change in meeting what is new and challenging in its environment. It is also a readiness to rethink what its environment is and its purposes in seeking renewal. The university should be, by definition, a learning organisation. Its critics have often, while respecting it as a learned organisation, challenged its capacity to reach out in new ways. Lord Melbourne's dictum, in establishing the nineteenth century commission on Oxford and Cambridge, was that 'universities never reform themselves'. The challenge for the Irish universities, now, is to disprove this dictum, and to demonstrate a capacity to recreate themselves. This means, first, to sustain and develop their role as primary agencies for the creation, interpretation, application and communication of advanced knowledge not only within Ireland but internationally as well. Second, the challenge is to become more closely and fully engaged with their environments, including the regions and communities they serve; and third, to address the great social, cultural and ethical issues of the day.

Re-creation is not destruction: there are values to preserve and the tradition of an academic community sharing a common purpose. Ireland has a relatively small population, not so many universities and they are not large by international standards. Is this scale an advantage or a weakness? That depends on how their governing bodies and presidents seek to position their institutions, either as minor players in a big league, or as a well co-ordinated system of both co-operating and competing institutions dedicated to achieving a frontier position, benchmarking themselves according to key, selected strengths,

growth points, and weaknesses which they determine to eliminate. Such a successful demonstration would be of greater interest internationally as universities everywhere struggle against mounting challenges to determine their own futures. The Irish universities have many advantages: the country has a thriving economy, stable social and political environment, a buoyant national mood, high regard, internationally. It is enjoying success on many fronts. For the universities themselves, there are: a reasonably secure if still narrow financial base, good if still insufficient facilities, well functioning internal organisation, well qualified staffs and able student bodies, and an effective national legislative and policy framework. Is this too rosy a picture? Do the universities really have the potential just outlined? Are the conditions of their operation still short of adequate? As already indicated, resources are insufficient and need to be further augmented. In considering the potential of the universities, if given the right lead, it is useful to observe the rapid rise, from modest beginnings of some of the world's major global enterprises and the successful re-positioning of universities elsewhere. True, the Irish universities are struggling to catch up with the budget cuts and constraints of the '80s and early '90s. Unbalanced funding which supports targeted programmes but not the infrastructure to sustain them over time, hastily assembled facilities and management structures and other inadequacies testify to the pressures. These and other inadequacies must be taken into account. But Ireland, in these respects, is no different from many other countries where rapid growth and rising expectations combined with constrained resources are putting universities severely to the test. The point is not that there are difficulties, but whether there is capability and a will to address them and an environment which is presenting major, new opportunities.

Is there an impetus to take the kinds of big steps familiar in a number of other national systems? For example, almost totally financed from public revenue sources, is there a sufficient challenge for the Irish universities to become more entrepreneurial: to co-operate in selling such services as undergraduate and post-graduate places and consultancies on the global market, as Australia, Japan, Switzerland and the UK among others now do so successfully and other countries are actively planning to do? Is the pressure of diminishing levels of unit cost funding encouraging the universities to greatly increase the proportion of non-formula-funded resources - as has happened in Australia, the UK and the USA? Are there opportunities for the universities, together with the institutes of technology to provide large-scale professional up-grading programmes - for engineers, systems analysts, designers, accountants, lawyers, doctors, public servants, and the staff of large enterprises? And, if so, are there incentives including incentives for university staff to take up these opportunities?

Ireland has the great advantage of a population fluent in a language of universal currency - English. This, together with social factors already mentioned, has proved to be a highly exploitable asset in the economic boom of recent years. It is a

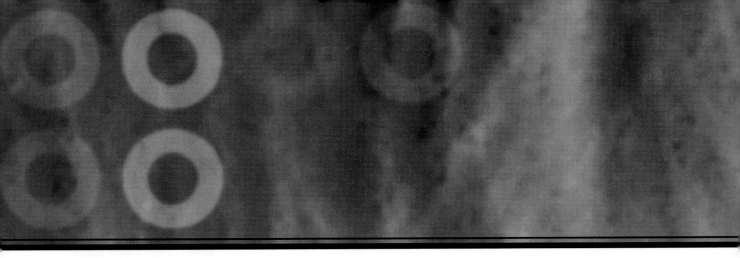

major selling point in the marketing strategy of countries which have greatly increased out-of-country enrolments. But, of itself, it is not sufficient. Universities seeking to greatly expand fee-paying enrolments from abroad need to ensure that there are very good programmes in language tuition, tutorial support, reasonably priced housing, a generally welcoming atmosphere, and the provision of high demand courses well backed with state-of-the-art facilities. They need to develop expert knowledge of the market and of the communities from which the students might come. These require long term planning, investment strategies, and an institution-wide commitment to what can amount to a very substantial change of direction. Facilities are needed not only for on-campus study, but for study in the country of origin and they might include a mix of distance education provision and joint teaching to a high standard with a country-of-origin institution or agency. There are working models of all of these and other arrangements from which Irish universities wishing to greatly extend their international role beyond the Western European theatre could take advantage.

The 'global' course is one direction to take; another is the regional. Not all universities are well placed to enter the highly competitive global market, and the costs of failure are high. Some institutions are far better placed to exploit local and regional advantage - although that cannot nowadays be taken to mean no national or international profile at all. Research, for example, if of sufficient quality will achieve an international profile whatever its focus or locale and such quality should be the target of any serious research endeavour in universities. However, a university might choose to focus its energies within a largely regional context - drawing the majority of its students from there, building local and regional partnerships with industry and the community, achieving a high regional profile, local loyalties and patronage, and setting as a principal target the growth and development of the region.

Recreating the Irish universities means that in broadening horizons to see themselves as global players they would aim to enhance their power and capability. It means, also, a readiness to see themselves as diverse, competing yet at the same time cooperating members of a system which concurrently gains in power and influence. Some may say, 'all is well, nothing beyond what is already being done is needed'. The rejoinder must be that the higher education policy environment in Ireland has set and is setting directions and challenges that are not being fully met, and that there is a burgeoning international higher education environment against which the Irish universities should be benchmarking themselves. There are other benefits, to countries when their universities play very prominent international roles: diplomatic and economic benefits from networking and students educated abroad returning to positions of influence in their own country, research collaboration, enriched staff and student experience.

In the past there has been a tendency to emphasise the drawbacks: overseas students taking places from home students, costs of networking and distraction from domestic missions and needs. Globalisation and Ireland's successful experience in the international programmes of the European Union put matters in a different light. The international environment is yet another of the challenges which present either opportunities or threats.

The strength and the quality of the universities will be shown through their readiness to reach deep into their familiar environments, but also to chart new territories and, like the migrating generations, to make their mark on the world.

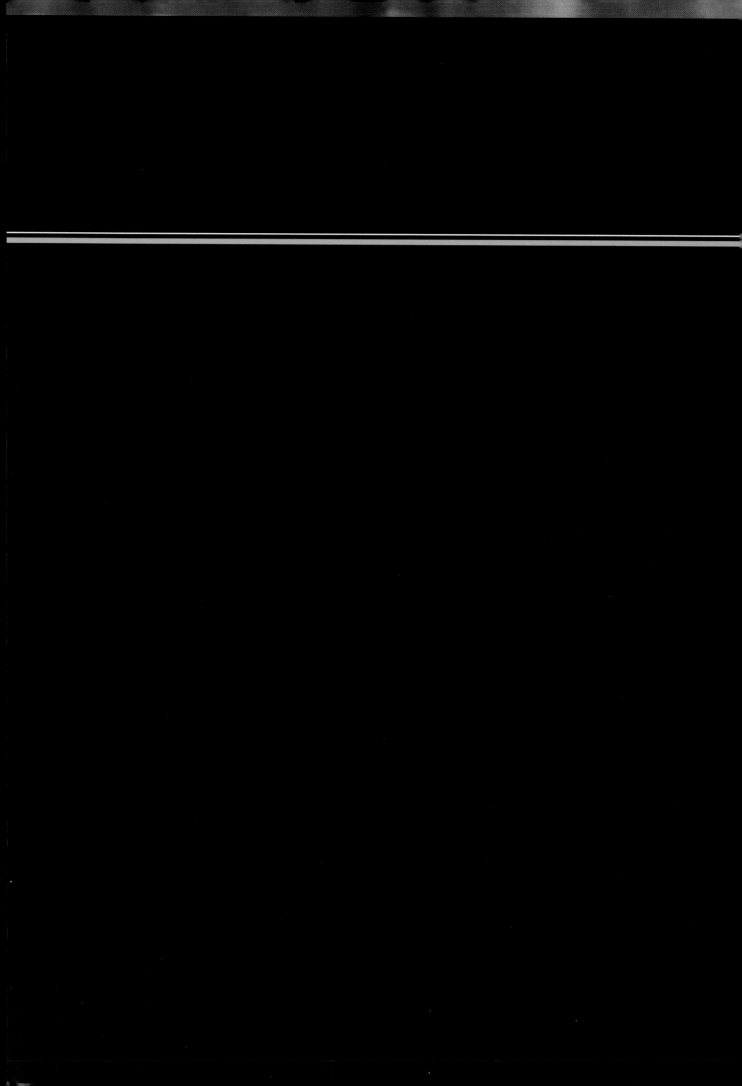

appendix

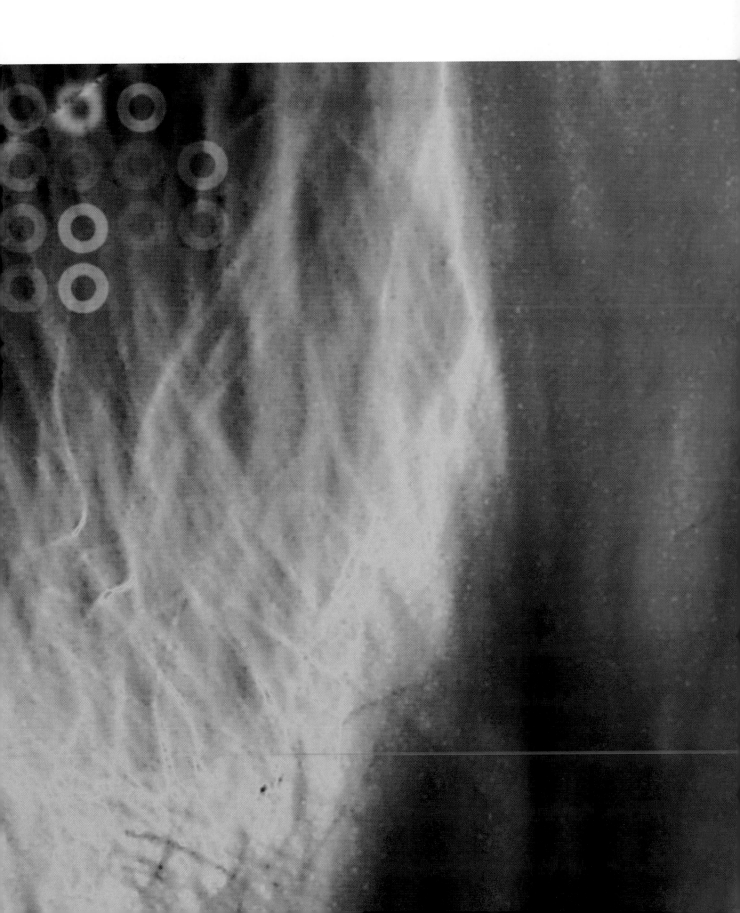

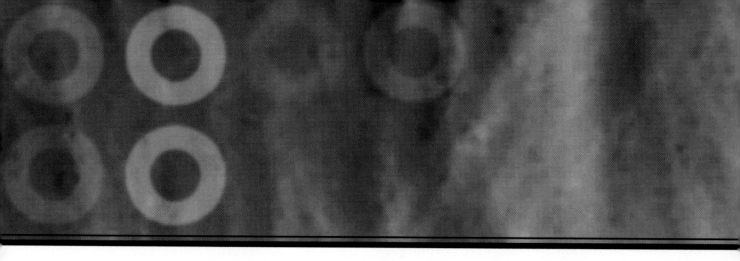

Net entry rates in tertiary education by gender and age distribution (1998)

	Tertiary-type B			Tertiary-type A					
	Net entry rates			Net entry rates			Age at:		
	M+W	Men	Women	M+W	Men	Women	20th percentile1	50th percentile1	80th percentile1
OECD countries									
Australia	m	m	m	53	45	61	18.4	19.5	27.9
Austria	8	7	9	28	25	31	19.1	20.5	23.8
Belgium (Fl.)	27	22	33	28	28	28	18.3	18.7	19.6
Canada	m	m	m	m	m	m	m	m	m
Czech Republic	13	10	17	22	26	18	18.7	19.8	22.4
Denmark	32	23	42	30	29	32	20.9	22.6	26.9
Finland	12	9	15	58	49	67	19.9	21.4	25.5
France	m	m	m	m	m	m	m	m	m
Germany	142	102	172	28	28	28	20.0	21.4	24.4
Greece	m	m	m	m	m	m	m	m	m
Hungary	m	m	m	45	41	49	19.2	21.1	27.9
Iceland	16	13	19	38	29	48	20.9	22.3	27.0
Ireland	25	23	26	28	27	30	18.0	18.6	19.4
Italy	1	1	1	42	37	47	19.2	19.7	20.7
Japan[2]	33	22	45	36	45	27	m	m	m
Korea[2]	46	49	43	43	48	37	m	m	m
Luxembourg	m	m	m	m	m	m	m	m	m
Mexico	m	m	m	21	22	21	18.4	19.7	23.7
Netherlands	1	1	1	52	50	54	18.6	19.9	23.3
New Zealand	36	28	44	68	56	79	18.7	22.0	>40
Norway	6	6	6	56	45	68	20.0	21.7	28.3
Poland	m	m	m	m	m	m	m	m	m
Portugal	m	m	m	m	m	m	m	m	m
Spain	9	9	9	41	36	46	18.5	19.3	22.5
Sweden	x	x	x	59	50	69	20.1	22.2	29.5
Switzerland	m	m	m	m	m	m	m	m	m
Turkey	11	12	10	20	25	15	18.3	19.7	23.2
United Kingdom	27	25	30	48	45	51	18.5	19.6	26.0
United States	14	13	15	44	40	48	18.4	19.6	26.4
Country mean	19	16	22	40	37	43	~	~	~

	Tertiary-type B			Tertiary-type A					
	Net entry rates			Net entry rates			Age at:		
	M+W	Men	Women	M+W	Men	Women	20th percentile1	50th percentile1	80th percentile1
WEI countries									
Argentina	27	15	38	48	44	52	19.9	22.6	27.7
Chile	13	14	12	32	34	30	m	m	m
China	7	m	m	4	m	m	m	m	m
Indonesia	4	3	4	8	9	7	17.9	18.7	19.7
Israel	29	28	29	49	43	55	21.2	23.5	27.3
Jordan	13	m	m	24	m	m	18.2	18.6	18.9
Malaysia	13	13	14	15	15	16	20.3	20.8	m
Paraguay	6	3	9	m	m	m	m	m	m
Philippines	a	a	a	49	39	59	17.2	17.5	17.8
Sri Lanka	m	m	m	3	m	m	m	m	m
Thailand	18	18	18	38	33	42	18.5	m	m
Uruguay	20	10	30	26	21	31	m	m	m

1. 20/50/80 percent of new entrants are below this age.

2. Gross entry rate

Source: OECD (2000) **Education at a Glance. OECD Indicators Education and Skills.** Paris. OECD. Table C3.1, p. 157.

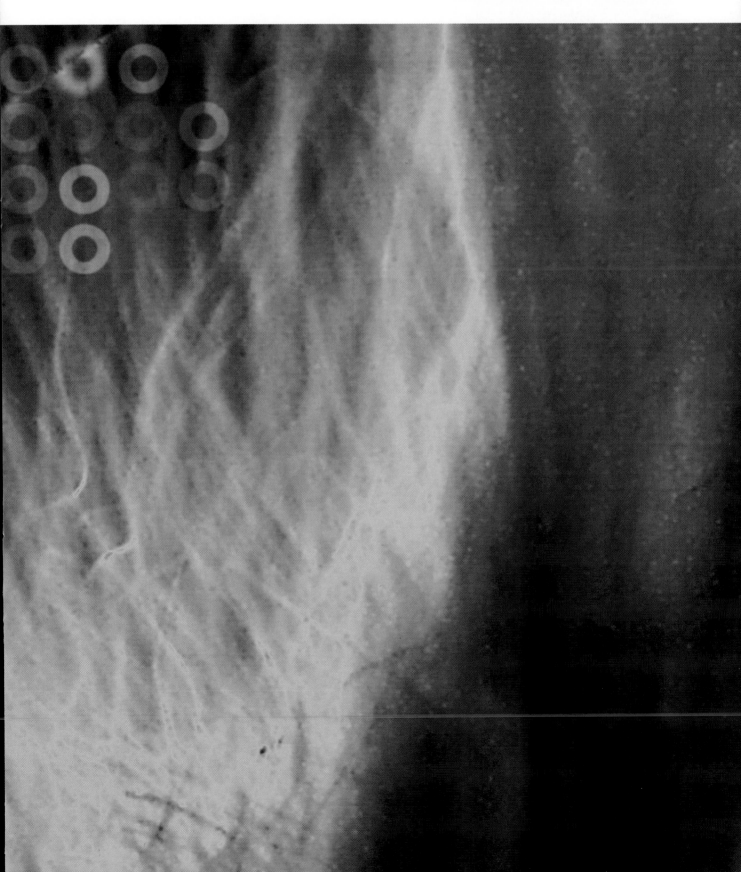

references and selected bibliography

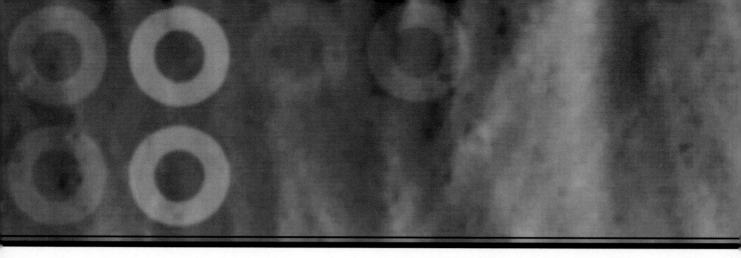

Aamodt, Per O. (1995) 'Floods, bottlenecks and backwaters: an analysis of expansion in higher education in Norway.' **Higher Education** 30 pp. 63-80.

Aamodt, Per O. (2000) Personal communication.

Abecassis, A. (1994) 'The policy of contracts between the state and the universities - a quiet revolution.' in Cazenave, P. (ed) **Evaluation and the Decision Making Process in Higher Education: French, German and Spanish Experiences.** Paris. OECD.

Adelman, C. (1992a) The Way We Are. **The Community College as American Thermometer.** Washington. US Department of Education.

Adelman, C. (1992b) Tourists in Our Own Land. Cultural Literacies and the College Curriculum. Washington DC. US Department of Education.

Adelman, C. (2000) 'A parallel universe.' **Change** 32. May/June. Pp. 20-29

Almond, G.A. and Coleman, J.S. (eds) (1960) **The Politics of the Developing Areas.** Princeton, N.J. Princeton Univ. Press.

Alpin, C., Shackleton, J.R. and Walsh, S (1998) 'Over- and under-education in the UK graduate labour market'. **Studies in Higher Education.** 23.1. pp. 17-34.

Altbach, P.G. (ed) (1996) **The International Academic Profession: Portraits of Fourteen Countries.** Princeton, N.J. The Carnegie Foundation for the Advancement of Teaching.

Altbach, P.G. (1998) 'Comparative perspectives on higher education for the twenty-first century.' **Higher Education Policy** pp. 347 - 356.

Altbach, P.G. and Chait, R. (eds) (2001) 'The changing academic workplace' - special issue of **Higher Education** 41, 1-2, January - March pp. 1-219.

Amaral, A.M.S.C. (1997) **The US Accreditation System and the CRE's Quality Audits.** Porto. University of Porto.

Anderson, D., Johnson, R. and Milligan, B. (in press) **Access to Postgraduate Courses: Opportunities and Obstacles.** Canberra. DETYA.

Anderson, M. (1992) **Imposters in the Temple: the Decline and Fall of the American University.** New York. Simon and Shuster.

Armytage, W.H.G. (1955) **Civic Universities. Aspects of a British Tradition.** London. Ernest Benn. Ltd.

Arnold, M (1999) 'Mainstreaming the digital revolution.' **Higher Education Quarterly**. 53.1. Jan. pp. 49-64.

Aronowitz (1985) 'Academic freedom: a structural approach.' **Educational Theory.** 35.1.pp. 1-13.

Ash, M.G. (ed) **German Universities Past and Future: Crisis of Renewal?** Oxford and Providence. Berghahn.

Association of European Universities (CRE) **A Strategy for Action** (1995 - 1998) Mimeo.

Astin, A.W. and Chang, M.J. (1995) 'Colleges that emphasize research and teaching: can you have your cake and eat it too?' **Change.** Sept/Oct.

Ball, C. (1996) 'Whose universities are they anyway - a review article of B. Salter and T. Tapper **The State and Higher Education** and M. Shattock **The U.G.C. and the Management of British Universities.' Oxford Review of Education.** 22.1.pp. 79-90.

Barblan, A. and Sadlak, J. (1988) 'Higher education in OECD European countries: patterns and trends in the 1980s.' Geneva. C.R.E. (Standing Conference of Rectors, Presidents and Vice-Chancellors of the European Universities).

Barnett, R. (1992a) **The Idea of Higher Education.** Buckingham. Society for Research in Higher Education and The Open University Press.

Barnett, R. (1992b) 'Linking teaching and research.' **Journal of Higher Education.** 63. Pp. 619-636.

Barnett, R. (2000) 'Reconfiguring the university' in Scott, P. (ed) **Higher Education Re-formed.** London and New York. Falmer Press. Pp. 114-129.

Bartolomo, E., Bataille, C. and Kreula, S. (1998) 'University graduates and the corporate sector: working together towards sustainable development.' in Ronning, A.M. and Kearney, M.-L. (eds) **Graduate Prospects in a Changing Society.** Paris. Inter-American Organization for Higher Education and UNESCO.

Becher, T. (1989) **Academic Tribes and Territories.** Milton Keynes. Society for Research into Higher Education and the Open University Press.

Becher, T. (1994) 'The state and the university curriculum in Britain.' **European Journal of Education.** 29.3.

Becher, T. (1999) 'Universities and mid-career professionals: the policy potential.' **Higher Education Quarterly.** 53.2. pp. 156-72.

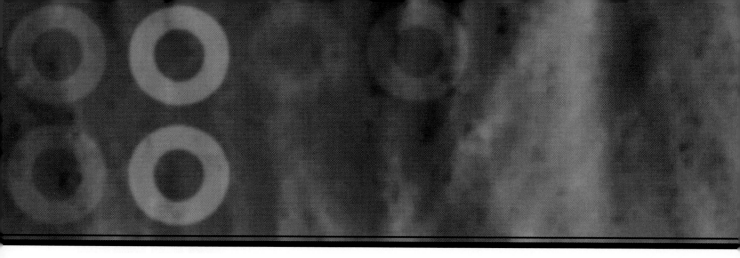

Becker, G. (1975) **Human Capital: A Theoretical and Empirical Analysis, with Special Reference to Education.** 2nd ed. New York. Columbia University Press.

Begin-Heick, M. (1999a) Guarding the Guardians: the meta-evaluation of an external quality assurance process. International Quality Assurance Association for Higher Education Conference on 'Evaluating Evaluation'. Santiago.

Begin-Heick, M. (1999b) Impact of program reviews on faculty, and faculty perceptions of them. International Quality Assurance Association for Higher Education Conference on 'Evaluating Evaluation'. Santiago.

Bell, C. (1994) 'More means different - expansion and quality.' in Hale, B. and Pope, N. **EHE - A Vision for Higher Education.** Report of 1993 Directors' Conference. Edinburgh. University of Edinburgh. Pp. 10-13.

Ben-David, J. (1972) **American Higher Education. Directions Old and New.** New York. McGraw-Hill Book Company.

Benson, R. (1996) **Assessing Open and Distance Learners.** Churchill, Vic.. Monash University.

Bereday, G.F (1973) **Universities for All.** San Francisco. Jossey-Bass. Inc. Publishers.

Berg, G.A. (1998) **Public Policy on Distance Learning in Higher Education: California State and Western Governors' Association Institutions.** Arizona State University.

Bertrand, G. (1994) 'Contractualisation and decision making in French universities: the experience of Burgundy University.' in Cazenave, P. (ed) **Evaluation and the Decision-Making Process in Higher Education: French, German and Spanish Experiences.** Paris. OECD.

Birnbaum, R. (1983) **Managing Diversity in Higher Education.** San Francisco. Jossey-Bass.

Bloom, A. (1987) **The Closing of the American Mind.** New York. Simon and Schuster.

Bok, D. (1982) **Beyond the Ivory Tower: Social Responsibilities of the Modern University.** Cambridge, MA. Harvard University Press.

Booth, W.C. (1989) 'Cultural literacy and liberal learnings: an open letter to E.D. Hirsch Jr.' **Change** 20.4. pp. 10-21.

Bourke, P. (1997) **Evaluating University Research: the British Research Assessment Exercise and Australian Practice**. Canberra. Australian Research Council and Higher Education Council.

Bourne, R. (ed) (2000) **Universities and Development.** London. Association of Commonwealth Universities.

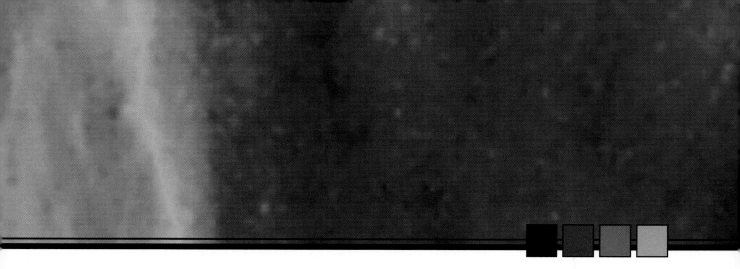

Bowen, N. and Shapiro, H. (eds) (1998) **Universities and their Leadership.** Princeton, N.J. Princeton Univ. Press.

Boyer, E. (1990) **Scholarship Reconsidered: Priorities of the Professoriate.** Princeton, N.J. The Carnegie Foundation for the Advancement of Teaching.

Boyer, E.L., Altbach, P.G. and Whitelow, M.J. (1994) **The Academic Profession: an International Perspective.** Princeton. N.J. The Carnegie Foundation for the Advancement of Teaching.

Boys, C.J. et al (1988) **Higher Education and the Preparation for Work.** London. Jessica Kingsley Publishers Ltd.

Bradshaw, D. (1992) 'Classifications and modes of transferable skills.' in Eggins, H. (ed) **Arts Graduates, Their Skills and Their Employment: Perspectives for Change.** London. Falmer Press. Pp. 39 - 115.

Brennan, J. (1997) 'Authority, legitimacy and change: the rise of quality assessment in higher education.' **Higher Education Management.** 9. 1. March. Pp. 7 - 25.

Brennan, J. (1999) 'Making an impact: experiences of quality assessment in 14 countries.' Paper presented at the International Quality Assurance in Higher Education Conference on 'Evaluating Evaluation'. Santiago.

Brennan, J. and Shah, I. (2000) **Managing Quality in Higher Education.** Milton Keynes, Bucks. Open Univ. Press.

Brew, A. and Boud, D. (1995) 'Teaching and research: establishing the vital link with learning.' **Higher Education.** 29. Pp. 261-273.

Burkhalter, B.B. (1996) 'How can institutions of higher education achieve quality within the new economy?' **Total Quality Management.** 72. 2. Pp. 153-156.

Callahan, R.E. (1962) **Education and the Cult of Efficiency.** Chicago. University of Chicago Press.

Camblin, L.D. and Steger, J.A. (2000) 'Rethinking faculty development.' **Higher Education.** 39.pp. 1-18.

Carnegie Commission on Policy Studies in Higher Education (1980) **A Summary of Reports and Recommendations.** San Francisco. Jossey-Bass Publishers.

Carnegie Commission for the Advancement of Teaching (1992) 'Trendlines: signs of a changing curriculum' **Change** 24.1. pp. 49-52.

Casey, R.G., Gentile, P.and Bigger, S.W. (1997) 'Teaching appraisal in higher education: an Australian perspective.' **Higher Education** 34.pp. 459-482.

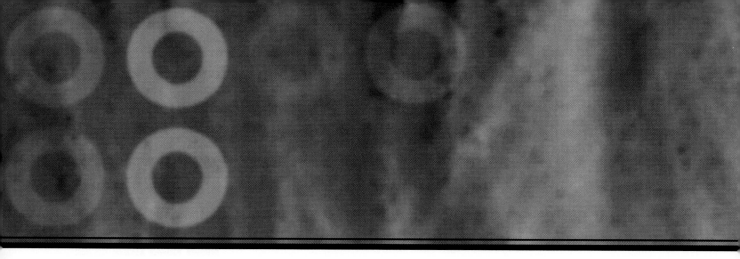

Casper, G. (1995) 'Come the Millennium Where the University?' San Francisco. American Educational Research Association. (Keynote address)

Cave, M., Dodsworth, R. and Thompson, D. (1991) **Regulatory Reform in Higher Education in the UK: Incentives for Efficiency and Product Quality.** Oxford. Oxford University Press and the Oxford Review of Economic Policy.

Chene, L. (1999) Evaluating evaluations: a case study. International Quality Assurance Association for Higher Education Conference on 'Evaluating Evaluation'. Santiago.

Cheney, L.V. (1989) **50 Hours: A Core Curriculum for College Students.** Washington DC. National Endowment for the Humanities.

Choy, S.P. (1999) **Findings from the Condition of Education 1998: College Access and Affordability**. Washington DC. US Department of Education.

Clancy, P. (1999) 'Participation of mature students in higher education in Ireland.' In Fleming, T. et al **Higher Education. The Challenge of Lifelong Learning.** Maynooth National University of Ireland. Pp. 29-44.

Clancy, P. and Wall, J. (2000) **Social Background of Higher Education Entrants.** Dublin. Higher Education Authority.

Clark, B.R. (1983) **The Higher Education System.** Berkeley. University of California Press.

Clark, B.R. (1995) **Places of Inquiry. Research and Education in Modern Universities.** Berkeley, CA. University of California Press.

Clark, B.R. (1997) 'Common problems and adaptive responses in the universities of the world: organizing for change.' **Higher Education Policy.** 10.3/4. Pp. 291-295.

Clark, B.R. (1998) **Creating Entrepreneurial Universities: Organizational Pathways of Transformation.** Oxford. Pergamon.

Clark, B.R. (ed) **The Research Foundation of Graduate Education: Germany, Britain, France, United States, Japan.** Berkeley. The University of California Press.

Cockburn, A. and Blackburn, R. (eds) (1969) **Student Power/Problems, Diagnosis, Actions.** Harmondsworth, Middlesex. Penguin Books in association with New Left Review.

Colclough, C., and Manor, J. (eds) (1991) **States or Markets? Neo-Liberalism and the Development Policy Debate.** Oxford. Clarendon Press.

Commission of the European Communities (1992) **Memorandum on Higher Education in the European Community.** Luxembourg. The Commission.

Commission of the European Communities (1993a) **The Outlook for Higher Education in the European Community.** Luxembourg. The Commission.

Commission of the European Communities (1993b) Quality Management and quality Assurance in European Higher Education. Methods and Mechanisms. Luxembourg. The Commission.

Commission of the European Communities (1995) **Key Data on Education in the European Union.** Brussels. Office for Official Publications of the European Communities.

Commission on the Points System (Ireland)(Chairperson Aine Hyland) (1999) **Final Report and Recommendations.** Dublin. The Stationery Office.

Committee of Inquiry (Australia) (Chair, David Hoare) (1995) **Higher Education Management Review.** Canberra. A.G.P.S.

Committee on Higher Education (UK)(1963) **Higher Education: Report of the Committee appointed by the Prime Minister under the Chairmanship of Lord Robbins, 1961-1963.** Cmd 2154. London HMSO.

Committee on Standards in Public Life (UK) (1996) **Report on Local Spending Bodies.** London. The Committee.

Committee to Review Higher Education Financing and Policy (Australia) (Chairman R. West) (1998) **Learning for Life. Final Report.** Canberra. Dept. of Employment, Education, Training and Youth Affairs.

Commonwealth Higher Education Management Service (CHEMS) (1998) **Benchmarking in Higher Education.** Paris. UNESCO.

Conference of the Heads of Irish Universities (CHIU) (1998) 'The Future Needs of Higher Education in Ireland.' Dublin. Mimeo.

Conference of the Heads of Irish Universities (CHIU) (1999) **Report on the Pilot Project.** Dublin. CHIU.

Conference of Heads of Irish Universities (CHIU) (2000a) **Guaranteeing Future Growth.** Dublin. CHIU.

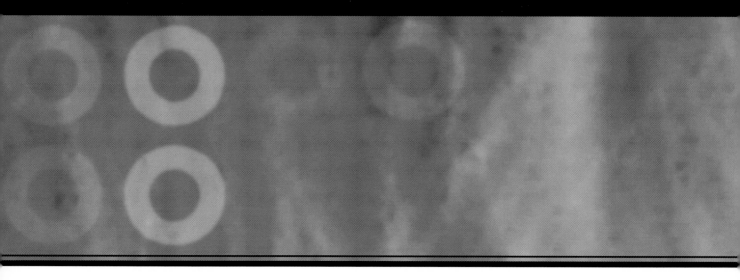

Conference of Heads of Irish Universities (2000b) **Technology Foresight and the University Sector.** Dublin. CHIU.

Cook, W.A. (1996) 'Managing for Excellence in Higher Education.' **Continuous Improvement Monitor International** HTTP://www.care.panam.edu/journal/library/Vol.1No1/mngexcel.html.

Coolahan, J. (2000) Personal communication.

Council of Europe (1997) 'Higher Education and Research Committee Round Table: the academic profession in Europe – status, prospects and remedies.' (Secretariat Memorandum) Strasbourg. The Council.

Cunningham, S. et al (1998) **New Media and Borderless Education: A Review of the Convergence Between Global Media Networks and Higher Education Provision.** Canberra. Department of Education, Training and Youth Affairs.

Daniel, J. (1992) 'A worldwide perspective on open learning.' Keynote address, Launching Conference of the South African Institute of Distance Education. Johannesburg. September.

Daniel, J. (1998) **Mega-Universities and the Knowledge Media: Technology Strategies for Higher Education.** London. Kogan Page.

Davenport, P. (2000) 'Development and the knowledge economy.' in Bourne, R. (ed) **Universities and Development.** London. Association of Commonwealth Universities.

Davies, G. and Tinsley, D. (eds) (1994) **Open and Distance Learning. Critical Success Factors.** Proceedings of International Conference. Geneva. Erlangen FIM.

Davies, J.L. (1996) 'The regional university: issues in the development of an organizational framework.' Paper prepared for IMHE General Conference 'Setting New Priorities for Higher Education Management' Paris. OECD/IIMHE.

Davies, J.L. (1998) The Public Role of the University: the Dialogue of Universities with their Stakeholders: Comparisons Between Different Regions of Europe. CRE (The Association of European Universities).

Davis, D. (1996) **The Real World of Performance Indicators: a Review of their Use in Selected Commonwealth Countries.** London. Commonwealth Higher Education Management Service.

Davis, P. (1995) **Adults in Higher Education: International Perspectives in Access and Participation.** London and Bristol PA. Jessica Kingsley Publishers.

Dearlove, J. (1998) 'Fundamental changes in institutions' governance structures: the United Kingdom.' **Higher Education Policy.** 11.2/3. Pp. 111-120.

de Boer, H. Maassen, P. and de Weert, E. (1999) 'The troublesome Dutch university and its Route 66 towards a new governance structure.' **Higher Education Policy** 12, 4, pp. 329-342.

de Boer, H., Denters, B. and Goedegebuure, L (1998) 'On boards and councils: shaky balance considered. The governance of Dutch universities.' **Higher Education Policy** 11, 2/3 pp. 153-164.

de Boer, H. Goedegebuure, L. and Meek, V.L. (1998) 'In the Winter of Discontent - business as usual' (Editorial) **Higher Education Policy.** 11. 2/3. Pp. 103-110.

Deloitte and Touche (1997) **Study on Governance and Management Structures of Irish Universities.** Dublin. Higher Education Authority.

Department of Education (Ireland) (1995) **White Paper: Charting Our Education Future.** Dublin. Stationery Office.

Department of Education and Science (Ireland)(2000) **Learning for Life: White Paper on Adult Education.** Dublin. Stationery Office.

Department of Education, Training and Youth Affairs (DETYA) (Australia) (1999a) **Higher Education - Report for the 1999-2001 Triennium.** Canberra. Commonwealth of Australia.

Department of Education, Training and Youth Affairs (DETYA) (Australia) (1999b) **The Quality of Australian Higher Education.** Canberra. The Department.

Department of Employment, Education and Training (DEET) (Australia)/ Organisation for Economic Co-operation and Development (OECD) (1993) **The Transition from Elite to Mass Higher Education.** Canberra. Australian Government Publishing Service.

de Weert, E. (1999) 'Contours of the emergent knowledge society: theoretical debate and implications for higher education research.' **Higher Education.** 38.pp. 46-69.

de Wit, H. (ed) (1995) **Strategies for Internationalisation of Higher Education.** Amsterdam. European Association for International Education/ OECD/IMHE; Association of International Education Administration.

de Wit, H. and Knight, J. (eds) (1999) **Quality and Internationalisation in Higher Education.** Paris OECD.

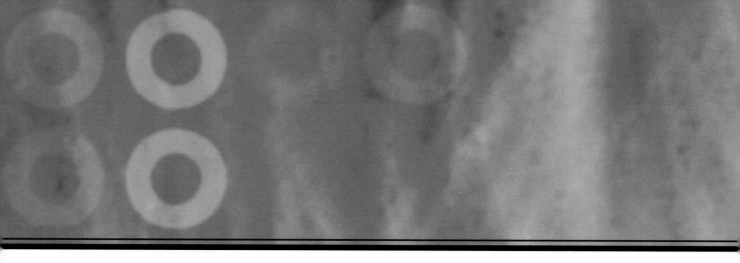

Dill, D.K. (1995) 'University-industry entrepreneurship: the organization and management of American university technology transfer units.' **Higher Education.** 29. Pp. 369-384.

Dill, D. (1996) 'Academic planning and organizational design: lessons from leading American universities.' **Higher Education Quarterly** 50, 1. January pp. 35-53.

Dill, D. (1997) 'Higher Education markets and public policy.' **Higher Education Policy.** 10. 3/4pp. 167-185.

Dill, D. (1999a) 'Academic accountability and university adaptation: the architecture of an academic learning organization.' **Higher Education.** 38. Pp. 127-154.

Dill, D. (1999b) 'Designing academic audit: lessons learned in the implementation of academic audit in Europe and Asia.' International Quality Assurance Association in Higher Education Conference on 'Evaluating Evaluation'. Santiago.

Dimmen, A. and Kyvik, S. (1998) 'Recent changes in the governance of higher education institutions in Norway.' **Higher Education Policy.** 11 2/3. Pp. 217-228.

Drucker, P. (1992) **Managing for the Future: the 1990s and Beyond.** New York. Truman Talley.

Drucker, P. (1993) **Post-Capitalist Society.** New York. Harper-Collins.

Dunne, M. (2000) Education for All Report: Ireland. Dublin. Department of Education and Science. Mimeo.

Ehrenberg, R. (1997) **The American University - National Treasure or Endangered Species?** Ithaca, New York. Cornell University.

El-Khawas, E. (1993) 'Demographic factors in the staffing of higher education: an international perspective.' **Higher Education Management** 5.2 April pp. 127-140.

Elliott, R. (2000) Personal communication.

Elton, L. (1986) 'Research and teaching: symbiosis or conflict.' **Higher Education.** 15. Pp. 299-304.

Embling, J. (1974) **A Fresh Look at Higher Education. European Implications of the Carnegie Commission Reports**. Amsterdam. Elsevier Scientific Publishing Company.

European Pilot Project for Evaluating Quality in Higher Education (1995) **European Report.** Brussels. Commission of the European Communities. November.

Farber, J. (1969) **The Student as Nigger.** N. Hollywood, CA. Contact Books.

Fleming, T., Collins, T. and Coolahan, J. (eds) (1999) **Higher Education. The Challenge of Lifelong Learning.** Maynooth. National University of Ireland Centre for Educational Policy Studies.

Flexner, A. (1908) **The American College. A Criticism.** New York. The Century Co.

Flexner, A. (1930) **Universities: American, English, German.** New York. Oxford University Press.

Frankel, C. (1968) **Education and the Barricades.** New York. W.W. Norton & Co. Inc.

Gardiner, R. and Singh, P. (1991) **Learning Contexts of University and Work. An Evaluation of the Effectiveness of Co-operative Education as a Skills Enhancement Process.** Canberra. Department of Employment, Education and Training.

Gaudemar, J-P (1996) 'The higher education institutions as a regional actor – some introductory thoughts.' Paper presented at IMHE General Conference. Paris. OECD/IMHE.

Geiger, R. (2000) 'University- industry research relationships: trends and issues drawn from recent US experience.' Paris. OECD. Mimeo.

Gellert, C., Leitner, E. and Schramm, J. (eds) (1990) **Research and Teaching at Universities.** Frankfurt. Peter Lang.

Gibbons, M. et al (1994) **The New Production of Knowledge.** London. Sage Publications.

Gibbons, M. (1995) 'The university as an instrument for the development of science and basic research: the implications of Mode 2 Science' in Dill, D.D. and Sporn, B. (eds) **Emerging Patterns of Demand and University Reform: Through a Glass Darkly.** Oxford. IAU Press.

Gibbons, M. (2000) 'Introduction' to Bourne, R. (ed) (2000) **Universities and Development.** London. Association of Commonwealth Universities.

Gibbons, M. et al (2000) **Rethinking Science: Knowledge Production in an Age of Uncertainties.** London Polity Press.

Gless, D.J. and Smith, B.H. (eds) (1992) **The Politics of Liberal Education.** Durham N.C. Duke University Press.

Goddard, J. et al (1994) **Universities and their Communities.** London. Committee of Vice Chancellors and Principals.

Goedegebuure, L.C.J., Kaiser, F. Maassen, P.A.M., Meek, V.L., van Vught, F.A. and de Weert, E. (eds) (1994) **Higher Education Policy. An International Comparative Perspective.** Oxford. Pergamon Press.

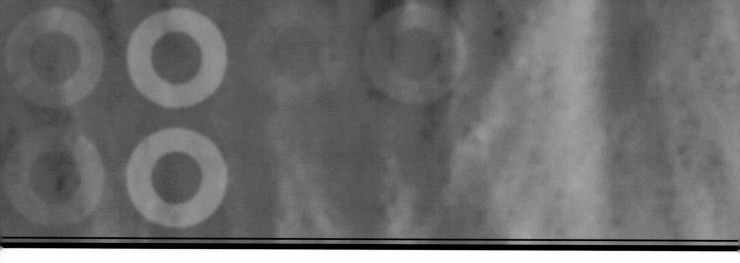

Goedegebuure, L. and van Vught, F. (eds) (1994) **Comparative Policy Studies in Higher Education.** Enschede. Center for Higher Education Policy Studies.

Gornitzka, A. Kyvik, S. and Larsen, I.M. (1998) 'The bureaucratization of universities.' **Minerva.** 36. Pp. 21-47.

Green, D. (ed) **What is Quality in Higher Education?** Buckingham. Society for Research in Higher Education and Open University.

Gumport, P.J. et al (1997) **Trends in United States Higher Education from Massification to Postmassification .** Palo Alto. Stanford University National Center for Postsecondary Improvement.

Hale, B. and Pope, N. (eds) (1994) **EHE – A Vision for Higher Education.** Report of 1993 Edinburgh Conference. Edinburgh. University of Edinburgh Enterprise Centre.

Halsey, A.H. (1992) **The Decline of Donnish Dominion: the British Academic Profession in the Twentieth Century.** Oxford. The Clarendon Press.

Hammons, J.O. and Nunn, W.H. (1994) 'Criteria for establishing two-year colleges in the United States.' **Higher Education Review.** 26.3 Summer.

Harayama, Y. (1998) 'The university system in Japan.' **Higher Education Management.** 10.1.pp. 69-85.

Harley, G.S. (1992) 'Distance education in South Africa: higher education.' Launching Conference of the South African Institute of Distance Education. September.

Harvard Committee (1945) **General Education in a Free Society.** Cambridge Mass. Harvard University Press.

Haug, G. and Kirstein, J. (1999) 'Project Report: Trends in Learning Structures in Higher Education.' Undertaken by the Confederation of European Rectors Conferences and the Association of European Universities (CRE) with financial support from the European Commission.

Heinonen, O-P (1997) 'What are national authorities expecting from higher education institutions?' **Higher Education Management.** 9,2 pp. 7-17.

Henkel, M. and Little, B. (eds) **Changing Relationships Between Higher Education and the State.** London. Jessica Kingsley Publisher.

Henkel, M. (2000a) 'Academic responses to the UK Foresight Programme.' **Higher Education Management.** 12.1 pp. 67-84.

Henkel, M. (2000b) 'Research education and research as a career.' Paper presented to OECD/IMHE expert meeting on Research Management at the Institutional Level. Jun 8-9. Paris. OECD. Mimeo.

Higher Education Authority (2000) **Report on Symposium on Open and Distance Learning.** Dublin. HEA.

Higher Education Quality Council (HEQC) (1997) **Graduate Standards Report. Final Report. Volume 1. The Report.** London. Higher Education Quality Council.

Hirsch, E.D. Jr. (1988) **Cultural Literacy. What Every American Needs To Know.** New York. Random House.

Hirsch, F. (1977) **The Social Limits to Growth.** London. Routledge and Kegan Paul.

Hoff, K.S. (1999) 'Leaders and managers: essential skills required within higher education.' **Higher Education.** 38. Pp. 311-331.

Holdaway, E.A. (1996) 'Current issues in graduate education.' **Journal of Higher Education Policy and Management.** 18.1 May.

Hughes, C. and Tight, M. (1995) 'Linking university teaching and research.' **Higher Education Review.** 28.1

Hughes, S. (1996) 'Vintage year for crÈme.' **The Times Higher Education Supplement.** 17 May.

Huisman, J. and Morphew, C.C. (1998) 'Centralization and diversity: evaluating the effects of government policies in USA and Dutch higher education.' **Higher Education Policy.** 11,1 pp. 3-13.

Husbands, C.T. (1998) 'Assessing the extent of use of part-time teachers in British higher education: problems and issues in enumerating a flexible labour force.' **Higher Education Quarterly,** 52.3. July. Pp. 257-282,

Husen, T. (ed) (1994) **The Role of the University. A Global Perspective.** Tokyo. United Nations University.

Hyland, A. (2000) Personal communication.

International Commission on Education for the Twenty-first Century (1996) **Learning: The Treasure Within.** Paris. UNESCO Publishing.

ICDE (International Council of Distance Education) (1993) **Distance Education for the World.** Inaugural Meeting

ICDE Standing Conference of Presidents of the Member Institutions. Presentations 25-26 October. Lisbon. ICDE.

IRDAC (1995) **Quality and Relevance – the Challenges of European Education.**

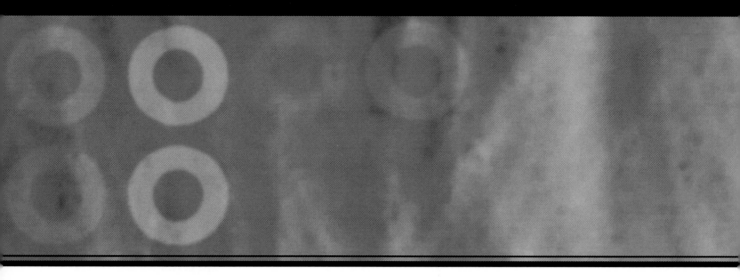

Jalling, H. and Carlsson, M. (1995) 'An attempt to raise the status of undergraduate teaching' (Sweden). **Studies of Higher Education and Research .** 1995. 2/3.

James, R. and Beattie, K. (1995) **Expanding Options: Delivering Technologies and Postgraduate Coursework.** Melbourne. University of Melbourne Centre for the Study of Higher Education.

Joint Working Group of the Council for Education in the Commonwealth and UKCOSA: The Council for International Education (2000) **Student Mobility on the Map. Tertiary Education Interchange in the Commonwealth on the Threshold of the 21st Century.** London UKOSA and CEC.

Jones, G.A., Skolnik, M. and Soren, B.J. (1998) 'Arrangements for co-ordination between university and college sectors in Canadian Provinces 1990-1996.' **Higher Education Policy.** 11.1.pp. 15-27.

Kanter, R.M. (1995) **World Class: Thriving Locally in the Global Economy.** New York. Simon and Schuster.

Karmel, T. (2000) Personal communication.

Kearney, M.L. (1998) 'Graduate employment in a changing society: a social responsibility for higher education. An overview.' in Ronning, A.H. and Kearney, M.-L. (eds) **Graduate Prospects in a Changing Society.** Paris. Inter-American Organization for Higher Education and UNESCO.

Kearney, M.L. (2000) Personal communication.

Keast, D.A. (1995) 'Entrepreneurship in universities: definitions, practices and implications.' **Higher Education Quarterly.** 49.3.pp. 248-266.

Keep, E. and Mayhew, K. (1996) 'Economic demand for higher education – a sound foundation for further expansion?' **Higher Education Quarterly.** 50 pp. 89-109.

Kells, H.R. (1999) 'National higher education evaluation systems: methods for analysis and propositions for the research and policy void.' **Higher Education.** 38.pp. 209-232.

Kenney-Wallace, G. (2000) 'Plato.com: the role and impact of corporate universities in the third millennium.' In Scott, P. (ed) **Higher Education Re-formed.** London and New York. Falmer Press. Pp. 58-77.

Ker, I. (1988) **John Henry Newman. A Biography.** Oxford. Oxford University Press.

Kerr, C. (1995) **The Uses of the University.** 4th ed. Boston. Harvard University Press.

Kershaw, A. and Safford, S. (1998) 'From order to chaos: the impact of educational telecommunications on post-secondary education.' **Higher Education.** 35. Pp. 285-298.

Kivinen, O. and Ahola, S. (1999) 'Higher education as human risk capital.' **Higher Education.** 38. pp. 191-208.

Kivinen, O. and Hedman, J. (2000) 'From loan-based to a grant-based student support system: Finnish experience.' **European Journal of Education.** 7

Koelman, J.B.J. (1998) 'The funding of universities in the Netherlands: developments and trends.' **Higher Education.** 35.2.pp. 127-141.

Kogan, M., Moses, I. and El-Khawas, E. (1994) **Staffing Higher Education. Meeting New Challenges.** London. Jessica Kingsley/ OECD.

Kogan, M. (1998) 'University-state relations: a comparative perspective.' **Higher Education Management.** 10.2.pp. 121-135.

Kyvik, S. and Smeby, J.-C. (1994) 'Teaching and research. The relationship between the supervision of graduate students and faculty research performance.' **Higher Education.** 28. Pp. 227-239.

Lamoure, J. (1999) 'Review of Brennan, J. de Vries, P. and Williams, R. (1997) **Standards and Quality in Education.** London. Jessica Kingsley.' **Higher Education Policy.** 12.3 pp. 277-279.

Lange, R. (1998) **Rethinking Higher Education. On the Future of Higher Education in Britain.** IEA Education and Training Unit.

LeVasseur, P. (1996) '1970-1995: An IMHE perspective on higher education in transition.' **Higher Education Management.** 8.3. Nov. pp. 7-14.

Levine, A. (1980) **When Dreams and Heroes Died. A Portrait of Today's College Student.** (Prepared for the Carnegie Council on Policy Studies in Higher Education) San Francisco. Jossey-Bass Inc. Publishers.

Liaison Committee of the Rectors' Conferences (1992) **Quality Assessment in European Higher Education - A Report on Methods and Mechanisms, and Policy Recommendations to the European Community.** Brussels. Commission of the European Communities.

Long, M. (1994) **A Study of the Academic Results of On-Campus and Off-Campus Students: Comparative performance Within Four Australian Tertiary Institutions.** Canberra. Australian Government Publishing Service.

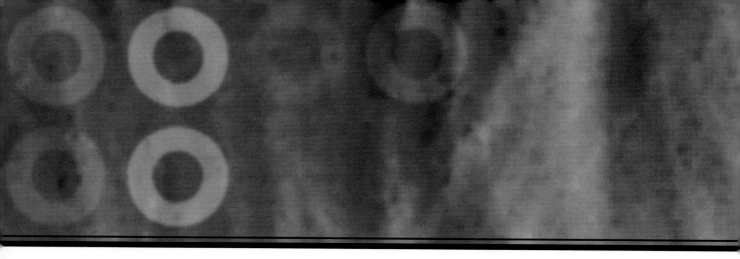

Lucas, C.J. (1994) **American Higher Education: a History.** New York. St. Martin's Press.

Lundvall, B.-A and Johnson, B. (1994) 'The learning economy' **Journal of Industry Studies,** 2, pp. 23-42.

Lutz, F.W. and Field, R. (1998) 'Business valuing in academia. The American University as a center for profit or inquiry?' **Higher Education** 36.pp. 483-419.

Lynton, E.A. and Ellman, S.E. (1988) **New Priorities for the University: Meeting Society's Needs for Applied Knowledge and Competent Individuals.** San Francisco. Jossey-Bass Publications.

Maassen, P. and van Vught, F. (1994) 'Alternative models of governmental steering in higher education.' In Goedegebuure, L. and van Vught, F. (eds) **Comparative Policy Studies in Higher Education.** Enschede. Centre for Policy Studies in Higher Education. Pp. 35-63.

McCann, D. et al (1998) **Educational Technology in Higher Education.** Canberra. Department of Employment, Education , Training and Youth Affairs.

McCarthy, P. and Humphrey, R. (1995) 'Debt: the reality of student life.' **Higher Education Quarterly**. 49.1. January pp. 78-86.

McDaniel, O.C. (1996) 'The paradigms of governance in higher education systems.' **Higher Education Policy** 9.2. pp. 137-158.

McDonough, P.M. (1994) 'Buying and selling higher education: the social construction of the college applicant.' **Journal of Higher Education.** 65.4. July/August.

McGivney, V. (1996) **Staying or leaving the course: non-completion and retention of mature students in further and higher education.** NIACE.

McGuiness, A.C. Jr (1994) **A Framework for Evaluating State Policy Roles in Improving Undergraduate Education: Stimulating Long-Term Systemic Change.** Denver COL. Education Commission of the States.

McGuinness, A.C. Jr. (1995) 'The changing relationships between the states and universities in the United States.' Higher Education Management. 7.3 November pp. 263-279.

McKinnon, K., Walker, S.H. and Davis, D. (2000) **Benchmarking. A Manual for Australian Universities.** Canberra. Dept of Education, Training and Youth Affairs.

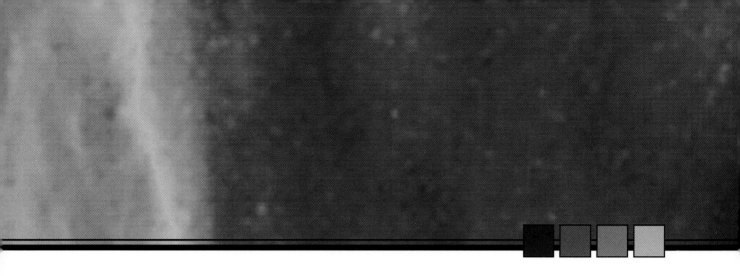

McNair, S. (1994) 'Editorial' **Education and Training.** 37.9 (Issue on Enterprise in Higher Education - EHE)

McNay, I. (1994) 'The regional dimension in the strategic planning of higher education.' **Higher Education Quarterly.** 48. 4 pp. 323-336.

McNicoll, I.H. (1995) **The Impact of the Scottish Higher Education Sector on the Economy of Scotland.** Glasgow. Committee of Scottish Higher Education Principals.

Maddison, A. (1995) **Monitoring the World Economy.** Paris. OECD.

Maddison, A. (2000) 'Perspective on global economic progress and human development. Economic progress: the last half century in historical perspective.' Canberra. Academy of the Social Sciences in Australia. Occasional Paper Series. 1/2000.

Marceau, J. (1993) **Steering from a Distance. International Trends in the Financing and Governance of Higher Education.** Canberra. Department of Employment Education and Training.

Marginson, S. (1992) 'Educational credentials in Australia: average positional value in decline.' Melbourne. University of Melbourne Centre for the Study of Higher Education.

Marginson, S. (1993) 'From the generalist courses to work: an annotated bibliography on generic skills.' Melbourne. University of Melbourne Centre for the Study of Higher Education.

Marginson, S. (1994) 'The transfer of skills and knowledge from education to work.' Melbourne. University of Melbourne Centre for the Study of Higher Education.

Meade, P. and Woodhouse, D. (1999) **Evaluating the Effectiveness of the New Zealand Academic Audit Unit: Review and Outcomes.** International Quality Assurance Association for Higher Education Conference on 'Evaluating Evaluation.' Santiago.

Meek, V.L., Goedegebuure, L.C.J., Krivinen, O., and Rinne, R. (eds) (1996) **The Mockers and the Mocked. Comparative Perspectives on Differentiation, Convergence and Diversity in Higher Education.** Oxford. Pergamon.

Meek, V.L. and Wood, F.O. (1998) 'Higher education governance and management: Australia." **Higher Education Policy.** 11. 2/3pp 165-181.

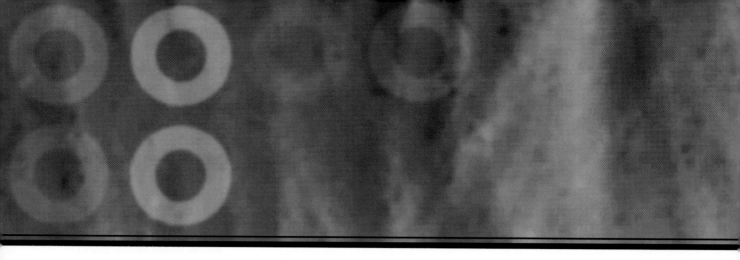

Meenan, J. (1980) **George O'Brien. A Biographical Memoir.** Dublin. Gill and Macmillan.

Middlehurst, R. and Gordon, G. (1995) 'Leadership, quality and institutional effectiveness.' **Higher Education Quarterly.** 49.3.July pp. 267-285.

Middlehurst, R. et al (2000) 'The Business of Borderless Education.' A project undertaken for the Committee of Vice Chancellors and Principals, UK. London. CVCP. Mimeo.

Millett, J. (1978) 'Planning and Management in National Structures' in Kerr, C. et al **Twelve Systems of Higher Education: Six Decisive Issues.** New York. International Council on Higher Education. Pp. 13-56.

Ministry of Education and Research, Denmark (1992) **Education Reform – a Danish Open Market in Higher Education**. Copenhagen. The Ministry.

Ministry of Education, Finland (1995) **Education, Training and Research in the Information Society. A National Strategy.** Helsinki. The Ministry.

Ministry of Education, Finland (1997) 'Developing Mass Tertiary Education: the diversification Response.' Background report for OECD/ Ministry of Education, Youth and sports of the Czech Republic international seminar on 'Mass Tertiary Education: the diversification Response.' Prague. November.

Ministry of Education, New Zealand (1998) **New Zealand Tertiary Education Sector: Profile and Trends.** Wellington. The Ministry.

Mjoes, O.D. (Chairman) (2000) **NOU 2000: 14. Freedom With Responsibility.** Report of the Higher Education Committee. Oslo. Ministry of Education, Research and Church Affairs.

Moodie, G.C. (1996) 'On justifying different claims to academic freedom.' **Minerva.** 34. Pp. 129-150.

Mortimer, K. (1994) 'Enterprise in higher education: reflections from the chair.' **Education and Training.** 37.9 pp. 20-24.

Muller, B. (1994) 'Evaluation of university research by the Deutsche Forschungsgemeinschaft.' in Cazenave, P. (ed) **Evaluation and the Decision Making Process in Higher Education. French, German and Spanish Experiences.** Paris. OECD. Pp. 129-141.

Myers, D. and Schirm, A. (1999) **The Impacts of Upward Bound: Final Report for Phase One of the National Evaluations.** Washington DC. US Department of Education.

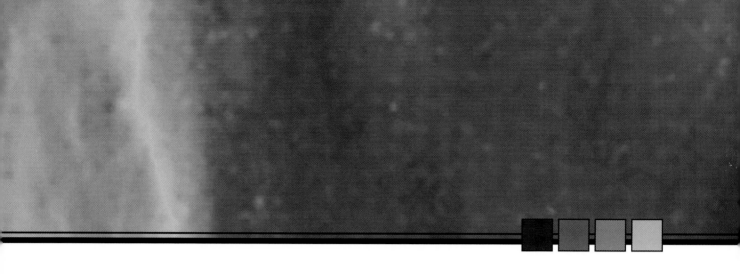

National Advisory Council for Education (ARO), the Netherlands (1994) **From Higher Education to Higher Learning** (Summary) Utrecht. The Council.

National Board of Employment, Education and Training, Australia (1994) **Credit Transfer and the Recognition of Prior Learning.** Canberra. AGPS.

National Board of Employment, Education and Training, Australia (1995) **Cross-Sectoral Collaboration in Post-Secondary Education and Training.** Canberra. Australian Government Publishing Service.

Neave, G. (1988) 'On the cultivation of quality, efficiency and enterprise: an overview of recent trends in higher education in western Europe, 1986-1988.' **European Journal of Education.** 23.1/2pp. 7-23.

Neave, G. and van Vught, F.A. (eds)(1991) **Prometheus Bound: the Changing Relationship Between Government and Higher Education.** Oxford. Pergamon Press.

Neave, G. (1995) 'On living in interesting times: higher education in Western Europe 1985 - 1995.' **European Journal of Education.** 30. 4. Pp. 377-393.

Neumann, R. (1992) 'Perceptions of the teaching- research nexus. A framework for analysis.' **Higher Education.** 23. Pp.159-171.

Newby, P. (1999) 'Culture and quality in higher education.' **Higher Education Policy.** 12. 3.pp. 261-275.

Newman, F. (1985) **Higher Education and the American Resurgence** (A Carnegie Foundation Special Report). Princeton, NJ. Princeton University Press.

Newman, J.H. (1856) **The Office and Work of Universities; on University Teaching considered in a Series of Historical Sketches.** Published as **University Sketches.** Introduced by G. Sampson. London. The Walter Scoll Publishing Coy. 1902.

Newman, J.H. (1943; originally 1852) **On the Scope and Nature of University Education.** London. Everyman.

Nilsson, K.-A. (1999) 'Institutional response to the Swedish model of quality assurance.' International Quality Assurance Association for Higher Education Conference on 'Evaluating Evaluation.' Santiago.

Nordic Council of Ministers (1996) **Evaluation of Higher Education in the Nordic Countries.** Copenhagen. Nordic Council of Ministers.

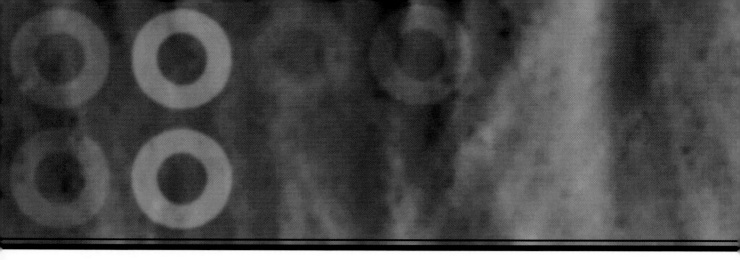

OECD (1966) **Investment in Education: Ireland.** Paris. OECD.

OECD (1974) **Policies for Higher Education.** Paris. OECD.

OECD (1981) **The Future of University Research.** Paris. OECD.

OECD (1983) **Policies for Higher Education in the 1980s.** Paris. OECD.

OECD (1987a) **Adults in Higher Education.** Paris. OECD.

OECD (1987b) **Universities Under Scrutiny.** Paris. OECD.

OECD (1990) **Meeting of Ministers of Education: Communique.** Paris. OECD.

OECD (1991) **Alternatives to Universities.** Paris. OECD.

OECD (1993) **From Higher Education to Employment. Synthesis report.** Paris. OECD.

OECD (1995) **Research Training - Present and Future.** Paris. OECD.

OECD/IMHE (1995) 'Seminar on Human Resources and Staff Development.' Hong Kong Baptist University. November.

OECD (1996a) **Employment and Growth in the Knowledge-Based Economy.** Paris. OECD.

OECD/CERI (1996b) **Internationalisation of Higher Education: OECD Documents.** Paris. OECD.

OECD (1996c) **Lifelong Learning for All. Paris.** OECD.

OECD (1997a) **Education Policy Analysis.** Paris. OECD.

OECD (1997b) Mass Tertiary Education: the Diversification Response. Report of an international seminar. Paris. OECD. Mimeo.

OECD (1998a) Country Note: France (prepared for the thematic review of the first years of tertiary education) Paris. OECD. Mimeo.

OECD (1998b) **Education Policy Analysis.** Paris. OECD.

OECD (1998c) **Human Capital Investment. An International Comparison.** Paris. OECD.

OECD (1998d) **Redefining Tertiary Education.** Paris. OECD.

OECD (1998e) **University Research in Transition.** Paris. OECD.

OECD (1999) **Education Policy Analysis.** Paris. OECD.

OECD/IMHE (1999a) **Internationalisation and Quality in Higher Education.** Paris. OECD.

OECD/IMHE (1999b) **The Response of Higher Education Institutions to Regional Needs.** Paris. OECD.

OECD (2000) **Education at a Glance. OECD Indicators.** Paris. OECD.

OECD/IMHE (2000a) General Conference. Paris.

OECD/IMHE (2000b) **Research Management at the Institutional Level: Report of Expert Meeting June 8-9.** Paris. OECD.

Ortega y Gasset, J. (1946; first pub. 1930) **Mission of the University.** Trans. H.L. Nostrand. London. Kegan Paul, Trench, Trubner and Co. Ltd.

Osborne, R.D. (1996) **Higher Education in Ireland North and South.** London and Bristol PA. Jessica Kingsley Publishers.

Osborne, R.D. and Leith, H. (2000) **Evaluation of the Targeted Initiative on widening Access for Young People from Socio-economically disadvantaged backgrounds.** Dublin. Higher Education Authority.

Ottenwaelter, M.-O. (1996) 'The European Pilot Project for Evaluating Quality in Higher Education' **QA** (International Network for Quality Assurance Agencies in Higher Education. 11 January. Pp. 1-3.

Parry, G. (1997) 'Patterns of participation in higher education in England: a statistical summary and commentary.' **Higher Education Quarterly.** 51. 1. January pp. 6-28.

Partridge, P.H. (1978) 'The universities and the democratisation of higher education' in The University of Adelaide: **The Defence of Excellence in Australian Universities: Proceedings of a national seminar.** Pp. 10-19.

Pechar, H. and Pellert, A. (1998) 'Managing change: organizational reform in Austrian universities.' **Higher Education Policy** 11. 2/3pp. 141-151.

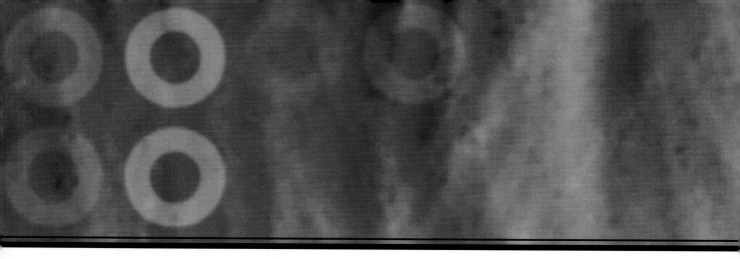

Perkins, J.A. (1966) **The University in Transition.** Princeton, N.J. Princeton Univ. Press.

Perry, W. and Rumble, G. (1987) **A Short Guide to Distance Education.** Cambridge. International Extension College.

Pickering, J.F., Matthews, D.M., Wilson, C. and Kirkland, J. (1999) 'The university: industry interface in the generation of intellectual property.' **Higher Education Quarterly.** 53, 1, Jan. pp. 6 -28.

Ping, C.J. (1997) 'Working paper: educational imperatives for a new era.' Regional Conference on Higher Education: National Strategies and Regional Co-operation for the 21st Century. Tokyo. July.

Powles, M. (1993) 'Postgraduates at the interface between higher education and industry.' Melbourne. University of Melbourne Centre for the Study of Higher Education.

Pritchard, R.M.O. (1998) 'Academic freedom and autonomy in the United Kingdom and Germany.' **Minerva.** 36. Pp. 101-124.

Pyper, I.F. (1998) 'A comparison of part-time higher education provision and participation rates in the UK: implications for Northern Ireland.' **Higher Education Quarterly.** 52.4 October. Pp. 365-377.

Ramsay, E. (1999) 'The national framework for Australian higher education equity: its origins, evolution and current status.' **Higher Education Quarterly** 53.2 April. pp. 173-189.

Ramsden, P. and Moses, I. (1992) 'Associations between research and teaching in Australian higher education.' **Higher Education** 23.pp. 273-295.

Ramsden, P. and Martin, E. (1996) 'Recognition of good university teaching: policies from an Australian study.' **Studies in Higher Education** 21.3 pp. 299-315.

Rasmussen, J.G. (1998) 'New rules of university governance in Denmark.' **Higher Education Policy.** 11.2/3pp. 183-189.

Renwick, W.L. (1996) 'The future of face-to-face and distance teaching in post-secondary education.' in OECD/IMHE **Information Technology and the Future of Post-secondary Education.** Paris. OECD.

Reponer, R. (1999) 'Is leadership possible at loosely coupled organizations such as universities?' **Higher Education Policy**. 12.3 pp. 237-244.

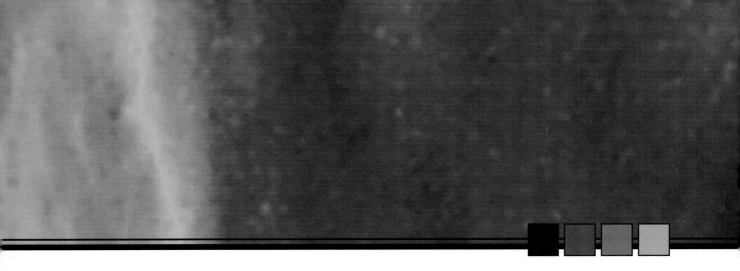

Rhoades, G. (1990) 'Political competition and diversification in higher education.' In J.C. Alexander and P. Colomy (eds) **Differentiation Theory and Social Change. Comparative and Historical Perspectives.** New York. Columbia University Press.

Rinne, R. and Kivinen, O. (1993) 'Adult education, the second chance: fact and fiction.' **Scandinavian Journal of Educational Research.** 37. 2. Pp. 115-128.

Robbins, D. (1993) 'The practical importance of Bourdieu's analyses of higher education.' **Studies in Higher Education.** 18.2 pp. 151-163.

Robbins, L. (1974) 'Foreword' to J. Embling. **A Fresh Look at Higher Education. European Implications of the Carnegie Commission Reports.** Amsterdam. Elsevier Scientific publishing Company.

Roberts, P. (1996) 'Critical literacy, breadth of perspective and universities: applying insights from Freire.' **Studies in Higher Education.** 21.2.pp. 149-163.

Ronning, A.J. and Kearney, M.-L. (eds) (1998) **Graduate Prospects in a Changing Society.** Paris. Inter-American Organization for Higher Education and UNESCO Publishing.

Rosenman, L. (1996) **The Broadening of University Education: An Analysis of Entry Restructuring and Curriculum Change Options.** Canberra. Department of Employment, Education, Training and Youth Affairs.

Roszak, R. (ed) (1969, first pub. 1967) **The Dissenting Academy. Essays Criticizing the Teaching of the Humanities in American Universities.** Harmondsworth, Middlesex.

Rothblatt, S. (1989) 'Conversazione: the idea of a university and its antithesis.' Bundoora, Vic. Seminar on the Sociology of Culture.

Rothblatt, S. (1999) 'Remembrance of things past.' **Higher Education Policy** 12.4.pp. 367-375.

Scheele, J.P. (1999) 'Evaluating evaluation in the Netherlands.' International Quality Assurance Association for Higher Education Conference on 'Evaluating Evaluation.' Santiago.

Schuller, T. (1995) **The Changing University.** Buckingham. Society for Research in Higher Education and The Open University Press.

Schuller, T., Raffe, D., Morgan-Klein, B. and Clark, I. (1999) **Part-time Higher Education: Policy, Practice and Experience.** London. Jessica Kingsley Publishers.

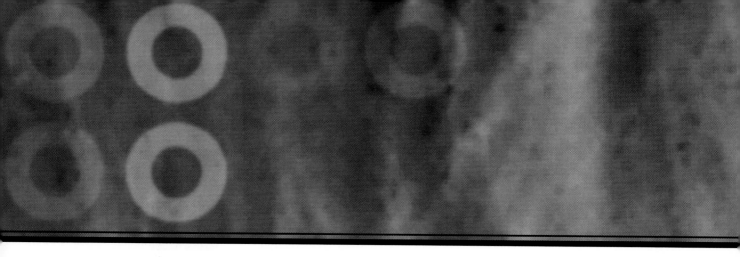

Scott, M.F. (1989) **A New View of Economic Growth.** Oxford. Clarendon Press.

Scott. P. (1984) **The Crisis of the University.** London. Croom Helm Ltd.

Scott, P. (1993) 'Response to R. Smith: The transition from elite to mass higher education: overview and current issues.' in DETYA/OECD **The Transition from Elite to Mass Tertiary Education.** Canberra. DETYA.

Scott, P. (2000) 'A tale of three revolutions? Science, society and the university.' In Scott, P. (ed) **Higher Education Re-formed.** London and New York. Falmer Press pp. 190 - 206.

Scott, P. (ed) (2000) **Higher Education Re-formed.** London and New York. Falmer Press.

Scottish Office (1994) **Higher Still: Opportunity for All.** Edinburgh. Scottish Office.

Seeley, J. (1867) 'Liberal education in universities.' In Farrar, F.W. (ed) **Essays on a Liberal Education.** London. Macmillan & Co. pp. 145-178.

Shattock, M. (ed) (1996) **The Creation of a University System.** Oxford. Blackwell.

Shattock, M. (1997) 'The managerial implications of the new priorities.' **Higher Education Management** 9. 2. pp. 27-34.

Skilbeck, M. (1998) Education in the OECD, 1990-2010. Paris. OECD. Mimeo.

Skilbeck, M. (2000) **Access and Equity in Higher Education. An International Perspective.** Dublin. Higher Education Authority.

Skilbeck, M. (2001) **Review of the Queensland Open Learning Network.** Report for the Government of Queensland. Brisbane. Department of Education.

Skilbeck, M. and Connell. H. (1996) 'Industry-university partnerships in the curriculum: trends and developments in OECD countries.' **Industry and Higher Education.** February.

Skilbeck, M. and Connell, H. (1998) 'The management and financing of higher education.' **Prospects** XXVIII 3. Sept/ pp. 411-427.

Skilbeck, M. and Connell, H.M. (in press) **Quality Assurance in Higher Education: Report of a National Seminar.** Canberra. DETYA.

Slaughter, S. (2000) **Intellectual Property and Academic Freedom - Appellate court cases, 1989 - 1999.**

Slaughter, S., Campbell, T., Holleman, M., Morgan, E. (2000) 'The 'traffic' in graduate students: graduate students as tokens of exchange between academe and industry.' Draft paper. Tucson. Center for the Study of Higher Education, The University of Arizona.

Smeby, J.C. (1996) **Evaluation of Higher Education in the Nordic Countries.** Copenhagen. Nordic Council of Ministers.

Smith, A. and Webster, F. (eds) (1997) **The Postmodern University? Contested Visions of Higher Education in Society.** Buckingham. The Society for Research into Higher Education and Open University Press.

Smithers, A. and Robinson, P. (1996a) **Post-18 Education: Growth, change, prospect.** London. The Council for Industry and Higher Education.

Smithers, A. and Robinson, P. (1996b) **Trends in Higher Education.** London. The Council for Industry and Higher Education.

Sodersten, B. (1994) 'Knowledge, economic progress and the state.' Stockholm. SWFS Skrit Serie VI.

Sorkin, D. (1983) 'Wilhelm von Humboldt: the theory and practice of self-formation (Bildung) 1791-1810.' **Journal of the History of Ideas.** January. Pp. 55-73.

Starpoli, A. (1994) 'Evaluating a French university.' In Cazenave, P. (ed) **Evaluation and the Decision Making Process in Higher Education: French, German and Spanish Experiences.** Paris. OECD. pp. 55-59.

Steering Committee (1995) **Report of the Steering Committee on the Future Development of Higher Education.** Dublin. Higher Education Authority.

Stensaker, B. (1999) 'External quality auditing in Sweden: are departments affected?' **Higher Education Quarterly** 53. 4 Oct. pp. 353-368.

Storper, M. (1995) 'The resurgence of regional economies, ten years later: the region as a nexus of untraded interdependencies.' **European Urban and Regional Studies.** 2, 3, pp. 191-221.

Sweet, R. (1992) 'Assessing, shaping and influencing demand for higher education.' Melbourne. University of Melbourne Centre for the Study of Higher Education. Mimeo.

Tait, H. and Entwhistle, N. (1996) 'Identifying students at risk through ineffective study strategies.' **Higher Education** 31. pp. 97-116.

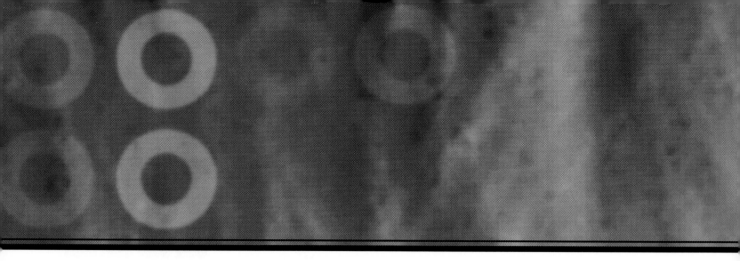

Task Force on Higher Education and Society (2000) **Higher Education in Developing Societies – Perils and Problems.** Washington DC. The International Bank for Reconstruction and Development/ The World Bank.

Taylor, W. (1987) **Universities Under Scrutiny.** Paris. OECD.

Taylor, W. (1996) The Early Years of Tertiary Education. A Selective Review of Recent and Current Literature. Paris. OECD. Mimeo.

Taylor, W. (2000) Personal communication.

Teichler, U. (1999a) 'Higher education policy and the world of work: changing conditions and challenges.' **Higher Education Policy.** 12. 4.pp. 285-312.

Teichler, U. (1999b) 'Lifelong learning as challenge for higher education: the state of knowledge and future research tasks.' **Higher Education Management.** 11.1.pp. 37-53.

Teichler, U. (1999c) 'Research on the relationships between higher education and the world of work: past achievements, problems and new challenges.' **Higher Education** 38. Pp. 169-190.

Teichler, U. and Kehm, B.M. (1995) 'Towards a new understanding of the relationships between higher education and employment.' **European Journal of Education**. 30.2 pp. 115-132.

Thomas, D. (ed) (1995) **Flexible Learning Strategies in Higher and Further Education.** London. Cassell.

Thompson, M. (1993) **Pay and Performance: the Employee Experience.** London. Institute of Manpower Studies.

Thune, C. Kristoffersen, D. and Wied, S. (1995) **A Comparative Analysis of Initiatives of Quality Assurance and Assessment of Higher Education in Europe.** Brussels. Commission of the European Communities.

Thune, C. et al (1999) Guarding the guardian: the evaluation of the Danish Centre for Quality Assurance and Evaluation of Higher Education.' International Quality Assurance Association for Higher Education Conference 'Evaluating Evaluation.' Santiago.

Tilak, J.B.G. (1998) 'Changing patterns of financing education.' **Journal of Indian School of Political Economy.** April – June pp. 225-240.

TQM (Total Quality Management) TWM in Higher Education Discussion Group. No. 09b 1996 at Listserv@UKANUM.CC.UKANS.EDU

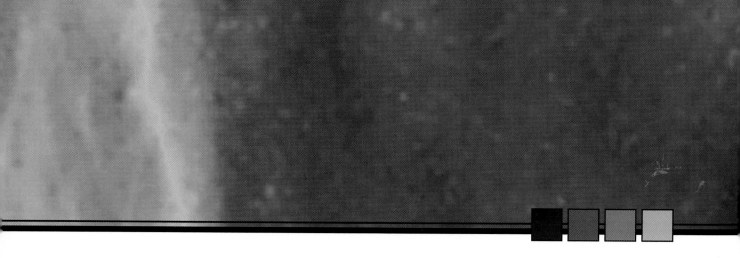

Trow, M. (1976a) 'Elite higher education: an endangered species.' **Minerva** 1

Trow, M. (1976b) 'Problems in the transition from elite to mass higher education.' in OECD **Policies for Higher Education**. Paris. OECD.

Trow, M. (1989) 'American higher education – past, present and future.' **Studies in Higher Education**.

Trow, M. (1994a) **Academic Reviews and the Culture of Excellence.** Stockholm. The Council for Studies of Higher Education.

Trow, M. (1994b) 'Managerialism and the academic profession: quality and control.' The Open University Quality Support Centre. **Higher Education Report** No.2

Trow, M. (1999a) 'From mass higher education to universal access; the American advantage.' **Minerva** 37. Pp. 303-328.

Trow, M. (1999b) 'Lifelong learning through the new information technologies.' **Higher Education Policy.** 12. 2. Pp. 201-217.

Truscot, B. (1951) **Red Brick University.** Harmondsworth, Middlesex. Penguin Books.

UNESCO (1996) **Higher Education in the 21st Century. A Student Perspective.** Paris. UNESCO.

UNESCO (1998) **Higher Education in the Twenty-first Century. Vision and Action.** World Conference on Higher Education Final Report. Paris. UNESCO.

United Kingdom Council for Industry and Higher Education (1996) 'Helping Students Towards Success at Work.' London. The Council.

University of London (2000) **Convocation News.**

van Dam-Mieras, R. (n.d. but 1998) 'The Open University of the Netherlands.' CRE/CEPES European Regional Forum for the UNESCO World Conference on Higher Education. Paris. UNESCO/CRE.

van Vught, F. (1994) 'Bigger but not better.' **The Times Higher** October 7, 1994, p. 5.

van Vught, F. and Westerheijden, D. (1993) **Quality Management and Quality Assurance in European Higher Education.** Enschede, CHEPS.

Vavoka, B. (1998) 'The new social contract between governments, universities and society: has the old one failed?' **Minerva.** 36. pp. 209-228.

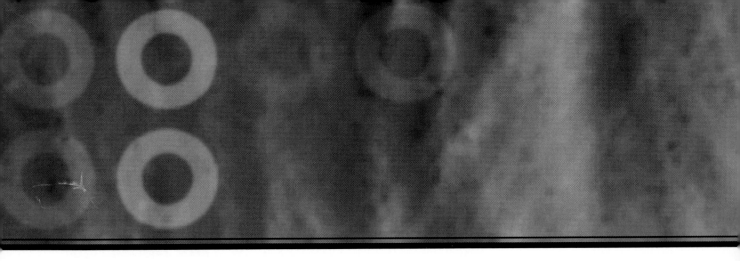

Veysey, L.R. (1965) **The Emergence of the American University.** Chicago. University of Chicago Press.

Vitale, M. (ed) (1998) **Science and Technology Awareness in Europe: New Insights.**European Science and Technology Forum. Science Research Development. Luxembourg. European Communities.

Volkwein, J.F. and Carbone, D.A. (1994) 'The impact of departmental research and teaching climates on undergraduate growth and satisfaction.' **Journal of Higher Education.** 65.2

vom Brocke (1991) 'Friedrich Althoff: a great figure in higher education policy in Germany. **Minerva.** XXIX. 3 Autumn. Pp. 269-293.

Vossensteyn, J.J. (1999) 'Where in Europe would people like to study? The affordability of higher education in nine Western European countries.' Higher Education. 37. Pp. 159-176.

Wasser, H. and Picken, R. (1998) 'Changing circumstances in funding public universities: a comparative view.' **Higher Education Policy.** 11.1.pp. 29-35.

Webb, G. (1996) **Understanding Staff Development.** Buckingham. The Society for Research into Higher Education and Open University Press.

Webber, G.C. (2000) 'U.K. higher education: competitive forces in the 21st century.' **Higher Education Management.** 12.1.pp. 55-66.

Weidmer, R.L. (1993) 'Perspectives on scholarship in education: undergraduate and graduate students' views on faculty scholarship.' Paper for Annual Meeting of the American Education Research Association. Atlanta GA.

Weimer, M. (1993) 'The disciplinary journals on pedagogy.' **Change.** Nov./Dec.

West, L.H.T., Hore, T., Eaton, E.G., Kermond, B.M. (1986) **The Impact of Higher Education on Mature Age Students.** Canberra. Commonwealth Tertiary Education Commission.

Westerheidjen, D. (1997) 'A solid base for decisions. Use of the VSNU research evaluations in Dutch universities.' **Higher Education.** 33. Pp. 397-413.

Whitely, T. (1995) 'Enterprise in higher education - an overview from the Department for Education and Employment.' **Education and Training.** 37.9. pp. 4-8.

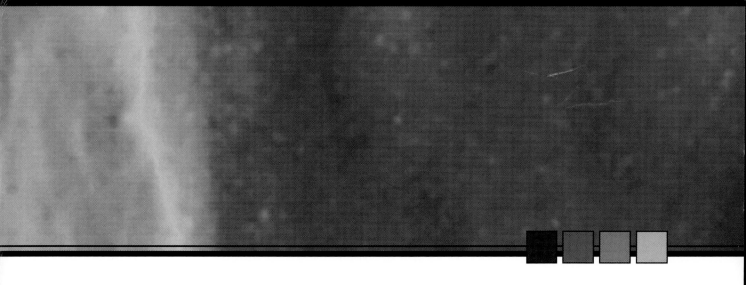

Will, A. (1998) 'Agronomy: an uncertain profession.' In Ronning, A.H. and Kearney, M.L. (eds) **Graduate Prospects in a Changing Society**. Paris. Inter-American Organization for Higher Education and UNESCO.

Williams, B. (1994) 'Higher education and unemployment.' **Higher Education Quarterly** 48.4. October pp. 277-292.

Williams, G. (1996) 'The many faces of privatisation.' **Higher Education Management.** 8.3.Nov. pp. 39-56.

Williams, G. (1997) 'The market route to mass higher education: British experience 1979-1996.' **Higher Education Policy.** 10. 3/4pp. 275-287.

Williams, G. (1999) 'What's in a Name?' (Editorial) **Higher Education Quarterly.** 53. 1. January. Pp.1-5.

Windolf, P. (1995) 'Selection and self-selection at German mass universities.' **Oxford Review of Education.** 21. 2.

Wissenschaftsrat (Science Council) (1988) **Recommendations of the Science Council on the Perspective for Higher Education in the 1990s.** Cologne. Wissenschaftsrat.

Woodhouse, D. (1999) 'Quality Assurance and the International Student Market' paper presented to Quality Assurance and Accreditation in Australian Higher Education Conference. Canberra. December.

Woollard, A. (1996) 'A national measure for minds.' **The Times Higher Education Supplement.** 3 May.

World Bank (1994) **Higher Education: The Lessons of Experience. Development in Practice.** Washington DC. World Bank.

Wright, W.A. (ed) (1995) Teaching Improvement Practice: Successful Strategies for Higher Education. Boston MA. Anker.